The

Business Case
Guide Second Edition

Cost of Ownership

Financial Justification

Return on Investment

Cost Benefit Analysis

Marty J. Schmidt

The Business Case Guide

2nd edition

Marty J. Schmidt

The Business Case Guide, 2nd edition

ISBN 1-929500-01-7

Published by Solution Matrix Ltd.
304 Newbury Street, N° 350
Boston, MA 02115   USA
www.solutionmatrix.com

Excel is a trademark of Microsoft Corporation
1-2-3 is a trademark of Lotus Development Corporation.
Crystal Ball ® is a registered trademark of Decisioneering, Inc.
@RISK is a trademark of Palisade Corporation

Contents

Acknowledgements

The contents of this Guide represent the contributions of many colleagues, clients, and friends. The systematic approach to case building and the tools that make it work come primarily from the hard-won experience of people in many fields, all of whom wrestled with the problem of estimating costs and benefits and learned something new in the process.

Over the years we have built upon each other's work. I am no longer completely clear on the distinction between my own contributions and the contributions of the very talented and generous people I have worked with. However, even though I am not sure who first came up with this or that specific idea, or when that was, I do know very certainly who deserves thanks and recognition:

Patty Pollard, Lyndon Wilkes, Bob Tapscott, Mary Russo, Martin Stark, Scott Trudo, and Joe Goodnough (greater Boston area)

Karen Nicholas and Al O'Connor (Clearwater, Florida)

Annika Hjelm and Susan Munns (Geneva)

Kari Tuovinen (Helsinki)

Johannes Ritter (Paris)

Hans Christensen, Jörgen Eklund, Gunnar Fröberg, Erik Hartikainen, and Madelaine Ledell (Stockholm)

Ralph Booth (Montréal)

Richard Kennedy (San Diego)

Special thanks are also due to Michael Doughty (St. Helena, California) for many improvements to the *Guide*.

Marty J. Schmidt
Boston, 3 May 2002

Chapter 1

What's a Business Case?

Everyone talks about the "business case" but few people understand clearly what that means. This chapter defines the term and presents a high level overview of what belongs in a case and why (the view from 39,000 feet).

The Nature of the Case

Y OU ARE embarking on a mission that is becoming increasingly critical in organizations of all kinds: to predict the results of a business decision, in terms that are clear, concrete, and credible. This is especially crucial when proposing action and you need answers to questions like these:

- Will new the design software justify the investment?
- Which product should we bring to market?
- Should we lease the service vehicles or buy them?

The *business case* is a tool for addressing questions like these: A business case is a decision support and planning tool that projects the likely financial results and other business consequences of an action.

Now, that much should surprise no one. This is probably close to what most people mean when they say "business case." The common understanding is true, as far as it goes, but that definition does not get at the heart of what make a business case different from such things as business plans or accounting statements. Nor does it address the issues that make the difference between a strong case and a weak case. Lack of understanding on these points, however, is one reason so many cases fail, i.e., they are not believed or they do not predict what actually happens. For that reason, Chapter 1 of this *Guide* focuses on the essential nature of the business case.

The terms business case and financial case are often used interchangeably, probably because people see financial results as the case's reason for being. The person who says "Bring me your business case!" usually means "Show me the numbers! Tell me what this means in real money!" Certainly there is a financial model at the heart of a good case, including projected cash flow and financial analysis. But there is more to a good business case than that.

Consider the second word in the term at hand, *case*. We also know the word in a legal context. In a criminal trial, for instance, a good lawyer makes the legal *case* by applying evidence and reasoning to

▣ A business case is a decision support and planning tool that projects the likely financial results and other business consequences of an action.

1

⊡ A good business case, like a legal case, uses evidence and reasoning to reach a conclusion.

support a conclusion ("Guilty!" or "Not Guilty!"). In the courtroom, it is not enough simply to put the gun and the fingerprints in front of the judge or jury. The lawyer must connect that evidence to the conclusion with a rationale that is compelling and legally sound. Judge and jury also need to know *how* the evidence was obtained, so they can decide for themselves whether it means what the lawyer says it means. And they also have to evaluate their own *certainty* on the conclusion.

Similarly, if you want to persuade your manager to loosen up the company purse strings and fund your proposal, or if you have to decide yourself between alternative actions, then your *business case* needs more than a few expected cash flow figures. You need to connect evidence (business impacts and estimates) to a conclusion ("A projected net gain of $1 million!") with a convincing rationale, and you have to present the rationale along with the projections. You also need to present the methods and assumptions behind the case: everyone involved needs to know how the evidence was developed and how to judge the certainty of projected results. Numbers alone do not make the case.

The Central Problem

⊡ Business case methods are rarely taught or explained, even in business schools or business books.

In many situations the need for good business case analysis is obvious and widely appreciated. Nevertheless, most business people feel challenged when they have to create or evaluate a case—even people with business degrees and backgrounds in finance and planning. They do not find many established standards for case content or structure. They discover that business case methods per se are rarely taught or explained, even in business schools or business books. They may be appalled at the lack of good business case examples in their own organization.

All of this is surprising because we know that a business case involves financial techniques that are well known and long established. Since the early 1900s, in fact, finance has developed as a discipline with methods of its own for decision support and planning. Financial metrics such as net present value (NPV) and internal rate of return (IRR), for instance, have been used for capital budgeting and asset management for many decades.

Well-known financial methods are central to a good business case but they are not the central problem in building the case. Ideally the case includes a financial model with a cash flow statement showing estimated costs and benefits for one or more scenarios. Decision makers will certainly want to see an NPV and maybe an IRR based on the cash flow summary. That much is standard finance. The central problem for case builders, however, is determining where the cost and

◙ The central problem for case builders is determining where the cost and benefit figures come from.

benefit figures come from in the first place. Which cost items should be included? What kinds of benefits belong in the case? How should these be assigned financial value? And what should be done with the business impacts that cannot be weighed in monetary terms? None of those questions are answered simply by naming the business case subject. Each of those questions can be answered in different ways.

This is why the business case author has to explain the methods and rationale behind the case, argue convincingly that evidence supports conclusions, outline the methods and assumptions underlying the case, and say something useful about the uncertainties and contingencies associated with the case results. All of these latter issues are beyond the scope of traditional financial practice. Building the case involves financial methods, but case building is something more than standard finance.

◙ This Guide covers the business case landscape from three levels:

- An overview at 39,000 feet
  Chapter 1
- A fly over at 3,000 feet
  Chapter 2
- A ground-level walkthrough
  Chapters 3-6

The Business Case Guide is designed to help you understand the structure and the content that make a business case compelling and useful. It is also designed to lead you through the steps in developing a solid business case: defining the case, designing the case, developing cost and benefit data, analyzing results, and packaging, presenting, and using the case. Think of the subject to be covered as a section of terrain, or landscape: we will cover the landscape several times, from several levels, bringing more detail into focus with each pass, while keeping the overall context in view.

This chapter presents a very high level overview of the best and worst kinds of business cases. Chapter 1 looks at these cases from 39,000 feet or 13,000 meters. Chapter 2 ("The Main Points") is another pass over the same terrain at, say, 3,000 feet or 1,000 meters: low enough to see the major landmarks, but high enough to keep the whole landscape in perspective. Think of the remaining chapters (3 through 6) as a ground level walk-through of the practical details.

Worst Case Scenario: The Double-List Business Case

Most people know that a business case anticipates business consequences of an action. For many, however, understanding does not run much deeper than that. Think of cases you have seen or produced and see if there is anything familiar in the following scenario:

A product manager proposes a new marketing program to the Marketing VP. In the written proposal, the manager builds a "case" for the program by referring to the competitive situation, the company's marketing strategy, and some projected improvements in sales.

The Marketing VP rejects the proposal. Why? The company's Financial Controller has just launched a campaign to improve financial discipline and accountability in all departments, including Marketing. Management wants to see a formal business case before taking action. The proposal in its present form is not a business case.

Product manager and staff meet, therefore, to start a case-building project. Half of those present are asked to find all the "costs" that go with the proposal and the rest are asked to find all the "benefits."

Two weeks later they meet again. The manager combines reports from individual staff members, carefully probing the reality of each contribution, taking care not to count any item twice. The resulting document is essentially two simple lists. One list has the cost items and an estimated value for each. The other lists the benefits and estimated figures for each of them. To bring it all together, the manager compares the sum of costs to the sum of benefits. Figure 1.1 shows the structure of this case.

If the benefits outweigh the costs, the conclusion seems obvious: even a child can see that funding the program is a good business decision. In the manager's mind, the case is made.

But is the case "made" in the Marketing VP's mind? What does the Financial Controller think? Probably you know instinctively this is a weak case. You may have seen or produced similar cases yourself and had the uneasy feeling that something is lacking. But what, specifically, is wrong? After all, isn't a business case supposed to summarize costs and benefits?

Double-list cases can be impressively detailed and complex. I have a 520 page example from a US Fortune 500 company on my desk, meant to evaluate several plant-closing options. Such cases may include excellent research and analysis. Nevertheless, when the essential structure is that shown in Figure 1.1, the case is inherently weak.

The double-list case illustrates some common case-building problems that are very real and very common today. A brief look at these

Figure 1.1 The double-list kind of case appears often in business today. Cost and benefit estimates are simply listed and totaled. Cases of this kind have limited value and are inherently weak.

Proposal	
Costs	**Benefits**
~~	~~~~~
~~	~~~~~
~~	~~~~~
~~	~~~~~
~~	~~~~~
Total Costs	**Total Benefits**

shortcomings will help clarify—by contrast—important qualities of a good business case.

Problem: Costs and Benefits Depend on Case Design

Once it is clear that a business case is needed, the natural response of many is to follow this manager's example and start collecting cost and benefit figures immediately. They assume that costs and benefits are ready to be measured when action is proposed, and that case-building is largely a matter of gathering these figures.

In fact, costs and benefits do not exist—they are not defined—until the case is designed. Properly designed statements of subject, purpose, and financial metrics, for instance, are prerequisites for setting case scope and boundaries along a number of dimensions. These elements are prerequisites for designing the cost model and benefits rationale. These, in turn, are the necessary basis for establishing the full range of expected benefits. Only when all these case design elements are in place is the inventory of costs and benefits defined and ready for evaluation.

Case design, in other words, determines which costs and benefits belong in the case, which do not, and how they should be estimated. When the case builder omits design steps as this manager did, there is no way of knowing whether the case represents its subject or meets its purpose.

Problem: The Case Does Not Have a Time Line

When the case report goes to recipients such as the Marketing VP, the foremost question on everyone's mind is: "What's the bottom line?" That is, how much can we expect to gain or lose if the proposal is implemented? Answering that question, however, immediately brings up others: What must we do to bring these results? Can we control or improve returns on this investment? In order to answer credibly and usefully, case data and results need to be organized along a time line. Case builders and case readers need to see the *timing* of individual cash inflows and outflows.

In the proposed marketing program, for instance, some cost items occur just once near the start of the program, such as initial planning and consulting, preparation of new marketing materials, or hiring a new program manager. Other cost items continue for months or years, changing level from time to time, such as continuing staff salaries or advertising costs. Still other cost items come in the middle or near the end of the program's life, such as special promotional events, or program phase out.

◙ Costs and benefits do not exist until the case is designed.

◙ Case readers need to know when financial impacts are expected to appear and how they will change in time.

Benefits also have time-dependent dynamics. Increased product sales should ramp up over time and then reflect changes in such things as market share and competitors' actions. Case readers need to know *when* all of these financial impacts are expected and how they will change in time. Otherwise, they cannot evaluate, coordinate, or optimize costs and benefits effectively.

Problem: The Case Lacks Self-Evident Validity

When a business case comes under review, an uninvited guest almost always comes along with it: the credibility question. We already know that numbers alone do not make the case. Readers also have to believe that the case is *valid*. They need to have some way of knowing that the case is:

- **Complete:** It includes everything relevant
- **Accurate:** It predicts what will happen
- **Objective:** Results are not biased by the author's motivations or limitations
- **Balanced:** Different case scenarios for competing options are truly comparable

The double-list kind of case provides no such assurance. The Marketing VP knows, for instance, that the author wants the proposal to be funded and has a strong interest in seeing that benefits compare favorably to costs. It is natural to ask, therefore, if personal biases operated to limit the "cost" findings or to overstate "benefits" estimates. How can anyone be sure, for instance, that all relevant costs in the proposed scenario made it into the case? One simply cannot tell from two simple lists.

Asking such questions, by the way, does not necessarily imply anything negative about the ethics of the business case author. Personal preferences and motivations color human judgment all of the time, often unconsciously and unavoidably, even when a person tries hard to be accurate and objective. Most people know this, and they also know that business cases involve arbitrary and subjective judgments.

Case builders and case readers need ways to ensure and communicate case validity. A good case explains its *methods* so that everyone knows why certain costs and benefits were chosen and how they were valued. The typical double-list case is very thin on "Methods."

Best Case Scenario

The double-list case is a weak but very common kind of business case. With some of its shortcomings in mind, we can better appreciate

> ▣ When a business case comes under review, an uninvited guest almost always comes with it: the credibility question.

its opposite, an ideal or best case approach. Even from a high-level, 39,000 foot overview, some defining characteristics of a good case are visible. In practical terms, a good case has some features that stand out even from a fast scan through the written report or a quick glance at the Executive Summary.

▣ A good case has several features that stand out, even from a 39,000 foot overview.

These six features in fact make a good checklist to apply when you have a business case in front of you. Think about cases you have seen, and cases you have produced. Ask:

☑ 1. Are the subject, purpose and scope, up front and clear?
☑ 2. Are cash flow projections organized along a time line?
☑ 3. Does the case present the assumptions and methods for identifying benefits and costs?
☑ 4. Does the case include all important benefits and costs, including those that are non-financial?
☑ 5. Does the case discuss critical success factors?
☑ 6. Does the case identify and measure risks?

▣ Does the case meet each criterion? A good case meets all six checkpoints.

A good business case passes all six checkpoints. The rest of this *Guide* covers these points in more detail—why they belong in the case, how they work together to make the case, how to develop them, and what they look like in different situations. For now, however, we can help set the context for all that follows by briefly considering each check point.

☑ Check Point 1: Are Subject, Purpose, and Scope Up Front and Clear?

A good business case report tells the reader immediately :

- The main components of the action or decision that is the subject of the case.
- Which business objectives are addressed by the subject.
- Why the case exists (the purpose).
- What is required to achieve the case purpose (financial metrics or other criteria).
- Whose costs and whose benefits are included, for which time period (the general scope of the case).

▣ Case builder and case readers need to know from the outset what the case is about, and whose costs and whose benefits are included, over what time period.

None of these points are adequately defined by simply naming the action, for example, "proposed marketing program," "computer system upgrade," or "choice of contractor." These elements of case design need to be specified before anyone can properly go looking for costs and benefits. Remaining chapters of this *Guide* show why these points need to be defined clearly, fully, and early in the case-building project and written early in the final report.

☑ Check Point 2: Are Cash Flow Projections Organized Along a Time Line?

A typical business cases looks into the future across a time period that covers a few weeks, a few years, or even longer. As you know already, readers need to see the timing of individual cost and benefit items across this period.

Figure 1.2 shows "bottom line" from a case that covers five years—perhaps for the proposed marketing program. Overall results (net cash flow) are shown, for each quarter year of the analysis period. The cash flow statement behind this graph would also show the contribution of each line item, for each quarter.

When data and results are viewed along a time line, management can begin to apply financial tactics (the arrows in Figure 1.2) to maximize or optimize returns from this investment: reduce costs, postpone costs, accelerate gains, and increase gains.

☑ Check Point 3: Does the Case Present the Assumptions and Methods for Identifying Benefits and Costs?

⬚ Case readers need to see the assumptions and methods behind the case.

We know already that numbers alone do not make the case. Readers need to judge for themselves whether data were obtained properly and whether they mean what the author says they mean. Case readers need to know the rules for including or excluding cost and benefit impacts and how the financial values were estimated. In other words, they need to see the assumptions and methods behind the case.

These topics are all covered in Chapters 3 and 4, but for now, it is enough to know that assumptions and methods—explicitly spelled

Figure 1.2 Business case results organized along a time line. Case readers need to see when results appear and how they change in time, in order to apply financial tactics (reduce costs, postpone costs, accelerate gains, and increase gains).

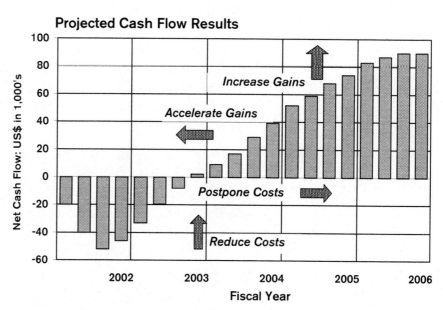

out for case builders and case readers—are the author's best means of ensuring that the case scores high in validity and credibility.

☑ Check Point 4. Does the Case Include All Important Benefits and Costs–Even Those That Are Non Financial?

Many cases are weak or misleading because they leave out important benefits and costs from the action under study. Why? You may know the reason already if you have heard people argue about "hard" and "soft" benefits or costs. The word *soft* usually means that someone doubts the reality or accuracy of certain line items in the case.

Case builders and case readers readily accept "benefits," for instance, when there is no question how to estimate their value. Benefits like "cost savings" and "increased sales revenues" usually fall into this category. These are sometimes called "hard" benefits because the rationale for estimating their worth is straightforward and easily defended.

In business, however, benefits like "improved customer satisfaction" or "enhanced branding," or "better employee morale," also have value, but some people see them as soft benefits that do not belong in a serious business case. For such benefits, the approach to making that value concrete is less clear, less prescribed. This makes some people uneasy and they drop such benefits from the case. Is this appropriate?

Leaving out a benefit or cost is not appropriate if the expected impact is both real *and* material to the purpose of the case. Every attempt should be made to assign financial value or, failing that, at least make the benefit tangible with some other measure. A benefit or cost omitted from the formal analysis will carry exactly zero weight in case results and zero weight in recommendations based on them. The irony is that some of the most important strategic benefits are often the hardest to quantify, and therefore omitted.

☑ Check Point 5: Does the Case Discuss Critical Success Factors?

A good business case is more like a management plan than a simple prediction. Yes, the case builder may predict net cash flow gain of $20 million if the marketing program is implemented, for instance, but that single result assumes that many things have to happen. Some of these assumptions concern factors that can be managed or controlled to some extent: these are *critical success factors* for achieving predicted results.

Staff may need training, new products may have to reach the market by certain dates, partnership agreements may need to be in place, and so on. Many of these "critical success factors" have to be managed to a specified result in order for the main prediction (net

Leaving out a benefit or cost is not appropriate if the expected impact is both real and material to the case purpose.

▣ A good business case describes who needs to do what, by when, in order for the predicted results to appear.

gain of $20 million) to appear. For that reason, the author's conclusions and advice should cover more than a simple recommendation to act on the case subject: "Fund my proposal because the benefits outweigh the costs!" Instead, a good business case for a complex subject has a "Recommendations" section that identifies critical success factors that are manageable or partially manageable. The section describes who needs to do what, by when, in order for the predicted results to appear.

☑ Check Point 6: Does the Case Identify and Measure Risks?

Your business case readers will want to know the predicted financial result, of course, but they also want to know the likelihood of other outcomes as well. Case readers, in other words, must know how to assess the risks underlying predicted results.

Suppose the case builder predicts a net gain of $20 million from the marketing program. In fact, everyone knows that the results will not be $20 million *exactly*. The actual net will certainly be something more or something less. But, will the overall result be close to the predicted value? Or could it be very different from that value? To answer such questions, the case builder performs a formal sensitivity and risk analysis.

▣ Case readers must know how to assess the risks underlying predicted results.

For the current example, the case projections (a net gain of $20 million) will depend on many assumptions about factors that *cannot* be managed or controlled. In order to make the financial projections concrete, the case builder had to make assumptions about such things as market size, market share, customer preferences, competitor actions, economic trends (e.g., inflation), and other things. All these assumptions contribute to projected results and all are uncertain to some degree. Sensitivity and risk analyses (major topics in Chapter 6) produce two kinds of information about uncertainties. They determine:

• Which assumptions are most important in controlling overall results. This is *sensitivity* analysis.
• The likelihood of other outcomes besides the most likely result. This is *risk* analysis.

The author's recommendations should address both points. For instance, if sensitivity analysis shows that predicted results depend heavily on assumed market size, then the audience should be warned to pay close attention to this factor over the program life. If market size turns out differently from the assumptions, then predicted business case results will change.

Or, if management says that any investment in programs must return benefits at least 100% greater than program costs, then the business case author should use the risk analysis to estimate the probability that returns will be at least that high.

Next steps

By now you should be getting the picture: A good business case predicts business outcomes, but in order to do so *credibly* it has to communicate much more than projected cash flow totals.

Cases that meet the six check points above tell the audience clearly what the case is about, where the projected results come from, and what has to occur in order for those results to appear. Now, in Chapter 2 we descend from 39,000 feet and take a closer look at some of the main points involved in producing such a case.

What's the Difference?

Business Case vs. Business Plan

Even those with a strong background in analysis or business planning sometimes have to ask: What's the difference between a business case and a business plan? It's a question you may have to answer many times for your colleagues and management. Table 1.1 summarizes some of the differences.

	A Business Case...	A Business Plan...
Is organized around...	A single action.	An organization or the whole enterprise.
Predicts...	Cash flow results and important non-financial impacts that follow from the action.	Business performance of the organization, especially in the main categories of the income statement.
Is based on...	A cost model and a benefits rationale, designed for the case and applied to one or more action scenarios.	The business model for the organization and expected trends.

Table 1.1. Important differences between a business case and a business plan.

In brief, a business case focuses on what follows from a single action, or decision alternative, while the business plan anticipates sales, expenses, margins, and profits for an organization.

Both tools, of course can play a role in decision support or financial planning, and one kind of tool can support the other.

A business case can support the business plan, by helping answer questions like this: "How will the proposed marketing program impact our business performance?"

A business plan can support a business case by helping case developers estimate costs and expenses, sales revenues, and expected changes in these areas.

In Summary

A BUSINESS CASE is a decision support and planning tool that projects the likely financial results and other business consequences of an action or decision.

A good business case is like a legal case in one sense: both use evidence and reasoning to support a conclusion.

A good business case— like a scientific research report—has a "Methods" section that shows clearly why cost/benefit line items were included or excluded and how they were assigned value.

The central problem for case builders is answering questions like these: Which cost items should be included? What kinds of benefits belong in the case? How should these impacts be assigned financial value? And what should be done with the business impacts that cannot be estimated in monetary terms?

The double-list kind of business case represents several case-building problems that are very real and very common:

- The case lacks design, and costs and benefits depend on design.
- The case does not have a time line, and readers need to know when costs and benefits are expected in order to manage them.
- The case does not have self-evident validity, largely because it does not reveal its methods.

A good business case:

- Defines the case subject, purpose and scope, up front, in clear practical terms.
- Shows expected cash flow consequences of an action or decision, organized around a time line.
- Presents the rationale and methods for identifying and estimating benefits and costs.
- Includes all important benefit and cost impacts, even those that are not easily described in financial terms.
- Discusses critical success factors that must be managed in order to bring predicted results.
- Identifies and measures risks.

Chapter 2

The Main Points

Building a solid business case requires good design principles and a well planned case-building process. This chapter is another overview of the case design and process terrain, this time from 3,000 feet: low enough to see the important design features and process steps in some detail, but high enough to keep the whole landscape in perspective.

Design and Process are Everything

S EVERAL YEARS ago I worked with the Director of Information Technology (IT) of a large commercial bank who had a problem: twice in a twelve-month period he had proposed a major IT project to the bank's Executive Committee, and twice the Committee had said "No" to his proposal. Now he was preparing a third, final attempt. Here was the situation:

To the IT Director, the rejections were mystifying and disturbing: mystifying because the proposal made very good sense on technical and operational grounds, and disturbing because his own job was on the line, depending on the outcome of the next submission. Why were the first two proposals rejected? What had to change in the next version?

A committee of senior bank executives turned down the earlier versions for business reasons, not technical reasons. They simply had no confidence in the financial justification that accompanied the proposals. Obviously, the next attempt had to score high in credibility.

The proposal included upgrades to local area networks in branch offices and the creation of a new "front end" to bank data and information feeds. These were designed to provide loan officers and professional sales people with easier and broader access to customer data, economic data, and the bank's own decision-support software. One goal was to improve the quality of decision making (reduce losses from bad loan decisions). Another goal was to reduce loan-processing time from an average ten days to three days. A third goal was to improve the sales team's performance selling the more profitable financial services. Hardware and software prototypes had already shown promise in pilot studies at two of the bank's busiest branches. These improvements, the Director estimated, would bring increases in net profits of about $140 million across five years.

Everyone agreed that the objectives were laudable, but few beyond the Director himself believed the financial projections.

Jumping to the end of the story, I can report that after another two months of case-building, the Director resubmitted his proposal with a new business case and won the Committee's "Yes." What is truly remarkable is that all three cases—two that failed and one that passed—predicted essentially the same outcome: About $140 million net increase in bank profits across five years, after recovering investment costs. The third case was believed, the first two were not.

▣ When building the business case, design and process are everything.

Why did the third case get different results? Two reasons are paramount and these are the main themes of this chapter:

- The successful case was designed properly.
- The case-building process was specifically planned to maximize credibility with its audience.

The clear lesson for everyone at the bank was this: when building the business case, design and process are everything.

The View from 3,000 Feet

▣ This chapter covers the business case landscape again, low enough to see the main points, but high enough to see the context.

Chapters 3–6 of this *Guide* cover the practical details of case analysis and case construction. As mentioned, those chapters are the ground-level walkthrough of the same terrain we saw from 39,000 feet in Chapter 1. The bank example taught us, however, that details have to be understood in the context of case design and the case building process. Before putting on the walking shoes, therefore, let us take one more overview of the business case terrain, this time low enough to see the main points of case design and process clearly, but high enough to keep the whole landscape in view. Think of this chapter as a fly-over at 3,000 feet.

The Natural Order of Case Design

When we first met the Director and his project team to plan a third version of the proposal, we started with a discussion of the important case design tasks ahead. We also had on the table an outline of the ideal business case structure. It so happens that important case elements appear in the case report in about the same order that we approach them in the case-building project. In a sense, the author has to take readers down the same road traveled by case-builders.

From 3,000 feet, we can see the main landmarks along the case design road. Table 2.1 presents the major sections in the business case structure. Think of this list as the *logical* structure for a strong case: your finished case report may use different headings, but no matter what labels and titles are used, a solid case addresses the purpose of each section.

Table 2.2 (next page) lists twenty design elements in the five major sections of a complete case. Detailed descriptions come in later chapters, but for now we highlight the importance of *order*—working through design decisions in the natural order. Most items in the table depend on the items above them. The outline of the business case-building project, in other words, is also an outline for the case report. Not every case needs all twenty design elements but most do need at least one item from each of the five major sections.

Near the beginning of the case report should be an inventory of the motivating factors behind the case: the business objectives, opportunities, threats, and problems that the business case subject may address. This material is necessary for developing much that follows, such as the scope and boundary statements (rules for determining whose costs and whose benefits are included, over what period of time). This material also helps determine which benefits can be included and how to assign financial value to them. At the end of the case, this material is the starting point for making specific recommendations for action.

The case subject (what the case is about) and the case purpose (why the case is being built) should also appear near the start of the report, in terms that are complete and precise. These too contribute

⊡ The outline of the case-building project is also an outline of the case report.

Business Case Structure

A. Introduction
Defines what the case is about (the subject) and why it is being built (the purpose). Also presents the business objectives addressed by the subject of the case.

B. Methods and Assumptions
Design elements fix the boundaries of the case (whose costs and whose benefits are examined, over what time period). Also outlines the rules for deciding what belongs in the case and what does not, along with important assumptions.

C. Business Impacts
The main business case results: financial and non financial business impacts expected in one or more scenarios.

D. Sensitivity, Risks, and Contingencies
Shows how results depend on important assumptions, as well as the likelihood that other results appear.

E. Conclusions and Recommendations
Recommends specific actions based on business objectives from Section A and the results from Sections C and D.

Table 2.1 Five major sections of the business case. Most cases need one or more design elements from each section.

BUSINESS CASE STRUCTURE AND PROCESS

A Introduction

Design elements

- Subject: What the case is about
- Purpose: Why the case exists and what it will be used for
- Situation and motivation:
  Objectives, opportunities, threats, problems,
  limitations and constraint

B Methods and Assumptions

Design elements

- Scope and boundary definitions
- Financial metrics and other decision criteria: information
  required for the case to achieve its purpose
- Major assumptions
- Scenarios to be developed and analyzed (scenario design)
- Case structure: incremental vs. full value data
- The cost impact model
- The benefits model and benefits rationale

C Business Impacts

Design elements

- Cash flow projections
- The dynamic financial model
- Financial analysis, development of financial metrics
- Rationale for including important non financial impacts

D Sensitivity, Risks, and Contingencies

Design elements

- Sensitivity analysis:
  Which assumptions are important in determining results?
- Risk analysis:
  How likely are the projected results?
  How likely are other results?
  Which factors must be watched?
- Contingency analysis:
  Which factors must be managed?

E Conclusions and Recommendations

Design elements

- Results rationale:
  linking case results to case subject and purpose
- Choice of scenario(s) for action
- Strategy and tactics for optimizing results

Table 2.2 Business case design elements for the completed case report. Each design element calls for choices or decisions from the case builder. Design elements should be approached in this order because most depend on elements above them.

to the scope and boundary statements, narrowing and sharpening the definition of what, exactly, belongs in the case.

When the other steps are completed in order, and when readers then move through them in the same order, the natural result should be a clear understanding of:

- The rationale for including or excluding items
- The quality of the data
- Implications of the financial results
- The likelihood of achieving predicted results
- Practical recommendations for achieving projected results

Understanding and credibility, in other words, come from a logical structure that is built up in stages.

The Core Team: Key to Credibility

The project team for the bank's business case was already formed when we started the final case project. These people would do most of the time-consuming hard work—digging into databases, budgets, business plans, vendor proposals, and the like, as well as interviewing internal specialists, external experts, ordinary IT users, and customers. Most of these people were on the Director's staff. A few were IT specialists from other departments. Our first action, however, was to recruit a *second* team for the case project—a group we called the "core team." This team played a critical role in improving the quality of the case and, more important, establishing credibility.

Core team members were recruited with an eye on the history of the two earlier proposals that failed. Those proposals had projected good financial results, but the Executive Committee did not fully believe them. One Senior Vice President had been especially negative during previous reviews. In his opinion, predicted benefits were "soft benefits," total costs were seriously underestimated, and there was little chance that everything could be installed, running, and delivering results on time. He expressed these views energetically during the earlier reviews, no doubt swaying other opinions on the Committee and generally souring the atmosphere each time.

That Vice President was the first person we recruited for the core team. We also went after high-level managers from Corporate Finance, Human Resources, and Marketing, as well as several branch managers and two members of the President's Strategy and Planning Group. The ten-member core team met three times during two-months of case building. By contrast, the project team poured many times more person-hours into the project. Both teams were essential to building a successful case, but the core team was indispensable for

> The core team plays a critical role in improving the quality of the case and, more important, establishing credibility.

ensuring that case results were understood and believed by the Executive Committee.

Effective use of a core team, in fact, can be the single most important step you can take to ensure the success of your own business cases. The importance of the core team cannot be overstated. It is very important that case project managers recruit effectively for the core team and then control team meetings carefully. A good core team, properly led, brings credibility and accuracy in at least four ways.

The Core Team Provides Cross-Functional, Cross-organizational Input

The core team can be a valuable source of information and guidance for the case designer. This is vital when the subject of the case has cross-organizational impact, or when the costs are focused in one organization but the benefits are realized more broadly.

Product proposals, technology proposals, and infrastructure proposals often fit that description. So do many other actions in a complex business environment. If the subject is bringing a new product to market, or closing a corporate site, or entering a new market, for instance, cost and benefit impacts may cross boundaries of many kinds—organizations, management levels, budget categories, and planning periods. In such cases, the core team can help define case boundaries and help fill in the cost model more completely and with more authority than a project team that is drawn from a single organization or function.

The core team can bring other critical expertise and information to the table:

- Line managers on the team can help in "costing" and "valuing" operational impacts in their own areas.
- Financial experts can connect the business case subject with the company's long-range business plan (a vital connection, when assigning financial value to strategic benefits). They can help explain budget issues, financial constraints, and how spending decisions are made.
- Human resource specialists can help assess the personnel impacts of a proposed action: job levels required, average salary and overhead costs, training requirements, hiring costs, for example. "HR" expertise is especially welcome when decision alternatives include, "hire from within," "hire externally," and "outsource."
- Senior managers from the highest levels can help identify and prioritize organizational objectives—business performance objectives, financial objectives, operational objectives, and still other objectives. This provides a solid basis for estimating benefit values and for recommending actions.

◙ Effective use of a core team can be the single most important step you can take to ensure the success of your business case.

◙ Cost and benefit impacts may cross boundaries of many kinds—organizations, management levels, budget categories, or planning periods.

In brief, the case will be a better case with cross-functional, cross-organizational input from the core team.

That much of the core team's role is obvious. Other roles for the team are less obvious but may be even more important.

The Core Team Spreads the Sense of Ownership

The core team can be the vehicle for spreading a *sense of ownership* for your business case, widely beyond the case-building project team. It is a simple reality that people who become involved in producing something, or contribute to the design of something, naturally begin to feel some ownership for it. In meetings and discussions, team members contribute to case design and development. Inevitably, it becomes their case coming up for review instead of just your case.

A shared sense of ownership is desirable: Most people do not want something they work on to fail.

The Core Team Communicates Methods, Rationale, and Expectations

You cannot assume that your audience will automatically appreciate your business case on its own merits simply from reading the finished document or listening to a presentation of results. A case is not successful until it is communicated successfully, and a complete business case has a lot to communicate.

In order to properly evaluate a case, the audience needs to understand the important points in each major section (see Table 2.1). It is not easy to gain that understanding from a single reading of a case report or a short presentation by the author. The author can meet some of this challenge by using the core team as a communications channel during the case-building project. There is no reason to wait until the final results are in, to begin communicating important methods and rationale behind them.

Why is complete communication so important? Business case results necessarily depend on many arbitrary judgments and assumptions, and these are natural targets for criticism, especially if they are revealed only in the final presentation or completed document. When bringing your case into a competitive or critical setting you do not want to have to announce and defend the arbitrary elements of your case at the same time. The core team can be an effective channel for communicating such things as case design, the rationale for including certain benefits, and important assumptions, long before the final results are in. When review day comes, critics may still argue your interpretation of case results, but you leave them little room to question your methods or data.

▣ The core team can be the vehicle for spreading a sense of ownership…most people do not want something they work on to fail.

▣ You do not want to have to announce and defend the arbitrary elements of your case at the same time.

21

The Core Team Can Turn Damaging Criticism Into Constructive Criticism.

Finally, you may need to use the core team as a vehicle for handling people who are seriously difficult critics of your proposal, such as the Senior Vice President I mentioned. If you face people who fit that description, you may want to bring one or more of them onto the core team at the outset.

As members of the core team, these critics will have objected and contributed everything they have to say before the final review. Through careful management of core team meetings, you can show them, respectfully, that they are "on the record."

Not every critic belongs on the core team, of course: there are some people who—to put it plainly—simply do not respect respect. However, when your critics actually do contribute to case design, they may even develop some sense of ownership for the case. This should lead to fewer critical surprises late in the game.

Recruiting and Managing the Core Team

Using the core team to maximum advantage requires discipline and careful management. Discipline is required, because it is simply easier not to bother with a core team at all. The natural inclination of many people, in fact, is to make sure that project building is done by their own groups, keeping everything under their own roofs, so to speak. Many omit core team formation altogether. Why?

Some feel this is the way to ensure that everything "comes out right." They may see the core team idea as a risk that might loosen the case owner's control of the project, or take case design and results in undesirable directions.

Case builders also avoid using a core team for simple practical reason: it is not easy to get the time and involvement of other managers and specialists, especially those high in the organization. It is easy to think: "What's in it for him, or her?" Why would they want to find time for my business case project?" Case builders may not feel confident they can recruit the kind of team members they need. When you ask people to serve on the core team, two principles are important:

- First, recruit only people to whom you can honestly say: "This business case is important to the organization (or company), and in order to do it right, we need your contribution."
- Second, be very clear that time requirements for core team members will be controlled and limited.

Depending on the length and scope of the business case project, core teams normally have two to four one-hour meetings. (In fact, core team members often develop an interest and a sense of owner-

◙ When critics contribute to case design, they may even develop some sense of ownership for it.

◙ Using the core team to maximum advantage requires discipline and careful management…many case builders omit core team formation altogether.

ship beyond initial expectations and then end up contributing much more time. But that is a decision for them to make, later.)

Incidentally, there is no reason the core team has to be called by that name. You may use terms like "Steering Committee," "Project Review Team", "Business Case Advisory Board," or anything else that fits better in your own organization's culture.

What does the core team actually do? One thing they do *not* do is completely redesign or take control of the case. Nor do they do the "heavy lifting" case-building work. They do make limited and controlled contributions. These contributions are important, and they have self-evident value to the team members, but remember, they are limited and controlled. This *Guide* identifies opportunities for core team contributions and suggested meeting agenda topics throughout Chapters 3 through 6.

Take the Long-Term Time Line View

One feature should stand out, even when scanning quickly through a business case report: the time line. Actions in a complex environment have many consequences and these unfold over time. The business case captures some of these across a finite "window", or segment of that period, that is, across an *analysis period*. Note that the analysis period is *not* the time required for the business case project. The analysis period is a designated number of weeks, months, or years, into the future, for which costs and benefits are estimated.

Chapter 1 argued that the presence or absence of a time line can make the difference between a strong case and a weak case. The time line adds credibility because it helps everyone understand the sources of cash inflows and outflows. Without a time line, it is difficult to provide practical management guidance on specific actions over the analysis period. That much makes sense to most people, when pointed out to them.

▣ Case results can depend heavily on the choice of analysis period.

Be sure, however, that your case-building team, your core team, and your case recipients, understand a little more about the role of the time line beyond the fact that the case needs one. Everyone involved with the case needs at least a "3,000 foot level" understanding of these points:

- The choice of analysis period is arbitrary.
- Case results can depend heavily on analysis period length.
- Longer analysis periods are usually preferable to shorter periods.

Companies and organizations sometimes prescribe standard analysis periods for business cases or planning work. This reasons for setting standard analysis periods may be to bring consistency to business case and planning work, or to ensure that competing cases are compared fairly. Those are laudable objectives, but remember, the fact remains that the analysis period length is purely arbitrary—whether chosen by case builder or policy maker. Sometimes the prescribed standard is appropriate for the comparison, decision, or planning needs at hand, and sometimes the standard is not appropriate.

▣ The time line helps everyone understand the sources of cash inflows and outflows.

Figure 2.1 below shows how the choice of analysis periods can shape case results. The figure is a very typical investment curve, with cash flow projections extending years after an initial decision. In this figure, inflow and outflow totals are shown separately for each quarter year of a five-year analysis. Cost and benefit profiles like this result from many kinds of business actions: introducing a new product, entering a new market, running a training program, buying new production equipment, or opening a new site, to name a few. Is this action a good business decision?

To answer that question, you might consider several financial criteria, or *financial metrics*. These are the results of analyses performed on the cash flow figures, and they are called *metrics* because they "measure" some aspect of the whole data set. Table 2.3 (below the figure) summarizes four of these financial metrics: Cumulative cash flow, net present value of the cash flow (NPV), internal rate of return (IRR), and a simple return on investment figure (simple ROI). These metrics are covered more fully in later chapters, but for now, it is enough to know that cost and benefit patterns typically change over time, and the message from a short analysis period can be quite different from

Figure 2.1 The early cash flow projections in a business case may look very different from cash flows late in the analysis period.

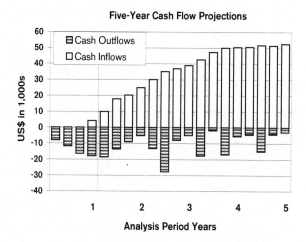

Table 2.3 Financial metrics for the case depend heavily on the length of analysis period.

| Financial Metric | At the end of . . . | | | | |
	Year 1	Year 2	Year 3	Year 4	Year 5
Cumulative Cash Flow	($57.1)	($30.4)	$57.0	$205.0	$391.6
NPV @ 10.0%*	($47.0)	($25.2)	$41.6	$144.7	$258.4
IRR	N/A	-11.1%	11.5%	18.8%	21.2%
Simple ROI**	-92.4%	-23.3%	41.3%	107.4%	174.7%

* 10.0% annual rate, discounted quarterly

** Simple Return on Investment = Incremental Gain or Loss / Total Cost

a long-term view. After two years this investment shows a net loss by all criteria. Each extra year in the analysis period improves the overall outlook substantially. Is this action a good business decision? That depends on whether you look two, three, four, or five years into the future.

The example also illustrates why longer analysis periods are usually more appropriate than shorter periods: today's actions have consequences that extend far into the future, sometimes long after the original assets are paid for and fully depreciated, or long after the people originally responsible for implementation and operation have departed.

Scenarios: The Future in Detail

▣ Business cases are built to answer questions…questions can be answered only if the logical structure of the case is designed to address them.

We just saw how business case results can be negative or positive depending on one arbitrary design decision: length of analysis period. Other design decisions are equally arbitrary and equally important in determining results. The choice of analysis period is a decision about business case *scope*. Now we turn to design decisions that create the business case *logic*.

Remember that business cases are built to answer questions like these: Which proposal represents the best business decision? Will the returns justify the investment? What will this action do for our business performance? Such questions can be answered only if the logical structure of the case is designed to address them. The logical structure of the case resides in the scenario design (introduced in this section), the cost model, and the benefits rationale (next section).

▣ The logical structure of the case resides in the scenario design, the cost model, and the benefits rationale.

The term *scenario* means, simply, a story showing one way that events might unfold. Chapter 1, for instance, used "worst case" and "best case" scenarios to compare weak and strong business cases. Scenarios in the business case itself, however, are more structured and more detailed. A properly built scenario makes it possible to find and make tangible every business impact that belongs in the case. The story may be told with information drawn from business plans, project plans, vendor proposals, pilot studies, prior experience, or other sources. Telling the story also requires an abundance of *assumptions* about things like market size, salary increases, the price of fuel, and anything else we need to specify in order to project cost and benefit impacts into the future. And, the scenario may incorporate formal models, rules, and logic (rationale) in order to leave no doubt about what belongs in the case and what does not. Together, all the scenario elements tell the story of one possible future, in concrete detail.

To see how the right choice of "stories," really makes it possible to answer questions about business decisions, consider again the IT Director for the bank, mentioned earlier. Scenario design begins with

25

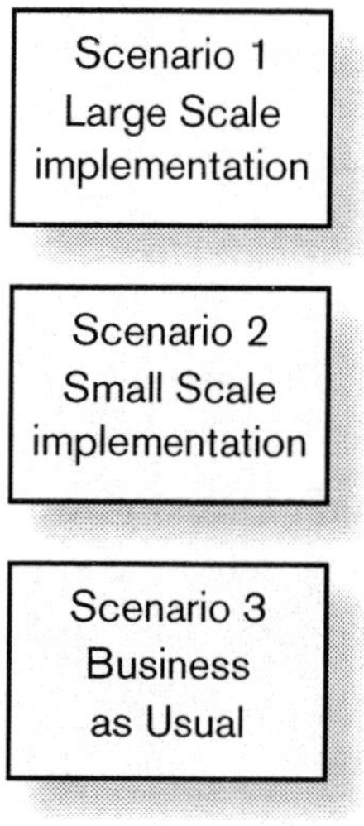

Figure 2.2 Scenario design for the IT Director's business case. Normally the case needs one scenario for each proposal or decision alternative, as well as a "Business as Usual" scenario as a baseline for comparison. (Business as usual and proposal scenarios are sometimes called "As Is" and "To Be" scenarios)

Scenario 1
Large Scale
implementation

Scenario 2
Small Scale
implementation

Scenario 3
Business
as Usual

the business case *subject*: what the case is "about." In this case, the Director proposed upgrades to local area networks in branch offices and the creation of a new "front end" to bank data and information feeds. As a rule, the case needs one scenario for each proposal or decision alternative. In fact, the director presented bank management with two quite different implementation alternatives: a "large scale" option and a "small scale" option. So, his business case included two proposal scenarios, one for each option.

Scenario design also considers the business objectives that motivate the proposal. Here, the Director and the bank had three objectives:

- Improve the quality of decision-making (reduce loan loss)
- Reduce loan-processing time
- Improve sales team performance

Notice the words "improve" and "reduce" in these objectives. These are relative terms. We have to ask: Improved, relative to what? Reduced, relative to what? In order to recognize improvements or reductions under either proposal scenario, the case also needs a baseline scenario for comparison. Thus, the Director's business case included a third scenario: "business as usual." This predicts key measures of business performance should *neither* proposal scenario be implemented. Each proposal scenario forecasts business impacts of an action. Whether or not these predictions represent improvements or reductions depends on how they compare to "business as usual." (Note that some people refer to "business as usual" and "proposal" scenarios as the "As Is" and "To Be" scenarios). Figure 2.2 represents the scenario design for the Director's proposal.

You may wonder at this point if just one scenario for each major alternative can really cover all the questions a business may want to ask. After all, the number of possible different futures is infinite. We may want to examine many different ways of implementing each alternative. The IT Director may want to know, for instance, the predicted business results under different assumptions about future business growth, or different assumptions about future prices. He may want to see how each alternative develops if deployment is executed quickly in a single phase, compared to slower deployment carried out in multiple phases. Usually, however, we do *not* need a different scenario for each "what if?" question or each combination of assumptions we want to test. Instead, we explore the relationship between many different assumptions and business case results all within the framework of a very few scenarios (such as we see in Figure 2.2), with

▣ We do not need a different scenario for each "what if?" question...instead we explore many different assumptions and case results with a thorough risk and sensitivity analysis.

a thorough risk and sensitivity analysis. We turn to those subjects later in this chapter and again in later chapters.

Business Impacts: Costs and Benefits

Deciding which scenarios to build and compare is one step in designing the business case logic so as to address decision making or planning questions. We need at least two scenarios, for instance, to compare business results from a proposed action to business as usual. In order to fully address the case purpose, however, we also need a rational system for structuring the internal content of the scenarios. In order to have confidence that case results address important questions, we need a means of knowing that scenarios:

- Include every important business impact

  and

- Different scenarios in the same case are truly comparable

To meet these needs, we turn to two scenario-building tools, the *cost model* and *benefits rationale*.

◻ Major actions in complex environments have lots of consequences....the cost model and benefits rationale make it possible to deal with hundreds or thousands of potential impacts.

When you first think seriously about finding all the consequences of a proposed action, and then deciding which impacts belong in the case and which do not, and then trying to assign financial values to them, the task may suddenly seem hopelessly difficult. Major actions in complex environments have lots of consequences. Implementing either of the IT Director's proposal scenarios, for example, would change the way hundreds of professionals sell, process, support, and make decisions about loans and other financial services. Practically speaking, can any human case-builder—with limited time and finite resources— expect to deal properly with hundreds or thousands of potential impacts for the case? The cost model and benefits rationale make it possible to answer "yes."

Both of these tools deal with the universe of business impacts. By *business impact*, we mean the important business consequences that follow from scenario assumptions and the specific action or conditions that the scenario represents (for example, "small scale implementation," "large scale implementation," or "business as usual."). Table 2.4 (next page) is one way to organize the universe of potential business impacts. The cost model and benefits rationale, together, help identify all the business impacts for the business case out of this universe.

Table 2.4 first puts all possible business impacts into two categories: "Direct financial impacts," and "Contributions to business objectives." The first category includes all the impacts show up immediately or directly in financial terms—money flowing in or out. Not surprisingly, these impacts include changes in cost items ("Increased travel expenses") and changes to cash inflows ("Sales revenues increase"). It may be less obvious, however, how the second business impact category covers *everything else* that belongs in the business case. Besides direct impact on cash inflows or outflows, the only business impacts that have value for the company or organization are those that contribute to business objectives.

"Contributions to business objectives" includes business impacts that are first measured or seen by some tangible evidence *other* than a change in cash flow. For example:

- When we do something meant to increase market share (the business objective), the first evidence that we are succeeding may be a change in the numbers of customers, sales transactions, or product units sold.
- If we redesign the engineering process so as to shorten new product development time (the business objective), the impact is measured first in terms of—no surprise—product development time.

Of course these impacts ultimately have financial consequences which we want valued as estimated cash inflows or outflows, but the

Business Impact	Example	Source
Direct Financial Impacts		
Cost Impacts		
• Cost increases	Increased travel expenses	
• Continuing costs	Staff salaries continue	
• Cost savings.	Lower equipment rental fees	Cost Model
• Avoided costs.	Additional hiring avoided	
Income Impacts		
• Income / inflows increase	Sales revenues increase	
• Income / inflows decrease.	External funding source stops	
Contributions to Business Objectives		
Contribution to:		
• Sales / marketing objectives	Increase market share	
• Financial objectives	Improve earnings per share	
• Operational objectives.	Shorten product development time	Benefits Rationale
• Image objectives.	Win award for service excellence	
• Internal objectives.	Improve employee morale	
• Product / service objectives	Improve product reliability	
• Other business objectives.	Establish strategic alliance	

Table 2.4 One way to list the full range of impacts that belong in a business case.

important point is that we first know the impact has occurred by some tangible evidence other than cash flow.

"Contributions to business objectives," by the way, can be negative as well as positive. Management actions can, for instance, hurt the company image, lower employee morale, or lengthen new product development time.

◙ We first know the impact has occurred by some tangible evidence other than cash flow.

With the universe of potential business impacts organized this way, we can now introduce the tools for finding specific impacts for the business case scenarios. Most people know that a business case typically includes "benefits" and "costs." However, these terms are often understood loosely as synonyms for "good things" and "bad things," and when it is time to build the business case, however, many people have trouble knowing exactly what is meant by "costs" or "benefits" in practical terms.

Direct Financial Impacts: Costs and The Cost Model

Consider first the *cost* impacts we need to identify and value for each scenario. Table 2.4 lists cost impacts as direct financial impacts, meaning that we can value these impacts rather directly in financial terms. Strictly speaking, "cost" for the business case means "cost item," not necessarily "bad thing." Cost items are the names of things the company spends money on, for goods, services, and resources of all kinds. Cost items appear in budgets and spending plans. They include expenses for continuing or short term expenses (salaries or office supplies, for instance), and the purchase of assets that go on the balance sheet.

◙ Cost items are the names of things the company spends money on, for resources of all kinds and for acquisition of assets.

In the business case, cost items are identified through the cost model and their impacts are summarized on the cash flow statement. A single cost item always begins as a cash outflow, that is, money that is spent. As table 2.4 suggests, however, we may compare cost items from different scenarios and find that an item has a lower cost in one scenario than it does in the other. A proposal scenario may have Year-1 salary costs of $250,000, while a business as usual scenario may have Year-1 salary costs of $350,000. There is a $100,000 cost savings in the proposal, relative to the business as usual. So, depending on how we compare scenarios, a cost item may result in a net cost increase, or as a continuing cost (same value in all scenarios), or as a cost savings (or avoided cost). In later chapters we take up the differences between these kinds of cost impacts. Now, from a 3,000 foot vantage point, we simply note that in building case scenarios, we determine first *which* cost items go into the case and then, later, how they behave over the analysis period. The cost model's first job is simply to help identify cost items that belong in the case. The cost model also helps us decide which items to exclude from the case.

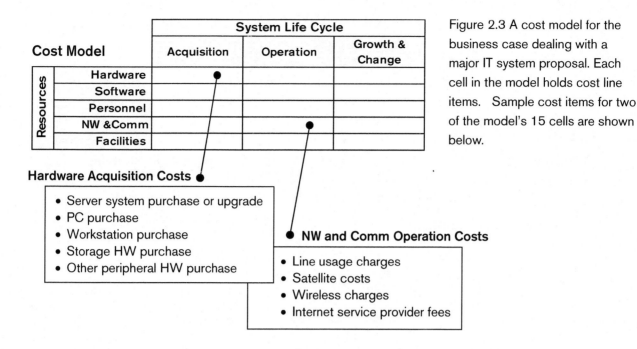

Figure 2.3 A cost model for the business case dealing with a major IT system proposal. Each cell in the model holds cost line items. Sample cost items for two of the model's 15 cells are shown below.

□ The cost model is really just an organized list. It groups together cost items that change together, which need to be planned and managed together.

The matrix at the top of Figure 2.3 is a cost model that works well for many IT-related business case studies. This model in fact was a central part of the IT Director's successful case mentioned earlier. The white cells are filled with individual cost items (sample cost items for two of the cells are shown). The Director had proposed system and network enhancements that were meant to increase staff productivity and effectiveness. This cost model includes every *cost* impact item that follows from that proposal.

The cost model is really just an organized list: potential cost items are organized into cells, rows, and columns. Each cell holds a group of cost items that change together, which need to be planned and managed together—usually because they have common cost drivers. The upper left cell, for instance, holds all "Hardware Acquisition Costs," (a call out shows what some of these cost items might be). Each of the fifteen cells in fact can have a long list of cost items.

Notice also that this cost universe is divided in two ways. The horizontal dimension groups cost items by "System Life Cycle" categories (Acquisition, Operation, and Growth and Change categories). Every IT cost item in the case fits into one of these categories. The scheme makes sense, because acquisition costs are planned and managed differently from continuing operational costs, which are planned and managed differently from growth and change costs.

The *vertical* dimension divides all costs into five different "IT Resource" categories (Hardware, Software, Personnel, Networking and Communications, and "Other" costs). This scheme also makes sense, because each resource category is planned and managed differently from the others.

Organizing cost items by categories in this way creates a surprisingly powerful tool for of identifying, analyzing, and communicating the "cost" side of the business case. Recall the problems with the "double-list" case from Chapter 1. Cost items were presented in one *unorganized* list. There was no way to tell from the list whether or not every relevant cost was included. And, the unorganized cost list gives no assurance that different case scenarios are compared fairly. With a cost model, however, case builders and case recipients have a simple, visual "rule" that shows which items belong in the case. If a cost item does not fit in one of the cells, the item does not belong in the case. When there are two or more scenarios in the case, we ensure comparability of scenarios by applying the same cost model to each scenario.

Finally, once we have the actual cost figures for each line item, the cost model becomes an analytic tool in its own right. Total costs for the items in each cell show clearly where money is being spent or saved. If we bring row and column totals into the picture, we can evaluate cost impacts by life cycle stages (column totals) or by resource categories (row totals). This gives management a unique picture of spending patterns that may not be quite so clear in the cash flow statement.

In summary, what is the cost model good for? The cost model:

- Serves as the definitive "authority" on which cost line items belong in the case and which do not
- Helps case builders identify every relevant cost item
- Assures case readers that every relevant item is included and that irrelevant items are excluded
- Ensures that different scenarios in the case are comparable with respect to cost coverage
- Provides management with an effective tool for cost planning and controlling costs

Different case subjects, of course, call for different kinds of cost models. The IT example in Figure 2.4 would not be suitable for business case analysis of a product life cycle decision, a program to improve the quality of patient care, or almost anything else other than an IT systems decision. Chapter 4 addresses the issue of making the cost model fit your subject and purpose.

Benefits Come From Business Objectives

There is more to business life than costs, of course. Business case scenarios need to capture impacts on *Income* (under "Direct Finan-

◙ The cost model is a simple, visual "rule" that shows which items belong in the case.

◙ When there are two or more scenarios in the case, we ensure comparability of scenarios by applying the same cost model to each.

cial Impacts" in Table 2.4), and they need to capture benefits that fall under the category *Contributions to Business Objectives.* While still at 3,000 feet, we view all these non-cost impacts simply as "benefits."

A good business case begins and ends with business objectives. Objectives provide motives for considering an action, and objectives are the basis for recommending action based on the analysis. Most important, objectives are the basis for bringing benefits into the case. You can take it as a matter of business case doctrine that business impacts are *benefits,* only if they contribute to business objectives.

Most companies or organizations in fact have many objectives. Some are explicitly written, others are implied but understood. When the case builder sets out to find all the business objectives that may be targets for the business case subject, the list may turn out to be surprisingly long. Here, for instance, are just a few of the kinds of objectives that may come within the business case scope:

▣ Business impacts are benefits only if they contribute to business objectives.

- Sales and Marketing Objectives
  - To increase sales revenues
  - To improve market share
- Financial/Business Performance Objectives
  - To increase cash flow, margins, or profits
  - To improve earnings per share
- Operational/Functional Objectives
  - To shorten new product development time
  - To increase order-processing capacity
- Product/Service Objectives
  - To improve customer satisfaction
  - To update the product line
- Image Enhancement Objectives
  - To be recognized as a provider of leading-edge technology
  - To be known as leader in environmental protection
- Internal Objectives
  - To improve employee morale
  - To provide a challenging career path for employees
- Other Business Objectives
  - To establish strategic alliances
  - To become a "total solution" supplier

When a proposed action contributes to such objectives, the impact might be recognized and measured directly in financial terms (increased sales) or it may be recognized and measured in some other terms (tangible evidence of improved customer satisfaction, for instance might appear as fewer complaints, or more repeat business, or even the results of customer satisfaction surveys). In order to bring any such impacts into the business case as benefits, however, the case builder develops a *benefits rationale* that establishes their validity and provides a basis for assigning financial value to them.

Suppose, for instance, that the bank's IT director believes that proposed system upgrades will help loan officers complete loan application processing in three days instead of the current average ten days. This impact (shorter loan processing time) might actually contribute to several business objectives, including lower operating costs, fewer bad loan decisions, and improved customer satisfaction. All of these contributions might belong in the business case, but to illustrate, consider just the benefit for the business case that has to do with "improved customer satisfaction." The rationale for such benefits can be built simply by answering a series of questions like these:

▣ The benefits rationale establishes the validity of benefits and provides a basis for assigning financial value to them.

- What are the business objectives for this company or organization?
  E.g., Improved Customer Satisfaction

- Can the proposed action (business case subject) contribute to the objective?
  Proceed only if "yes." At this point, we may not have worked out the cause and effect chain of events that lead from action to tangible contribution. We only ask if it seems reasonable that the action might contribute to the objective.

- Is this business objective a targeted objective for the company? If "no," is it still an important objective?
  Proceed only if "yes" to one of the above. The purpose of this step is to make sure the business objective is truly recognized as important in the company.

- What is the tangible evidence for reaching this objective?
  Progress toward the objective "improved customer satisfaction," can be reasonably inferred from tangible measures such as:
  ○ Improved repeat business rates
  ○ Fewer complaints, lower customer service costs
  ○ More referral business
  ○ Customer satisfaction survey scores

- What is the targeted level for the objective (in terms of the tangible measure above)?
  E.g., Improve repeat business rate by 100%, or
  Reduce the number of complaints per month by 50%

- Does reaching the target have value for the company?
  Proceed only if "yes."

- What is the overall value of reaching the target? (in $, £, €, ¥, or some other monetary unit)

The value of reaching the target may be estimated as:
- ° Percentage improvement in sales revenues/margins/profits
- ° Percentage reduction in current cost of sales/cost of service
- ° The cost of achieving the same end by another means
- ° Simply the value senior management would agree to "pay" to achieve the target
- ° The known cost of not reaching the target
- ° An arbitrarily assigned value

⊡ The legitimacy of most benefits for the business case has to be established with a benefits rationale.

- • What percentage of the overall value (for reaching the objective) should be credited to this action?
  - ° Use larger percentage if the action is a requirement for reaching the objective
  - ° Use smaller percentage if the action is one of many contributors.

Chapter 4 and 5 cover the benefits rationale and its use more fully. What is important to remember, now, is that the legitimacy of most benefits for the business case has to be established with such a rationale. Also, we note that it is important to establish and agree on the benefits rationale with your case audience or readers as early as possible in the case building process, well before the final case report is delivered. This is the best possible way to avoid later disagreements about so-called "soft benefits."

The Financial Model Part I: the Cash Flow Statement

It is time to see where scenario design, the cost model, and the benefits rationale are heading: to the financial model. For some people, the financial model *is* the business case. This is where the cost and benefit impacts come together with the time line and with numbers that represent real money.

Begin with the best most visible part of the financial model: the *cash flow statement*. What most people say "Show me the numbers!" this is what they want to see. The financial data in the case are expressed as cash inflows and cash outflows in a statement like the one shown schematically in Figure 2.4 on the next page.

⊡ The financial data in a business case are expressed as cash inflows and cash outflows, brought together in a cash flow statement.

Cash flow by the way, is not the same thing as income. *Cash flow* always refers to a real inflow or outflow of money. *Income* is an accounting convention that does not always represent real money coming in or going out. Business case analysis is *cash flow* analysis.

Near the center of Figure 2.4 is a schematic diagram showing the overall structure of a cash flow statement. Individual cost and benefit line items appear in the three top sections: "Benefits" (usually inflows), "Expenses" (usually outflows), and "Assets" (usually outflows). A "Summary" section at the bottom shows the net flow for each time segment.

EXPENSES	Year 1	Year 2	Year 3	Year 4	Year 5	Total
Cash inflows (outflows)						
$ in 1,000s						
Hardware maintenance expenses	(120.5)	(120.3)	(150.7)	(150.7)	(150.7)	(692.9)
Software maintenance expenses	(16.7)	(16.7)	(16.7)	(16.7)	(16.7)	(83.5)
End user applications - expensed	(23.0)	(23.7)	(24.4)	(25.1)	0.0	(96.2)
System staffing - operations	(320.0)	(356.2)	(396.5)	(441.3)	(491.2)	(2,005.1)
System staffing - programming	(348.0)	(412.2)	(496.7)	(588.3)	(716.5)	(2,561.7)
Electrical power	(6.5)	(6.5)	(6.7)	(6.7)	(7.0)	(33.4)
Insurance premiums	(4.2)	(4.3)	(4.5)	(4.6)	(4.7)	(22.3)
Security costs	0.0	(268.2)	(276.3)	(260.4)	(293.1)	(1,098.0)
Total expense item impacts	(838.9)	(1,208.1)	(1,372.4)	(1,493.8)	(1,679.9)	**(6,593.1)**

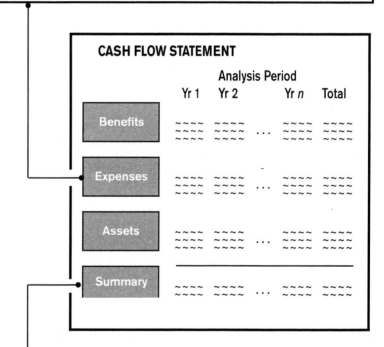

Figure 2.4 The cash flow statement (right) holds the financial impacts expected under one or more case scenarios. It is the place most people look to see overall case results, and it source of financial metrics such as net present value or internal rate of return. The cash flow statement will normally have the four major sections shown in the schematic version at right.

SUMMARY	Year 1	Year 2	Year 3	Year 4	Year 5	Total
Cash inflows (outflows)						
$ in 1,000s						
Benefit impacts	1,811.5	1,753.1	2,007.1	2,246.7	2,493.1	10,311.5
Expense item impacts	(838.9)	(1,208.1)	(1,372.4)	(1,493.8)	(1,679.9)	(6,593.1)
Net operating inflow(outflow)	972.6	545.0	634.7	752.9	813.2	3,718.4
Tax savings (tax) on operating income	(330.7)	(185.3)	(215.8)	(256.0)	(276.5)	(1,264.2)
Asset purchases	(712.3)	(47.6)	(175.6)	(84.4)	(28.2)	(1,048.1)
Tax savings from depreciation expense	48.4	73.3	67.4	64.0	60.4	313.5
NET CASH FLOW	**(22.0)**	**385.4**	**310.7**	**476.5**	**568.9**	**1,719.5**
Cumulative net cash flow	(22.0)	363.4	674.1	1,150.6	1,719.5	
Cash flow discounted at 9.0%	(20.2)	324.4	239.9	476.5	568.9	1,589.5
Cash flow discounted at 15.0%	(19.1)	291.4	204.3	272.5	282.8	1,031.9

▣ The cash flow statement may represent a single scenario, or it may represent the incremental differences between two scenarios.

▣ Line items in the cash flow statement come from the cost model and from the benefits rationale.

Statements like this are essentially just tables: rows hold line items and their cash flow data, while columns represent time segments (usually years, quarters, or months). Of course the natural medium for building a cash flow statement is a spreadsheet, unless you have financial software that builds it for you.

Whose costs and benefits does the cash flow statement represent? What exactly does it picture? Cash flow statements sometimes represent a single scenario. This one might show, for example, what to expect if an IT infrastructure upgrade is implemented. Another statement like it might show what happens under a business as usual scenario (no upgrade). The decision to upgrade or not upgrade might be based on a comparison of those two cash flow statements.

Other times, a single cash flow statement represents the differences between two scenarios, or incremental changes that would come under a proposal. More on that subject is coming Chapter 4 (when to use incremental data and when not to). For now it is important simply to see that cash flow statements like this one are the source of the case's main financial results, or the basis for developing financial metrics.

The grand total (bottom right) is a significant financial metric in its own right. It says that the proposed action should result in a net gain of $1,719,500 over 5 years. Financial managers would also want to see the results expressed on a discounted cash flow basis. The example summary includes two sets of discounting calculations as well. Other case results come directly from cash flow streams on this statement. Other financial metrics like "internal rate of return" or "payback period" (not shown here) would be based on these summary numbers.

Where does the all-important cash flow statement come from? The cost model and benefits rationale, already described, contribute line items to the cash flow statement. Think of the cost model and benefits model as the parents of the cash flow statement. Some of their line items go into the cash flow "Benefits" section, while others go into the "Expenses" or "Assets" sections. However, the cash flow statement has other "ancestors" as well. The cost and benefit estimates that go with each line item are influenced or controlled by other factors, including assumptions made during case design (for example, assumptions about prices, wage levels, inflation, business growth, and so on).

In the business case, the cash flow statement is indeed the high point of the financial analysis—but it is not the end point. The statement shows the most likely results under one or more scenarios, certainly the first item of interest for case readers. Everyone knows, however, that the real outcomes will not be *exactly* as shown here. The grand total, for instance, may be less, it may be more, but almost certainly it will be something different from the number sitting on the cash flow statement today. As a result, business case builders have to be ready to deal with the issues of uncertainty and risks.

The Financial Model Part II: The Dynamic Approach

Financial predictions are uncertain. As soon as the cash flow statement appears, questions arise such as:

- How likely are other results? What are the chances that we only see half the gain predicted here?
- What can management do to maximize results?
- What are the main risks to achieving the projected gain?

And so on. To answer such questions, you have to look beyond the cash flow statement itself, back to the assumptions and models underlying the case. Ideally, you would like to answer such questions easily and with confidence. Your ability to do so will depend to a large degree on how the cash flow statement is implemented. The recommended approach is to implement your cash flow statement as part of a larger financial model—a model that is truly dynamic. This section simply explains what that means (remember, this is still a 3,000 foot overview). Detailed practical guidance comes later.

We are talking about the source of the actual numbers, the cost and benefit cash flow estimates that go with each line item. For each line item (like "System staffing - operations" in Figure 2.4) there is a cash flow figure for each time segment of the analysis period. (Some of these can of course be zero). Consider the "Year 3" figure for that item in the example. The author estimates a cash *outflow* (indicated by the parenthesis) of $396,500. Where did that come from?

The number comes from *assumptions*. Strictly speaking, in fact, every data point in the business case comes from assumptions. In order to produce a "Year 3" cash flow estimate, the author had to make concrete assumptions about such things as:

- The number of people (or full-time equivalents) required
- The job levels or titles of each person
- The average salary for each job level, today
- The average overhead or burden rate per staff member
- Average salary increases for the next five years
- Average inflation rate for the next five years
- Average training cost per staff member per year

Depending on the situation, the list of assumptions behind a single cash flow estimate could go on and on. It might also bring in hiring costs, relocation costs, travel expenses, and other things not covered by "overhead." There might be expected changes in staff-

> ▣ As soon as the cash flow statement appears, questions will arise…to answer, you have to look back to the assumptions and models underlying the case.

> ▣ Every data point in the case comes from assumptions.

ing levels coming in the future. In any case, these assumptions are estimates in their own right, each involving more or less uncertainty. Nevertheless, in order to reach a concrete expense item estimate for Year 3, each assumption has to be expressed in concrete terms. Even though no one knows exactly what the average salary increase will be two years from now, some figure has to be used. All the uncertainty behind all the assumptions contributes to the uncertainty behind the single cash flow estimate.

In order to address questions about risks and uncertainty—the likelihood of different business case results—you need some practical way to look into the way that assumptions control overall results. One common way to do this is to create "best-case/worst-case" scenarios. A worst case scenario is created, based on very pessimistic (but still realistic) estimates for all the assumptions. A best case scenario is built from optimistic assumptions. The idea, presumably, is that reality will fall somewhere between the two extremes. That approach is sometimes acceptable for simple situations. When the case is complex, it is entirely too imprecise to be useful.

The better vehicle for answering questions about risk and uncertainty in a useful way is the dynamic financial model. The most visible part of this model is still the cash flow statement, but the difference between static and dynamic models has to do with the way the cash flow estimates are created for the statement. In the static approach, we estimate the numbers somewhere outside the cash flow spreadsheet, and then insert the number itself as a data point. In the dynamic approach, we insert a formula into the spreadsheet instead of a cash flow data point. The spreadsheet formula calculates the cash flow estimate, based on other numbers and other formulas somewhere else in the spreadsheet system. Those other numbers and formulas represent assumptions.

Figure 2.5 (next page) illustrates the dynamic principle. The financial model includes a cash flow statement, but also a Table of Assumptions, and many formulas and background calculations. All of these parts belong to a single spreadsheet system (i.e., cells in one part of the model can be linked to cells in other parts of the model). The model is *dynamic* if the data points in the cash flow statement are controlled by assumptions. On the cash flow statement here, for instance the user did not enter 312,000 directly into the staffing cost Year 1 cell. That cell instead contains a formula (shown below as it would appear in a Microsoft Excel spreadsheet). In a larger cash flow statement, dozens or hundreds of other data points could also be derived from a few assumptions.

Now, if assumptions change (say, the author decides that 8 people are called for instead of 6, and the overhead rate turns out to be 35.0% instead of 30.0%), all that has to change are two figures in the

> ▣ In order to reach a concrete expense item estimate...each assumption has to be expressed in concrete terms.

> ▣ In a dynamic model, we insert a formula into the spreadsheet instead of a cash flow data point.

Figure 2.5 The principle underlying the dynamic financial model. The model is implemented in a single spreadsheet system. It includes the cash flow statement, a table of assumptions, and formulas. Each "Value" cell in the table of assumptions has a name that can be used by the spreadsheet formulas. Cash flow estimates (like Year 1 Staffing costs) are produced by formulas, not by direct entry from the user. When an assumption is changed, all data points that depend on the assumption change.

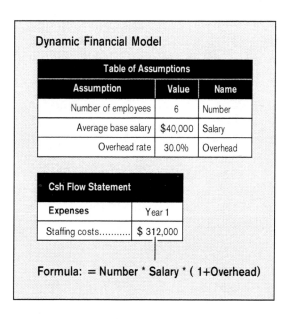

Dynamic Financial Model

Table of Assumptions		
Assumption	Value	Name
Number of employees	6	Number
Average base salary	$40,000	Salary
Overhead rate	30.0%	Overhead

Csh Flow Statement	
Expenses	Year 1
Staffing costs...........	$ 312,000

Formula: = Number * Salary * (1+Overhead)

☑ A dynamic model is a requirement for any serious form of sensitivity, risk, and contingency analysis.

table of assumptions. The staffing cost figure changes automatically to $432,000. All other data in the cash flow statement that depend on the assumption also update automatically.

Assumptions can be changed throughout the case building project as new information develops. Later, when the model serves as a management and control tool, assumptions need continuous updating. A dynamic model obviously lets the case builder deal with changing assumptions more easily than a static model. A cash flow statement built on live links and formulas is more than a simple convenience, however. A dynamic model is a requirement for any serious form of sensitivity, risk, and contingency analysis.

Uncertainties: The Devil is in the Assumptions

In the business case report, I recommend putting the main predictions in a major section of their own called something like "Business Impacts" (Section C in Tables 2.1 and 2.2). That section includes the cash flow statement, financial metrics derived from it, and any important non financial impacts. In that section, the numbers "speak for themselves." It is roughly comparable to the "Results" section in a scientific report.

Something else is required, however, in order to fully understand those results and to put them to good practical use. Everyone needs to understand what controls the results and what else may happen. Those issues are best addressed in another major section, "Sensitivity, Risks, and Contingencies." There are more numbers here, but also more analysis and the case builder's interpretations.

Sensitivity Analysis: What Happens if Assumptions Change?

Sensitivity analysis asks the question "What happens to predicted results if the assumptions change? It also asks "Which assumptions have a strong influence on results? Which assumptions are relatively unimportant? Providing answers to these questions adds substantially to the credibility and practical value of case results.

Remember that the financial model and its cash flow statement may incorporate some costs and benefits whose values are known with near certainty. However, the final results will probably also depend on some assumptions that are less certain. The previous section mentions a few typical assumptions (average salary level and average inflation rate for example), but in most business cases there will be dozens, if not hundreds of individual assumptions.

Questions about assumptions need to be addressed on an assumption-by-assumption basis, because some assumptions may impact results profoundly, while others may change greatly with little effect on results. Sensitivity analysis examines how the financial model's primary outputs change when certain input assumptions change.

The theory, methods, and subtleties of sensitivity analysis are addressed more fully in Chapter 6. For now—from a 3,000 foot vantage point—it is enough to know that there are different approaches to examining sensitivity.

The fast, easy way is to ask questions about sensitivity is to hold all assumptions constant except one, change that assumption to its lowest reasonable value, see what happens to predicted results and

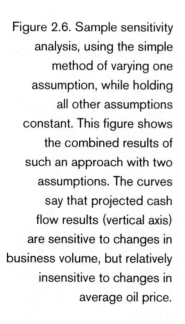

Sensitivity analysis asks: "What happens to predicted results if the assumptions change?

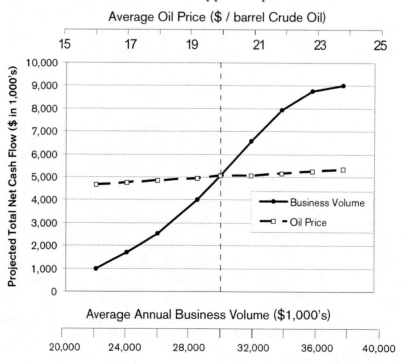

Figure 2.6. Sample sensitivity analysis, using the simple method of varying one assumption, while holding all other assumptions constant. This figure shows the combined results of such an approach with two assumptions. The curves say that projected cash flow results (vertical axis) are sensitive to changes in business volume, but relatively insensitive to changes in average oil price.

then change the assumption to other higher values, across a reasonable range, all the while watching how business case results respond.

Figure 2.6 shows what can come out of that approach. Suppose our model has only two assumptions: "average business volume per year" and "oil prices." The outcome that we watch is "net cash flow."

Here, to cover the entire range of reasonable possibilities, nine different values for each assumption are plugged into the table of assumptions in the dynamic model. This covers the horizontal axis of Figure 2.6 (The horizontal axis is of course scaled differently for each assumption). For each new assumption value, we plot the resulting net cash flow figure (the vertical axis). For this example, the cash flow results are clearly more sensitive to "business volume" than to "oil prices." We infer this because the "business volume" curve covers a wider range on the vertical axis. That is a signal to case developers and case readers that the assumptions about forthcoming business volume deserve especially thorough research.

Simple sensitivity analysis serves several purposes. It gives a rough but immediate guide to case builders or critics who may have reservations about some of the assumptions. Those who disagree with your assumptions can insert their own preferred value for an assumption and see immediately how that affects results. As a case builder you will naturally exercise your model this way often, to test the validity of the dynamic model itself (in a rough way), and to help make arbitrary judgments when estimating assumptions.

This fast and easy approach to sensitivity analysis, has some limitations, however. In the real world many assumptions are going to change together. In statistical terms, assumptions are often correlated. Prices, salaries, inflation, sales revenues, and other factors that have to be assumed for your case may go up or down, more or less together, as the economy becomes stronger or weaker. A test situation where only one assumption changes at a time (the fast and easy approach, described above) can be quite misleading. As a result, all but the simplest of business cases really require a more rigorous, statistically proper sensitivity analysis. Chapter 5 of this *Guide* shows how this is done. What is involved, essentially, is another exercise in applied statistics. A more rigorous sensitivity analysis uses correlation coefficients to describe the way that case results change when individual assumptions change. Fortunately, good sensitivity analysis is not difficult with some inexpensive software available today. It is not difficult, that is, if you have a dynamic financial model.

▣ Good sensitivity analysis is not difficult if you have a good dynamic financial model.

Risk Analysis: How Likely are Other Results?

Assumptions play a key role in answering other questions about the certainty of predicted results. From the cash flow statement, the case author derives a "most likely" estimate of net cash flow and other financial metrics, such as net present value or internal rate of return. Questions naturally follow, such as: How likely are *other* results? What are the chances that we realize, say, only 50% of what is predicted? What are the chances that we do much better? Risk analysis addresses such questions.

There are simple ways and complex ways to address "risk" in the business case, as well, but the better methods all have this in common: they keep individual risks in view. More precisely, good risk analysis relies on understanding the individual assumptions and how each contributes to overall results.

This *Guide* covers risk analysis in Chapter 6, along with sensitivity analysis. However, a brief glimpse now of what is coming should be helpful. For risk analysis, this Guide focuses on Monte Carlo simulation. This technique shows how "bottom line" results (like net cash flow) change when all of the important input factors (or assumptions) change at once.

Very briefly, the Monte Carlo approach works with a dynamic financial model, in which cash flow data depend on underlying assumptions. The process begins by identifying the most important assumptions—the assumptions that have the most control over results. (That is what we did in sensitivity analysis). For each important assumption, we describe the range of possible values for the assumption. In statistical terms, we describe a probability density function for each input assumption (statistical terms are unavoidable, but fortunately, the statistics involved should be within reach of anyone who passed an elementary statistics course in secondary school or university).

Based on this information, the Monte Carlo software program essentially "runs the future" (tries out combinations of assumptions) a few thousand times. Monte Carlo's main output is a probability curve based on thousands of such trials, like Figure 2.7 (next page). From this we can make statements like these: "We have an 80% chance of realizing a net gain of at least $1 million, we have a 50% chance of gaining $5 million, and we have a 30% chance of gaining at least $8 million."

This kind of information is more useful to management than a single "best estimate." If a gain of $1 million is as a "good" result, and there is an 80% chance of achieving it, the decision to go forward with the proposal may be easy. However, if the action absolutely must return $5 million or more, than a 50% risk may be unacceptable. It is possible to develop this kind of information about overall results only when you know something about the individual risk factors (assumptions) and analyze their collective behavior.

Figure 2.7 Sample results from Monte Carlo simulation with the financial model. The curve shows the probability that cash flow results will total at least to the level indicated on the vertical axis.

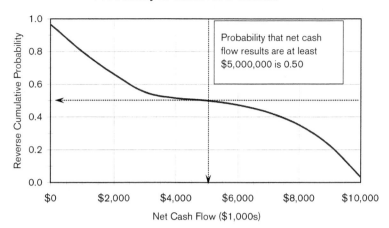

Probability of Cash Flow Results

Probability that net cash flow results are at least $5,000,000 is 0.50

Contingencies: What Must Happen?

Sensitivity and risk analysis show what the results depend on. Just as important, they also show what they do not depend on. Your case readers or audience will be most interested in the contingencies—what must happen in order for the predicted results to appear.

To turn this information into practical guidance for management, I recommend classifying your case assumptions as shown in Figure 2.8. Based on your sensitivity analysis, you first distinguish between important assumptions (those that have significant impact on results) and those that are unimportant (those that have little impact on results). Then divide the important assumptions into two groups:

• Assumptions about factors that *cannot* be managed or controlled
• Assumptions about factors that *can* be managed or controlled

This classification becomes important when you write the final section of the report, the "Conclusions and Recommendations." The important assumptions about factors beyond your control show what must be watched carefully. These might include assumptions about such things as:

Figure 2.8 Sensitivity and risk analysis allow the case builder to divide assumptions into groups shown in the figure. Management attention should be directed to the two kinds of "Important" assumptions.

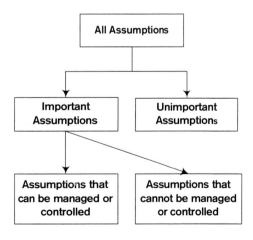

43

- Rate of inflation
- Actions of competitors
- Prices of commodities or raw materials
- Foreign currency exchange rates
- Government regulation
- Natural disasters

Unexpected changes in any of these signal that the case predictions need to be modified and the risk analysis should be reevaluated.

It is even more important for management to understand the role of assumptions about factors that can be managed or controlled, at least to some degree. This list might include such things as:

- Software development time
- Employee skill levels
- Recruitment and hiring of key individuals
- Discounts and pricing policies
- Employee pay raises

The list of manageable contingencies can be quite long when the business case crosses functional or organizational boundaries.

▣ The author has an obligation to show where responsibility lies for making the predicted results appear.

Putting the spotlight on these items sends a message that case results depend on many people meeting specific commitments. If the case assumes certain employee skill levels, by a certain time, for instance, then the training manager or others responsible have their assignments clearly spelled out. If the case assumes that pay raises will be held to a certain level, then management is on notice that raises beyond that level call for a change in business case predictions. In brief, the case author has an obligation to show where responsibility lies for making the predicted results appear.

Non Financial Benefits Belong in the Case

At the beginning of this chapter, I described the experience of an IT Director at a large commercial bank who had an urgent need to build a credible business case. The case was meant to support an IT proposal that had already been turned down twice. I also mentioned that the proposal was approved on the third try by the same Executive Committee that had said "no" to the earlier versions. Success finally came, largely from attending to the points highlighted in this chapter, essentially proper case design and a case building process that effectively communicated case design as well as results. What I have not mentioned yet is the role of non financial benefits in "selling" the case. The Executive Committee indeed accepted the financial predictions, but what tipped the scale in the right direction, I believe, was a solid demonstration that some large non financial benefits were also real and also important. Before coming down from 3,000 feet, we will take a brief look at what this involved.

By non financial benefits, I mean positive business impacts that cannot be evaluated immediately in cash flow terms. Such impacts often appear when a proposal contributes to strategic business objectives, such as improved corporate image, customer satisfaction, or employee morale. These may represent major corporate objectives, and reaching them should ultimately translate into lower costs and increased revenues. Nevertheless, you and your audience simply may not be ready to accept value estimates for them with confidence. These non financial benefits will not enter the financial model, cash flow results, or financial metrics, but they may still deserve consideration in the proposal. What can or should you say about them?

When non financial results are real and large enough to matter, and when they clearly impact a business objective, I recommend taking the following three steps for each such impact in your case:

1. Be sure the expected impact is recorded.

Identify the impact immediately after the cash flow statement and its analysis in the "Business Impacts" section, in the Executive Summary, and in Conclusions and Recommendations.

2. Make the impact tangible

Even if the impact is not valued in financial terms, describe its effects in ways that can be observed and verified. You may expect a real "improvement in staff professionalism," for instance, but not be able to evaluate the value of that in monetary terms. You can, however, describe the likely effects of that benefit in other observable terms, such as lower staff turnover, easier recruiting, less absenteeism, and so on.

3. Compare the impact directly to the financial impacts of the case, but in non financial terms.

Non financial benefits belong to the area that some people call "soft benefits," and these benefits need to be handled firmly and properly. You cannot assume that case recipients will automatically know about the benefit unless you tell them (Step 1). You cannot expect them to accept its reality unless you show them concretely how it shows up (Step 2). And, you need some way to say "This benefit is as important as the financial benefits." (Step 3). Chapter 6 takes on these topics in more detail, but for now, we will look briefly at the way the bank's IT Director handled the comparison of financial and non financial benefits.

There were in fact five major benefits we expected from implementing the Director's proposal:

Non financial benefits do not enter the financial analysis, but they may still deserve consideration.

- Increased revenues.

  From increased sales productivity and more success selling the bank's higher-priced services.

- Increased customer satisfaction.

  From decreased loan processing time and better support of customer service staff.

- An enhanced corporate image.

  By promoting the improved customer service, and by "repackaging" the bank's product line.

- A more professional work environment.

  By enabling professionals to give more attention to the creative aspects of their jobs.

- Cost savings.

  By reducing a range of information-gathering communications costs, by avoided hiring of new staff, and by reducing losses from bad loans.

Of these five benefits, only two actually made it into the financial model and cash flow statement. Recall that we had cross-functional, cross-organizational input from a high-level core team. On the team was an outspoken Senior Vice President with a low tolerance for "soft benefits." This group helped create a very solid case for the cash flow estimates of increased revenues and cost savings. Those were the two financial benefits in the case. The value of that core team contribution cannot be overstated. But the same group could not accept cash flow estimates for increased customer satisfaction, an enhanced corporate image, or a more professional work environment. They agreed these benefits were likely and they agreed the benefits were important. But they could not agree on their monetary worth.

In order to show how important these benefits were without using cash flow numbers, we focused again on the bank's business objectives. The complete list of objectives ran to some twenty four different entries, but highest on the list were those that had to do with competition. This bank competes intensely with several other banks for market share. Not surprisingly, some of the highest priority objectives were those that set goals for corporate image, winning the competitor's customers, reaching first time customers, and improving repeat business. Now, the important questions became these: Do the non financial benefits contribute substantially to important business objectives? How do the financial and non financial benefits compare to each other in this respect?

The core team debated and then answered the questions above, using a rating system instead of cash flow numbers (the technique is called "score-and-weight" and it is explained in Chapter 6). Figure 2.9

▣ Do non financial benefits contribute substantially to important business objectives?

summarizes the core team consensus results. There is a bar for each of the five benefits. The horizontal axis represents the relative importance of the benefit's contribution to all business objectives.

Surprisingly, the two top ratings went to non financial benefits: "Improved customer satisfaction" and "Improved corporate image," while the two benefits that had been quantified in cash flow terms (increased revenues and cost control) finished third and fifth out of the five benefits considered. Such results do not say how many dollars, euro, or yen "improved customer satisfaction" is worth, but they do say that the impact on customer satisfaction contributes more to all the bank's business objectives—in the view of this core team—than increased revenues (which have been estimated in financial terms).

Next steps

In order to establish the credibility of business case predictions, case recipients have to travel the same road covered by case developers. Chapter 2 was a 3,000 foot overview of that road and some of the major landmarks along the way. Now it is time to put on the walking shoes, and travel through the business case landscape at ground level. Put another away, Chapters 1 and 2 introduced the "what" and "why" of business case structure and content. The rest of this *Guide* addresses the practical details that explain the "how."

Consensus: Importance of Benefit

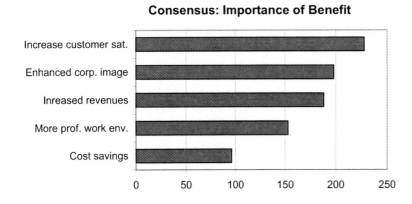

Figure 2.9 The core team consensus view of as described in the text. A score-and-weight rating method was used to evaluate the relative importance of benefits in contributing to overall corporate objectives. The chart includes financial and non financial benefits.

What's the Difference?

Cost/Benefit vs. ROI vs. Justification vs. TCO

You will hear business cases called by different names: cost/benefit analysis, return on investment (ROI), financial justification, and total cost of ownership (TCO). These are all terms for different kinds of cases. Each implies a slightly different approach to the general question: What are the consequences of an action or decision?

Whether developing your own case or evaluating someone else's, remember that none of these expressions has a single universally agreed definition.

The term **Cost/Benefit Analysis** is used in planning, decision making, program evaluation, proposal evaluation, and other activities, even though the term itself has no precise definition beyond the implication that both positive and negative impacts are going to be summarized and weighed against each other.

Return on Investment is used when deciding whether or not to invest in something, or make an acquisition. It is natural to ask how the expected returns compare to the required investment. ROI is not, however, a precisely defined method or calculation.

In financial circles ROI sometimes means "Return on Invested Capital," a measure of company performance: The company's total capital is divided into the company's income (before interest, taxes, or dividends are subtracted). Alternatively, ROI sometimes means "Return on Assets:" a company's income divided by the value of assets used to produce that income (for more on ROI, see Appendix B).

Most people, however, use ROI simply to mean the "Return" (incremental gain) from an action, divided by the cost of that action. This is "simple ROI." By that reckoning, an investment that costs $100 and pays back $150 after a short period of time has a 50% ROI.

ROI is an appealing concept because the meaning seems self-evident. Several factors complicate ROI calculation and interpretation, however, and many business cases do not attempt to present ROI as a quantitative result itself, but focus instead on financial metrics such as net cash flow, discounted cash flow, internal rate of return, or payback period, all of which *are* well defined concepts in finance.

One problem with simple ROI in a complex setting is the difficulty of finding the appropriate investment cost. This may call for arbitrary cost allocation judgments or the addition of "opportunity costs," for instance. The passage of time is also a problem. Investment costs typically come early, while returns may come years later. Thus, the time value of money (discounting) may have to enter the ROI equation. Sometimes it is especially difficult to match specific returns with specific costs.

In brief, the simple ROI concept is probably appropriate only when both the investment cost and the return occur in a short time period, are clearly tied to each other, and can be derived simply and unambiguously.

The term **financial justification** refers to the purpose of the case (why it is built or what is to be done with the results). The term does not prescribe specific methods. The basic idea is that an action is justified if it leads to better financial results than the alternatives. Or, sometimes those who ask for justification want assurance that an action or investment will "pay for itself."

Total cost of ownership usually means: the total cost of acquiring, installing, using, maintaining, changing, and getting rid of something across an extended period of time. TCO, in other words, is a life cycle cost estimate. It is often developed for computer systems, medical test equipment, and other expensive capital items.

TCO supports decision making when it is likely that all options come with about the same benefits and the only likely differences are on the cost side. TCO analysis also shows what an acquisition implies for future spending or budgetary planning. Note especially the following:

- TCO for most assets is more than purchase price, sometimes many times more. Five-year TCO for computing equipment, for example, can be three to ten times the original purchase price.
- Naming the TCO subject does not fix the boundaries of the analysis. You must still decide and communicate which costs belong in the analysis and why.
- TCO can be taken from the "cost" side of a broader cost/benefit analysis, but cost figures alone do not capture "benefits" except in a very limited way. If the TCO figures for different options are compared (perhaps a "business as usual" scenario and a "change" scenario), one may show cost savings relative to the other.

This *Guide* usually prefers the term *business case* to any of the four alternatives above. When you are asked for an ROI (or TCO summary, financial justification, or a cost/benefit analysis), it is prudent to respond with questions like these (expressed diplomatically, of course): "How is that to be calculated? "Which financial criteria are important to decision makers? Sometimes people who ask for these things assume they are precisely defined (but they are not). Sometimes case recipient and case author have different methods in mind. There is no reason to avoid the terms—just be sure that everyone involved agrees on what they mean.

In Summary

Building a successful business case requires an understanding of case design and effective management of the case-building process.

- Important case elements appear in the finished case report in about the same order they are approached in the case-building project. In a sense, the case author takes readers down the same road traveled by the case project team.
- Business impacts are business case benefits only if they contribute to business objectives.
- The case-building project manager can add credibility and accuracy by effective use of a core team. The core team:
  - Provides cross-functional, cross-organizational input to case design.
  - Spreads the sense of ownership for the case.
  - Communicates methods, rationale, and expectations.
  - Helps turn damaging criticism into constructive criticism.
- A good business case is organized around a time line extending across the analysis period.
  - The choice of analysis period is arbitrary.
  - Case results can depend heavily on the choice of analysis period.
  - Longer analysis periods are often preferable to shorter periods.
- Future business impacts are developed in the context of scenarios. A scenario illustrates the future in concrete detail. Most cases need at least two scenarios: one to represent a proposal or action, and a second to serve as a basis of comparison (a "business as usual" scenario).
- The cost model helps identify and organize all cost impacts in the case. These become line items in the cash flow statement. When the cash flow statement is completed, the cost model helps communicate what is included in the case and what is not. It also provides management with an effective cost management tool.
- The benefits rationale helps establish the legitimacy of benefits for the business case, and it provides a reasonable approach for estimating their values.
- The financial model contains the cash flow predictions that most people consider to be the heart of the case.
- Sensitivity and risk analysis of the financial model show how results are controlled (or not controlled) by different assumptions, and the likelihood that case results will differ from the predicted results. These analyses also show management which contingencies have to be managed in order to bring the expected outcome.
- It may not be possible to value all impacts in cash flow terms. These still belong in the case if they contribute to important business objectives.

Chapter 3

Case Design I:
The Introduction

This chapter begins the step-by-step walkthrough of the business case-building process. We start by recruiting a core team, gathering important background information, and then addressing the initial steps in case design.

The Road Ahead

WE ARE READY to cross the business case landscape again, this time at ground level, on foot. Some of the touring party left us at the last stop, by the way. For them, a conceptual overview of what belongs in a case, and why, was enough. Those of us still here, lacing up the walking shoes, really want to understand the "how" as well. If some of the technical detail ahead looks daunting, take heart: we've mastered the underlying principles already, and there will be rest stops along the way.

To keep things simple, I will use the term "case owner" from now on to mean the person responsible for managing the case-building project and for delivering a case report or presentation. Those who read the report, listen to the presentation, or make decisions based on its contents will be called "recipients."

Finally, one last word from your tour guide before we move on: pay attention to details! It is tempting to skip over seemingly minor items below like "Date" or "Disclaimer," in a rush to get to the more interesting points. In the long run, that can cost you more in lost credibility and impact than you might expect. Remember that the case is more than numbers, and even the small details contribute to quality of the finished structure.

First Things First

This chapter covers the first section in a case report, the Introduction. Figure 3.1 (page 55) identifies the case elements in this section, and this list will be our itinerary for today.

The Introduction, naturally, is the first section of the case report recipients see. Keep in mind that some of them in fact may not get beyond this section (there are people who read only Executive Summaries). For that reason alone, material here must represent the case in terms that are terse, clear, and accurate.

The case-building project team has to begin with these elements as well because the complete case design and all that follows depend very directly on the definition of subject, purpose, and choice of financial metrics for this section. These design items should be developed fully and carefully, and then reviewed and agreed by core team and case recipients as early as possible. You may continue to refine them through the project, but major changes late in the project may mean having to start over. Be sure the introductory items are solid and stable for all concerned before beginning "Methods and Assumptions" (The subject of Chapter 4).

Case owners typically start a business case project knowing roughly what the case is about and what it will be used for. They usually know something about the recipients, how much time there is to complete the case, and which people are available for the work. But how, exactly, should they get started?

Several tasks should start simultaneously, but completing a project plan for building the case is not one of them. At this point no one knows specifically which data belong in the case and which do not, or which assumptions need to be researched, and many other things. Remember that you must design the case before you can plan its construction in detail. In order to start moving toward that end, I do recommend starting several tasks immediately.

▣ The complete case design and all that follows depend very directly on the definition of subject, purpose, and choice of financial metrics.

Recruiting the Core Team

The core team was introduced in Chapter 2 as a review and advisory group that helps

- Provide cross functional, cross-organizational input.
- Spread the sense of case ownership.
- Communicate expectations and methods, broadly.
- Manage critics and criticism.

Review pp. 19–23 for more on how the team works in this way, along with some suggestions on recruiting and managing the team. Recruiting for the core team should start as soon as the case-building project is known. Once you have first-draft versions of the case design elements in this chapter, convening a core team meeting to review and refine them is advisable (See p. 71).

Gathering Background Information

Now is the time to start gathering documents, data, and other information that will be useful throughout the case-building project.

There is in fact a long list of items that could be helpful or necessary for your case-building project. If you have staff or project team support, you can start your people gathering this kind of information immediately, while you focus on planning the design phases of the case project. Here are a few of kinds of information to look for:

Previous Business Cases

If your organization or others in your company have done business cases on the same or similar subjects before, it is important to know what they found, and why they either succeeded or failed.

This should guide you in determining which financial metrics and other criteria your own case has to demonstrate in order to succeed. It may also alert you to what is unacceptable in your situation (assumptions, presentation format, or the rationale for valuing costs or benefits, for instance).

⊡ There is a long list of documents, data, and other information that will be useful throughout the case building project...start gathering necessary background information immediately.

Vendor Proposals and Pricing Information

If the case subject includes the acquisition of assets or other expensive goods or services, you will need price quotations from the vendors. Or, if the acquisitions are commodities or other things with established prices, you will need the best available information on prices that will be in effect during the period of time covered by the case analysis.

This information will be necessary for building the cost model and making cost estimates.

Business Objectives

Case owner, project team, and core team will need the most complete list of business objectives possible, for all levels of organizations in the scope of your case. It is especially crucial to find important, high priority objectives that may be impacted by the subject of your case. These may come from many sources, some written, some understood but unwritten, some public, some private, some given in financial terms, others stated in operational, functional, or other terms.

Business objectives are crucial for deciding which business impacts to include in the case, for evaluating the results of your analysis, and for making recommendations (see pp. 65–68)

Budgets and/or Resource Planning Information

If your proposal includes spending or funding requests (and it almost certainly will), it is important to know how they impact current and planned spending. It is also important to know how spending levels are set, how spending decisions are decided (especially with capital budgets), by whom, and by which criteria.

Knowledge of your organization's budgets and budgeting practices, or "resource planning," is necessary in order to be sure that your proposal is realistic, to know whether it fits existing budgets or requires them to change, and to ensure that you address conclusions and recommendations to the issues that concern decision makers.

Business Plans

Business plans starting with the present and extending several years into the future reveal the organization's business model, including such things as the cost structure, expected margins, spending areas that are problematic, and areas that are targets for change. They also show what the organization expects or wants in terms of business volume and growth in the immediate future.

This information will be the basis of many assumptions underlying case scenarios. It is helpful for predicting changes in costs and benefits over the years, and it is also helpful in valuing and prioritizing benefits.

Financial Policy and Practices

Your financial analysis and your recommendations will have to conform to local policy and practice, unless of course, you explicitly want to argue for a change in the way things are done. In any case, you need to know how the organization and your financial specialists currently approach such things as depreciation of capital assets and discounting cash flow. In developing case scenarios, you will need to know if there are local policies that prescribe leasing instead of buying, doing some kinds of work "in-house" vs. outsourcing, hiring full time employees vs. contract workers, and so on.

Planning Case Design

◙ Case design works best when the design elements are approached in the order they appear in the case report.

The first two sections of the case report ("Introduction" and "Methods and Assumptions") include the business case elements that should be designed before the rest of the case project can be planned in detail. These sections are the focus of this chapter and the next. Designing the case is a project in its own right and works best when the design elements are approached in the order they appear here (see "The Natural Order of Case Design, pp. 16–19). It also works best when all the people who will do the data gathering and analysis later, also understand and/or participate in case design. Accordingly, the author's project plan for case design should anticipate:

Business Case Structure
A. Introduction
B. Methods and Assumptions
C. Business Impacts
D. Sensitivity, Risks, and Contingencies
E. Conclusions and Recommendations

Table 3.1 The introductory section of the business case.

A. INTRODUCTION
- **Title and Subtitle**
- **Authors and Recipients**
- **Date**
- **Executive Summary**
- **Disclaimer**
- **Subject:** What the case is about
- **Purpose:** Why the case exists and what it will be used for
- **Situation and Motivation:** Objectives, opportunities, threats, problems, limitations and constraints

- Educating the project team on the "what" and "why" of case design elements.
- Project team meetings to develop design elements.
- Any research necessary for case design itself.
- Core team meetings, to review, adjust, and agree on case design.

The Introductory Section

Table 3.1 (above) lists the elements in the introductory section of a typical business case. Our task now is to consider these items, one by one. Your own case report may not actually use the same headers or subdivision names in this *Guide*: you may not want to use a formal section heading called "Subject Statement," or "Purpose" for instance. Shorter cases in fact are fine without subsection titles, or the outline format implied. It is the content that is important.

Title and Subtitle

Recipients expect the case title to identify briefly the proposed action or case subject and the general nature of the analysis. For example:

Competitive Marketing Program: Business Case Analysis

or

Cost/Benefit Study of Planned Employee Recreation Facility

or

Return on Investment Analysis of Proposed Infrastructure Upgrade

In other words, some part of the title needs to say: "This is a business case!" Of course you can say that with words other than "Business Case" such as:

- Return on Investment Analysis.
- Financial Justification.
- Business Impact Analysis.
- Projected Cash Flow Impacts.
- Total Cost of Ownership.
- Impact on Business Performance.

Given a choice, I prefer to call the work a "business case" instead of some of the other terms here (see "What's the Difference? Cost/Benefit vs. ROI vs. Justification vs. TCO, " pp. 48–49). However, you may have been asked to produce an "ROI" analysis, or "Total Cost of Ownership" summary, and if so, that is probably what you should call it. When you use any term (including "Business Case Analysis") be sure to set expectations properly. Take care to describe "Financial Metrics" in the Introduction so that recipients know exactly what is coming (see pp. 69–71).

A title is essential, of course, but you may also have the option of adding a *subtitle* to let recipients know more precisely what the case is about. A subtitle can add interest and clarity by identifying up front such things as:

- The time period analyzed.

Projections for Fiscal Years 2003 - 2007

- The specific action under study (when several similar actions have been proposed).

October 2002 Upgrade Proposals From IBM

- Special characteristics of the method

Five year projections based on historical data from 1993-2000

Subtitles should cover no more than one or two lines—otherwise they begin to take over the role of Executive Summary.

▣ A subtitle can add interest and clarity...it can let recipients know more precisely what the case is about.

Note that business case subtitles are not like the "tag lines" after titles in magazine or newspaper articles. There, authors use subtitles to add interest by revealing conclusions or making editorial comments ("Read the fine print before you sign a service contract!"). For the formal business case, however, conclusions or editorials in the title or subtitle would strike most recipients as unprofessional. They make your case look nonobjective.

Authors and Recipients

▣ Real names add credibility and psychological impact. They also set expectations and help others judge whether or not the case met its purpose.

Imagine two business case documents on your desk, ready for review. The first is written by "Anonymous" and addressed to no one in particular. The second has the owner's name and is addressed to a real person, or to a group whose members you know. Other things being equal, which case immediately has more credibility? Which is more likely to get your attention? And, if *you* are the named recipient on the second case, which case do you think is more likely to cause you to act?

Putting *your* name on the case sends a bold message: "I take responsibility for this!" Putting the *recipient's* name on the case sends a message, too: "OK, the ball is in your court now, so do something!"

Besides the credibility and psychological impact that come from naming names, there is practical value in stating clearly who wrote the case and for whom. Yes, it may be true that when a case is submitted, everyone involved knows the recipient and author. But cases often circulate far outside the originating organization. They may be reviewed or consulted long after the decision or action is taken. Those who read the case later may very well want to know more about the methods or results, or even the case-building project. If there is no identifiable author, there is no one to ask. Also, knowing for whom the case was written helps set reader expectations; it helps others judge whether or not the case met its purpose.

The business case differs in this way from standard accounting reports or budgets, where authorship may or may not be known and where credibility is rarely an issue. Readers probably do not care specifically which accountant put the final touches on the income statement, or which senior executive made the final adjustment to the capital budget ceiling. Everyone knows, however, that business cases reflect arbitrary and subjective judgements, that projections are uncertain, and that no two analysts are likely to produce exactly the same case results. For credibility reasons alone, it is necessary to show who is responsible for the report.

An address with both "To" and "From" is especially appropriate if the case is prepared by consultants, sales people, or anyone outside the receiving company or organization. "To" (or "Submitted to, or

Prepared for") may address an individual—in which case title and company (or organization) should be included:

> To: Mr. Arnold Willows, President
>   The Rochester Manufacturing Company

Or, the report may be addressed to a specific committee or group:

> Submitted to:
>   The Capital Review Board,
>   Colosseum Financial Services, Inc.

or

> Prepared for:
>   Project 2004 Steering Committee
>   Acme Diesel Corporation

Ownership (or authorship) may be indicated by "From," "Prepared by," or "Submitted by."

> Submitted by:
>   Marcus T. Cicero
>   Strategic Action Committee

Ownership is often attributed simply to committees or groups:

> Submitted by:
>   Strategic Planning Group
>   Edgewise Industries, Inc.

▣ Authorship/recipient information can show that a number of people contributed to the content.

Writing "to" or "from" committees or groups is fine if the actual individuals can be identified elsewhere, preferably in the case report, perhaps in a footnote or appendix.

Finally, authorship/recipient information can also serve to show at the outset that a number of people contributed to the content. As the head of a study group or project team, it can be important to remind readers that contributions came from individuals across many functional areas—maybe including finance, human resources, marketing, strategic planning, line management, and so on. As an outside consultant or sales person, it is important to register the involvement of any contributors *inside* the company or organization. For instance:

Submitted to:
    The IT Steering Committee
    Acme Diesel Corporation
Submitted by:
    W. Loman, Account Executive
    Arborway Systems, Inc.
With assistance from:
    Glenn Johnson, Acme Diesel Corporation
    Amanda Jones, Acme Diesel Corporation

Date

The cover page of the case report should show the date the report was completed and submitted. Both dates should appear if there is any substantial difference between them:

Completed: 16 October 2002
Submitted: 30 December 2002

Why such concern for "detail" like dates? Remember that business case data and assumptions can be highly time-sensitive. Prices, economic conditions, salaries, business performance—all can change many times before and after the case is completed. A "completed" date on the report helps recipients know just which values were used.

Also, cases are often revised and reissued through several cycles. Completion and submission dates on the first page make it easy to tell which of several versions is the latest.

While on the subject of dates, think beyond the Introduction for a moment and note that other text in the report body should indicate when the data were gathered or developed (especially in the Methods and Assumptions section):

Cost estimates reflect vendor prices in effect during August, 2002

or

Estimated expenses are based on customer service request patterns for the years 2000 and 2001.

Dating this way throughout the case report is important because cases use sources and assumptions that change, and these changes may impact case results. Dating source data this way lets the recipients know exactly which data were used, avoiding potential confusion later.

▣ Business case data and assumptions can be highly time-sensitive. A date on the report helps recipients know which values were used.

Executive Summary

Readers expect to find an executive summary very early in the report. (It may be called "Abstract" or simply "Summary"). Unlike other parts of the introductory section, the Executive Summary is the last part of the case to be written.

"Last" does not mean "afterthought" or "hastily written just before turning in the report," however. This small block of text often plays a key role in the way recipients judge a case and it has to be done right. The executive summary deserves careful preparation and your best writing. Why?

Some recipients will read *only* the executive summary. That is a reality in the age of information overload. Others will read some or all of the case report but miss the main conclusions, misunderstand the subject and scope, or otherwise misinterpret your case, unless you make these elements crystal clear in the executive summary.

The remaining recipients—those who read the case report carefully and completely—will still want to know the essence of the whole case from the outset. The report should not be a mystery story, where recipients have to push through to the end to find the conclusion. Let them know from the start. Think of the executive summary as a proposition ("Here is what I propose to demonstrate."), which the rest of the case then supports, elaborates, and proves in detail.

The best executive summaries contain the whole case in miniature. This means that a few terse, well-written sentences convey:

- The subject, purpose, and scope, of the case.
- Important business objectives addressed by the case subject.
- Key financial results from the analysis.
- Significant non financial impacts that may be expected.
- Major assumptions that control results.
- Conclusions and recommendations.

Obviously this cannot be done in just two or three short sentences. It can often be done, though, in roughly one-third of a page to a full page. Long and complex cases may require several pages or more. Obviously this calls for careful, skillful writing. How long should the executive summary be? The answer is: as short as you can make it while still including all the elements listed above.

The appropriate length really depends on the length and complexity of the case. I mentioned in Chapter 1 a 520-page business case report dealing with several plant closing options. That case has a 20-page executive summary, and that is appropriate, given the complexity and important differences between six scenarios that have to be

> Some recipients will read only the executive summary. Even those who read the report completely still want to know the essence of the case from the start.

> The best executive summaries contain the whole case in miniature.

communicated (and you can be sure that many recipients of that case read only the executive summary).

Disclaimer

Including a disclaimer in your case report is advisable if you are preparing the case for recipients outside your own company or organization. The disclaimer helps set recipient expectations properly. That is one of its purposes, but just as important, the disclaimer is there to provide some legal protection for the case author. That advice may at first sound overly paranoid, but experience shows it is just good common sense.

The message of the disclaimer is, in effect, something like this: "I built this case carefully and professionally, *but*...

- Do not hold me legally responsible for the accuracy of these predictions.
- Estimates of future financial results always include some uncertainty.
- The results depend on some factors beyond my control.
- The results are based on information that may change.
- The results may depend on important information that is unknown to me.
- The results depend in part upon information that you furnished to me.
- Do not mistake this business case for professional tax planning guidance (unless, of course, you are qualified and licensed specifically to provide tax planning guidance).

In a real business case, of course, the phrasing is more formal and diplomatic. Here, for instance, is the disclaimer used by one IT system integration consultant of the firm "Vantage Associates:"

> This report provides approximations of important financial consequences that should be considered in decisions involving the purchase, installation, and configuration of computing hardware and software. The analysis is based on information provided by you as well as information believed by Vantage Associates to be accurate. Price information is subject to change at any time. We recommend that you use this analysis only as an aid to develop your own cost and benefit analyses. The actual tax impact can only be determined accurately by consultation with tax advisors.

If you even suspect that a disclaimer might be advisable in your work, then by all means check with your legal department or find a qualified lawyer who can discuss your potential responsibilities,

🔳 A disclaimer is advisable if you prepare the case for recipients outside your own company or organization.

vulnerabilities, and liabilities from a legal standpoint. Verify that your disclaimer text is appropriate from a legal standpoint.

When you use a disclaimer, either give it a text section of its own early in the report or set it off from other text in some unmistakable way (e.g., with a different typeface or indentation). Also be sure to bring it to the attention of your recipients at least once. Do not bury it in the footnotes or appendixes.

Of course, a disclaimer will not fully protect you from the legal consequences of incompetent work, misrepresenting your qualifications, or misusing case results. However, if you do your best in good faith, it can provide some protection against a client or customer who later makes unfair claims against you or your organization.

Subject Statement

▣ The subject statement helps define or shape almost everything else in the case.

▣ To a certain extent, the results are determined (but not yet visible) when the subject is stated properly.

Every business case needs an explicit subject statement describing what the case is about. The statement is critically important because it helps define or shape almost everything else in the case. The subject statement may have a text subsection of its own or it may appear within an introductory section that has no subsections. What is important is that the subject statement be defined and agreed to at the beginning of the business case project. The case-building project team needs it for everything that follows. And, the subject statement should be written early in the case report, preferably on the first page or two. Recipients need it in order to evaluate all that follows.

Why is the subject statement so important? Two good analysts can work independently on the same business case subject and arrive at different business case results, but they should be very similar results if they start from the same subject statement, if it is defined fully, concretely, and precisely. On the other hand, if the subject is defined incompletely, vaguely, or imprecisely, they may arrive at quite different results. To a certain extent, the results are determined (but not yet visible) when the subject is stated properly.

The starting point for identifying the case subject is usually a proposed or planned action. Here, for instance, are some proposed actions that might prompt a request for business case analysis:

- An acquisition or replacement
- A construction project
- An investment in new capabilities or capacity
- A change in organization, operations, or product offerings
- A move into a new market

As suggested, the title should briefly identify the proposed action e.g., "Competitive Marketing Program: Business Case Analysis" or

"Return on Investment Analysis of Proposed Infrastructure Upgrade". However, the subject statement itself needs to describe the primary action and related actions more fully and precisely. A good subject statement actually has *two* components:

- The subject statement describes the action in the title at the next level of detail. It should present the six to ten most important parts, or sub actions of the overall action.
- The subject statement should also contain, in kernel form, the scope and business objectives behind the action.

The subject statement will require several sentences, at least. A "Reservation System Enhancement" in the title might appear like this in a subject statement:

> This business case examines the likely costs and benefits that follow from a proposed upgrade of the reservation system at Ferien Resorts, Incorporated. The upgrade is designed to increase transaction capacity by 150%, a level that should support Ferien's reservation-processing needs through the end of fiscal year 2006. Current system capacity is projected to be adequate only through mid 2002. The proposal calls for several major actions, including hardware upgrades to Ferien's four Model 900 servers, increasing data storage capacity by 300%, migrating to the UNIX operating system, acquiring thirty additional phone lines, and providing professional training for sixty reservation agents. This analysis covers the estimated business consequences of these actions, as they impact Ferien Resorts during fiscal years 2002 through 2006.

Now we really know what the case is about. We know which important actions are involved and we know the underlying objectives.

There is more to the subject than actions, however. Good subject statements are built around *objectives*—business objectives, financial objectives, functional objectives, or operational objectives (in this case, increasing transaction capacity by 150%, and meeting reservation processing needs through the end of 2005. Why move the focus from action to objective? Reaching objectives has financial and other business value that can be made tangible. The value of actions by, themselves (upgrading four Model 900 servers or training 60 agents) is much harder to quantify if the objectives are absent.

In brief, when a proposed action supports an objective (and all proposed actions do, in a rational environment), the appropriate subject for the business case is the full range of resources and actions required to reach the objective.

▣ The subject statement describes the action as well as the business objectives behind the action.

▣ Reaching objectives has value that can be made tangible.

The Purpose Statement

The title may suggest the general approach ("Total cost of ownership analysis"), and it may point to the central action ("Server systems upgrade") but it will probably not mention the *purpose* of the case itself, directly. An explicit purpose statement is essential, because the business case purpose must be known and understood alike by the case author and recipients.

The general purpose may be to support decision making and planning but the developer needs to know specifically what the case will be used for and how it will be used. For instance, the case purpose may be to:

- Help decide the timing of a planned action/acquisition.
- Help choose between different proposed capital acquisitions.
- Support next year's budgetary planning.
- Support a specific budgetary request.
- Help choose financing methods or vendor.

⊡ An explicit purpose statement is essential. The business case purpose must be known and understood alike by author and recipients.

The author should also know from the outset which financial criteria will be used to evaluate results, and what it will take in terms of these criteria achieve success (e.g., obtain funding). If the purpose is to support a proposed capital acquisition, for instance, and if the Capital Review Committee evaluates proposals with criteria such as internal rate of return (IRR), payback period, and net present value (NPV) of the cash flow stream, it is important to know that before beginning to build the case. If the Committee never funds anything with a payback period over, say, two years, it's important to know this, too. This is especially important if the case represents one of several alternative actions competing for the same funds or management attention. (See the discussion on Financial Metrics, pp. 79–81 AND Appendix B).

Why? Because the manner in which the case will be used and its purpose will influence case design and case methods in many ways. When different cases support competing proposals, for instance, the scope of cost and benefit coverage for all cases should generally be the same.

Note that first-time case builders often confuse the purpose and subject statements. They are quite different (see "What's the Difference? Subject vs. Purpose", p. 71).

Situation and Motivation

The subject and purpose statements really define the case, but authors and recipients alike generally need to know more about the context of the case than they learn from just those two rather terse statements. A subsection in the Introduction called something like "Situation," "Motivation," or "Background" is the ideal place to provide the rest of the essential contextual information.

This subsection completes the job of fully articulating what the subject of the case is supposed to accomplish and why, as well as other important realities or issues that have to be considered in order make sense of the case results and recommendations. Recommendations and conclusions at the end of the report point back to the subject statement, and they also point to the main issues raised in this subsection.

Recommendations and conclusions at the end of the report point back to main issues raised in this subsection.

Objectives

Remember that business objectives are the reason for considering an action or decision in the first place. The case is really "about" meeting business objectives. The subject statement introduces the main business objectives addressed by the action, but now, before leaving the introductory section of the case, we need to identify *all* business objectives that *may* be addressed by the case subject—including those that were not behind the original motivation for considering the action. We also need to identify objectives that might conflict with the subject of the case. This list of business objectives becomes the basis for assigning value to case benefits and it provides reasons for making recommendations and conclusions from case results.

Whose objectives, specifically is the case about? If you ask many middle level managers what their "objectives" are, the answer is often something like this: "My objectives are to finish projects on time and stay within budget." Or, the answer might be even simpler: "My objective is to keep my boss happy." Those sentiments might honestly reveal that manager's real concerns, and it is important to keep those objectives in mind when building the case, but a proper business case recognizes a broader set of business objectives:

Business objectives become the basis for assigning value to case benefits and for making recommendations and conclusions from case results.

- In profit-making companies, the business objectives in view are normally the company's objectives.
- In non-profit or educational organizations, the case considers objectives for the population or membership served, as well as organizational performance and financial objectives.
- In government organizations, the case considers objectives for the whole population under the government's jurisdiction, as well as organizational performance and financial objectives.

Table 3.1 (next page) lists some of the many possible objectives that may be important, which may be impacted by the subject of a business case. No such list could ever be complete, and your own organization almost certainly has objectives not listed there. When

Business Objectives

- Financial and Business Performance.
  - To increase sales revenues.
  - To increase cash flow.
  - To increase margins or profits.
  - To reduce costs.
  - To keep spending within budget.
  - To improve return on assets (ROA).
  - To improve or return on equity (ROE).
  - To improve return on investment (ROI).
  - To avoid costs in certain areas.
  - To increase inventory turns.
  - To reduce days sales outstanding.
  - To reduce debts or liabilities.
  - To reduce risks or exposure.
  - To improve stock price.
  - To improve earnings per share.

- Strategic Position and Ownership.
  - To establish/enhance strategic alliances.
  - To acquire key technology.
  - To prevent or to facilitate merger.
  - To prevent takeover or outside purchase.

- Competitive Marketing.
  - To increase market share.
  - To take market leadership.
  - To improve market position.
  - To increase repeat business.
  - To win first-time customers.
  - To win business from competitors.
  - To counter competitive threats.
  - To increase competitive strengths.
  - To differentiate products from the competition.

- Operations and Functions.
  - To shorten product development time.
  - To shorten distribution time.
  - To reduce administrative paperwork.
  - To increase productivity of professionals.
  - To increase productivity of the labor force.
  - To increase transaction capacity.
  - To reduce the accident rate.
  - To improve internal communications.
  - To deliver loan decisions within 24 hours.
  - To shorten order processing time.
  - To reduce the number of change orders.
  - To provide online account information.

- Products and Services.
  - To update the product line.
  - To introduce more competitive products.
  - To enter new product markets.
  - To create achieve technology leadership.
  - To improve customer satisfaction ratings.
  - To provide better quality customer service.
  - To provide new service offerings.
  - To permit more customized customer service.

- Employees and Work Environment.
  - To recruit top quality professionals.
  - To retain high quality employees.
  - To minimize absenteeism.
  - To promote from within.
  - To base promotions on ability and merit.
  - To improve professionalism of the work environment.
  - To foster professional development of employees.
  - To provide a rewarding work environment.

- Image.
  - To be recognized as a technology leader.
  - To be recognized as a leader in environmental protection.
  - To be recognized for community service.
  - To be recognized for facilitating employee participation in community service.
  - To be recognized as a contributor to industry standards or industry cooperation.
  - To be recognized as a producer of quality products or reliable products.
  - To be recognized for outstanding customer service.
  - To be recognized as the performance leaders.
  - To be recognized as the low price leader.

- Sales Performance.
  - To shorten the sales cycle.
  - To lower the cost of sales.
  - To increase the size of the average order.
  - To increase unit sales.
  - To increase the close rate.
  - To increase sales productivity.

Table 3.1. Some common kinds of business objectives. The case-building project team should identify those that may be addressed by the subject of the case.

identifying business objectives for consideration in the business case, it may not be easy to classify objectives under the categories used in Table 3.1. That is not a problem: the categories are there only to help you think of objectives you might otherwise overlook. Your task is to identify objectives, not classify them.

You may find that some objectives overlap ("Increase sales revenues" and "Increase profits", for instance), and that some objectives really support other objectives ("Improved customer satisfaction" supports "Increase repeat business," which, in turn, supports "Increase sales revenues"). You may even find that two or more "official" objectives are really just different ways of saying the same thing. All of that is not a problem at this point in the case-building process or at this point in the business case report. What is of first importance now is to identify business objectives that may be addressed by the subject of the case. This list may be, and often is, longer than expected when a proposed action is first discussed.

Where do you look, to find all of your organization's objectives (so that you can select those that might be impacted by the case subject)? The best answer for most organizations is probably: "Many places."

In public companies (those that sell shares of stock to the general public), the company's quarterly and annual reports are an excellent source of business objectives. Financial objectives are often presented along with targets (e.g., "Our objective remains to grow sales revenues by 10% per year," or "Our objective is to maintain an operating margin of 20%"). However, annual reports are also rich in non financial objectives, relating to customer satisfaction, market position, image, environmental impact, employees, and many other areas. Before building your business case, you will find that going through your company's annual report and culling out objectives is time well spent. The most important objectives for non-profit and government organizations are often summarized in their charter statements, or mission statements, or periodic performance reports.

Objectives also appear in press releases, management directives, employee handbooks, and formal mission statements (some organizations even have these framed, on display in public areas). Some objectives may be unwritten but universally understood because they derive from commonly held values (e.g., "Attract and retain talented employees"). Some objectives may be temporary ("Return to profitability") and others relatively permanent ("Be recognized as the industry leader in customer satisfaction"). In brief, the search for all your organization's objectives will require energy and imagination to look through many different sources.

After you have identified your organization's objectives, and once you have selected those that may be addressed by the business case subject, the next step for the business case author is to *prioritize* them.

▣ The task at this point is to identify objectives, not classify them.

▣ Annual reports are an excellent source of business objectives.

Not all objectives are equally important to the organization, and you do not want to build a case that tries to extract value from contributions to low-value objectives. From your list of business objectives that may be addressed by the case subject, identify these that are truly important and of real interest to management or (in the case of non-profit or government organizations) the organization's constituency. The business case should focus only on objectives that have real value to those groups. Many organizations, to be realistic, superficially acknowledge a wide range of laudable objectives, while in fact only a few actually drive behavior in the organization. When selecting the truly important objectives, you do not need to be cynical, but you do need to be honest.

Identify the objectives that are truly important and of real interest to management.

Honesty also requires that you identify any objectives that might *conflict* with the proposed action of the business case subject. A proposed across-the-board salary freeze, for instance, might serve the objective to "Reduce expenses" and "Maintain operating margin at 15%," but it could very well work against other objectives like "Retain talented employees and provide them with a rewarding career path." In the final analysis, working against an important objective may well have to be counted as a "cost" that goes with the subject of the case.

Later in the case, we will need to describe how progress toward each objective is measured, in tangible terms, identify target levels for the objective, and describe the value of reaching the objective. For the Introduction, however, it is enough simply to identify the complete set of important objectives that may be addressed by the business case subject.

Other Important Contextual Information

Authors and recipients alike also need to understand from the outset, any significant opportunities, threats, problems, historical factors, limitations, or constraints in the current situation that should be considered when evaluating business case results. In brief, this part of the introductory section is the place to collect all other important information that authors and recipients need to know.

Here are just a few suggestions of the kinds of information that might be important enough to deserve mention here:

- **Opportunities**
  - Recent changes in laws or regulations that open new business opportunities.
  - Competitor weaknesses, competitor problems.
  - Recent events resulting in favorable prices or lower costs.
  - Synergy with other plans or projects.

□ Collect all other important information that the authors and recipients need to know.

- **Threats**
  - Expected competitor actions (e.g., product announcements).
  - Increasing competition.
  - Unfavorable changes in laws or regulations.
  - Anticipated law suits or legal problems.
  - Requirements to act or else face penalties.
- **Problems**
  - Cash flow problems.
  - Company image problems.
  - Product quality problems.
  - Customer satisfaction problems.
  - Schedule slip problems.
  - Employee turnover problems, staffing problems.
  - Supplier/vendor availability problems.
  - Current economic conditions.
  - Shrinking market, or currently poor market performance.
  - Product obsolescence, decreasing length of product life.
- **Historical factors**
  - Previous business cases on the same or similar subjects.
  - Success or failure of similar actions taken in the past.
  - Feasibility studies or pilot projects underway or completed.
  - Important trends (e.g., price trends, population growth or shrinkage in geographical markets, or changing customer preferences).
- **Limitations or constraints**
  - Budgetary or spending constraints.
  - Expiration of patents, contracts, or partnership agreements.
  - Time-to-market constraints (e.g., new product year or seasonal sale dates that cannot be missed).
  - Limited time in which to complete the action.

The list of possible "other" information that should be considered in building or evaluating business case results could extend indefinitely. However, the examples above should be enough to help you and your case-building team know what to look for.

Next Steps: Bring in the Core Team

When you have completed first draft versions of the subject statement, purpose statement, and other case design elements in this chapter, it is a good time for a core team meeting (you may wish to review pp. 19–23 on the value and role of the core team). The team need do nothing more than review these elements, make suggestions for changes, and reach consensus agreement on the form they should have as you move into the next phases of case design.

This meeting provides a very necessary "sanity check" on the direction the case-building project is going and the expected form of results. If there are differences of opinion on the core team, or between core team and case authors, it is very important to resolve them now, before moving on. And, by giving core team members the chance to contribute to case design, you have started the very important process of transferring a sense of ownership to important players outside the case-building project team.

What's the Difference?

Subject vs. Purpose

This chapter strongly emphasizes the primacy of *subject* and *purpose* statements: these two elements of business case design determine and direct all that follows.

Subject and purpose statements address quite different issues and both are required if a credible, usable business case is to be built. Even though they have relatively simple definitions, people often confuse the two. Before leaving the chapter on the introductory section of the business case, it is worth summarizing once more the differences between subject and purpose.

	Business case subject...	Business case purpose...
Describes...	• The action or decision whose consequences will be analyzed • The business objectives addressed by the action	• Why the business case is being developed, for whom, and how it will be used.
Answers these questions...	• What action or decision alternatives are being considered? • What are the main components of the primary action? • Which business objectives are addressed by the action?	• Who will use the results? For what purpose? When?

Table 3.2 Important differences between the business case subject and the business case purpose.

In Summary

The case-building project begins by recruiting the core team, gathering important background information, and then addressing the initial steps in case design.

- The gathering of background information should begin immediately. It is helpful or necessary to gather previous business cases, vendor proposals and pricing information, business objectives, budgets and resource planning information, business plans, and statements of financial policy and practice.

- Case design begins with the first elements in the case report because all that follows depends very directly on the definition of subject, purpose, and choice of financial metrics.

- Recipients expect the case title to identify briefly the proposed action or case subject and general nature of the analysis.

- A subtitle for the case can add interest and clarity.

- Naming the author and recipients adds credibility and psychological impact.

- Business case data and assumptions can be highly time-sensitive. A date on the report helps recipients know which values were used.

- Some recipients will read only the executive summary. Even those who read the report completely still want to know the essence of the case from the start. The executive summary should contain the entire case in miniature.

- A disclaimer is advisable if you prepare the case for recipients outside your own company or organization.

- The subject statement helps define or shape almost everything else in the case. To a certain extent, the results are determined (but not yet visible) when the subject is stated properly.

- The subject statement describes the action as well as the business objectives behind the action. Reaching objectives has value that can be made tangible.

- A subsection in the Introduction called something like "Situation," "Motivation," or "Background" is the ideal place to provide important contextual information not included in the subject or purpose statement.

- When first draft versions of the subject statement, purpose statement, and other case design elements in this chapter are completed, a core team meeting is advisable to check on the direction the case is going, and to begin the process of transferring ownership beyond the case-building project team.

Chapter 4

Case Design II:

Methods and Assumptions

This chapter continues the step-by-step walkthrough of the business case building process. After defining the case subject and purpose (Chapter 3), we are ready to design the tools that determine which costs and which benefits belong in the case.

Who Needs a "Methods" Section?

⧉ Every case report needs a methods section so that recipients can fully understand case results.

IN ORDER TO SET the context for today's trek through the business case landscape, recall something we learned while still at 39,000 feet (Chapter 1): most people think of the business case essentially as an exercise in financial mathematics, but the central problem for case builders is not really a financial issue. The central problem is determining where the cost and benefit figures come from. Which cost items should be included? What kinds of benefits belong in the case? And, what values should they receive? The design elements in this chapter provide the methods for answering such questions.

In fact, understanding methods is crucial to case building and case reading, and every case report needs a *methods* section so that recipients can fully understand case results. A little history might help explain why we have to deliver more than "the numbers."

Business case analysis was born in the first decades of the early twentieth century, during the same years that finance became a discipline in its own right. It was first applied to investments in assets used in manufacturing, such as buildings, factory machines, and vehicles. The idea was to develop common criteria for comparing potential investments in different kinds of assets, when they compete for the same funds. Decision criteria like "net present value" and "internal rate of return" can be used for choosing between a proposed machinery purchase and a proposed building (for more on decision criteria, see pp. 79–81 in this chapter and Appendix B, "Financial Metrics").

By the 1950s, financial decision criteria and business case analysis had become well accepted tools in asset management and financial planning. Finding costs and benefits and calculating decision criteria are straightforward activities, as long as the case deals with production-related assets. Think of the "cost" picture for a large assembly line machine, for instance. The purchase price is easily known, and so are its requirements for maintenance, power, and labor. Factor in the set-up costs as well, and no one doubts that you have the costs covered. The benefits estimates are similarly easy: we know what the production rate is *without* the machine, and we can probably estimate very precisely what the production rate will be *with* the machine. Increased production has a value that can be assigned easily (in terms of cost savings and increased sales, for instance). The business case for production-related assets is clear and unambiguous.

By the 1960s, however, organizations were spending large sums on newer kinds of assets, namely computers and communications systems. When technology started claiming larger and larger portions of capital and operating budgets, business people naturally attempted to apply business case analysis to these investments as well. With technology spending, however, neither the cost nor the benefits picture is quite so clear. The full range of computing costs, for instance, often extends across organizations and functions. Many such costs are "hidden" (that is, not obvious). And, the business benefits from computing hardware and software may not be tied directly to production capacity. True, they might improve efficiency and productivity, but they might also contribute to other business objectives such as improved customer service, or improved product design. Deciding which costs and which benefits belong in the case and how to value them, were no longer simple, unambiguous tasks.

Today, business case analysis is applied (or attempted) for all kinds of subjects, including environmental improvement projects, marketing programs, welfare programs, research programs, product development reviews, and reorganization plans. The results of such cases depend heavily on the choice of costs and benefits, but for that, case builders often find little guidance within their own organizations.

Nevertheless, there is certainly a growing emphasis on *accountability* in business, government, and non-profit organizations everywhere. People are asked or required, increasingly, to treat all decisions as *business* decisions, to document their decision criteria, and to *show* they have used good judgement. How do they do that, credibly, when everyone knows that case authors have considerable freedom to select or ignore costs and benefits and to shape the structure of the analysis?

To deliver business case results that others can understand and use with confidence, the author must follow the lead of research scientists, who always include a "methods" section in research reports. When reporting scientific results or business case results, the recipient needs to know more than just the outcome of the experiment or the values of financial criteria like net present value. Recipients need to know *how* the data were obtained and analyzed, in order to judge for themselves whether the results mean what the author says they mean.

◻ With computers and communications systems, deciding which costs and which benefits belong in the case, and how to value them, were no longer simple, unambiguous tasks.

◻ Recipients need to know how the data were obtained and analyzed.

When different authors analyze the same subject and come up with different case results, recipients should be able to see the reasons for the difference in the methods section.

Who needs a methods section in the business case report? The author needs it to explain and defend, if necessary, his or her conclusions. Recipients need it in order to understand and evaluate case results for themselves.

The rest of this chapter describes business case methods—case design elements—that you, as case author, will first apply and then report. Table 4.1 lists these elements.

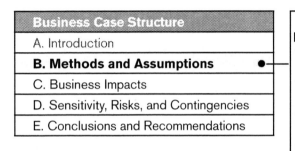

Business Case Structure
A. Introduction
B. Methods and Assumptions
C. Business Impacts
D. Sensitivity, Risks, and Contingencies
E. Conclusions and Recommendations

Table 4.1 Design elements in the Methods and Assumptions section

B. METHODS AND ASSUMPTIONS
- **Scope and boundary definitions**
- **Financial metrics and other decision criteria**
- **Major assumptions**
- **Data sources**
- **Scenario design**
- **Data structure: incremental vs full value data**
- **The cost impact model**
- **The benefits model and benefits rationale**

Scope and Boundary Definitions

▣ The case building team needs to agree on and fix the scope and boundaries, in order to design the rest of the case.

Once you have the case subject and purpose statements in hand (and not before then), it is time to answer questions like these: *Whose* costs, and *whose* benefits belong in the case? And, how far into the future should we project business results? Answers to these questions define the scope and boundaries of the case, and they are used as rules for deciding which data belong in the case and which do not.

The case building team needs to agree on and fix the scope and boundaries, in order to design the rest of the case. Recipients of the finished report need to see them early in the methods section, in order to know exactly what the case covers. "Scope" is the range of coverage encompassed by the case along several dimensions; "boundaries" define the scope precisely. A case might have a four-year analysis period (the time scope), beginning on 1 January 2003 and ending on 31 December 2006 (the time boundaries).

Just which scope and boundary statements have to be defined varies from case to case. Some categories below might not apply for your own cases. On the other hand, you may have to add some kinds of statements not listed here. In brief, scope and boundary statements contain all the information required for determining whose costs and benefits are in view, over what time period.

Time

Time is one dimension that has to be defined for every case in the form of the *analysis period.* This identifies the weeks, months, or years into the future for which costs and benefits will be estimated. The time line of the analysis period becomes the backbone of the cash flow summary.

Obviously, choosing the analysis period is a matter of choosing a length of time and a starting date. The resulting time period is stated with two calendar dates:

1 January 2003 through 31 December 2006
or
15 August 2003 through 14 August 2006

Recall from our 3,000 foot overview of the business case terrain (Chapter 2, pp. 23–25) that the choice of analysis period is arbitrary (unless your organization has established a standard analysis period, in which case you have to use someone else's arbitrary choice). There is no universal "right" analysis period, but here are some guides to making the choice:

- Find out if the case recipients expect or require a certain analysis period coverage.

If the Product Management Review Committee wants to see the expected costs and benefits for a six-year product life cycle, you do not want to produce a case with a two-year analysis period.

- Remember that business case results can depend heavily on the choice of analysis period.

We saw in Chapter 2 that one cash flow stream can produce positive or negative financial results, depending on the analysis period in view (Figure 2.1 and Table 2.3, p. 24). Insofar as you can foresee the general pattern of expected cash flow results, do not cut short the analysis period before important benefits or costs are likely. This is one reason that longer analysis periods generally provide more usable results than shorter periods.

- Determine if there is a "natural" or "logical" choice for analysis period.

If your case deals with a purchase decision for machinery, vehicles, computer hardware, laboratory equipment, or anything else that has

▣ Time is one dimension that has to be defined for every business case, in the form of the analysis period.

▣ Business case results can depend heavily on the choice of analysis period.

a roughly predictable life-expectancy, you may choose an analysis period that covers the useful life of the item. Or, if the subject of the case is a *program* with a pre-determined life span, that may be the obvious choice for analysis period.

- The organization's long-range planning horizon may be a good choice of analysis period.

If your organization looks, say, three years into the future for its long-range planning, you may already have available good estimates of business performance, costs, prices, and other significant trends over this period. The quality of available information beyond the planning horizon may be poor.

- Do not extend the analysis period so far into the future that prediction is meaningless.

An organization deciding which of several different retirement plans to offer employees, might reasonably look forward 30 or 40 years into the future. If the same organization is deciding which computer hardware to purchase, the analysis period has to be much shorter: estimates of hardware and software prices or capabilities more than 4 or 5 years into the future do not come with much credibility.

- If you are still uncertain about the best analysis period, choose the longest period that might be necessary.

It is easy to shorten the period, later, if that becomes appropriate.

Whose Costs? Whose Benefits?

The rest of the scope and boundary statements deal with the questions "Whose costs?" and "Whose benefits" belong in the case. These statements have to be detailed enough to identify the real organizations and individuals who are being analyzed. We may not actually know them by name ("Amanda C. Jones"), but we do need to know how many there are and their positions ("2 Account Executives, 3 Senior Sales Representatives").

Some people (your business case recipients, perhaps) may be surprised to learn that the two questions (Whose costs? Whose benefits?) may have different answers. It is entirely possible that the appropriate scope for costs might be narrow, covering for example a single service organization (e.g., an IT department, or a training group), whereas the benefits scope for the same case could be very large. Business cases for government organizations, for instance, are usually mandated to consider benefits for the whole population served. In any case, if the scope of costs and the scope of benefits differ, you will need two sets of scope and boundary statements.

◙ If you are uncertain about the best analysis period, choose the longest period that might be necessary. It is easy to shorten the period later.

◙ The questions "Whose costs?" and "Whose benefits" may have different answers.

To reach the level of concrete specificity needed, the author may have to define scope and boundaries in terms of the organizations, functions, geography, technology, and other categories that should be included in the case. Answering the questions in the subsections below should help you decide whether or not to include scope and boundary statements of each kind.

Organizations

Does the subject and purpose of the case concern the whole company? (Or enterprise, institution, or agency). If so, simply state that.

Are some organizations to be included, but others not included? If, the case concerns one or two specific divisions, but not others, then a statement is needed here. E.g.,

This scope of the case is limited to the Consumer Products Division .

The same kind of statement might identify specific departments, product units, agencies, military command units, branches, or other organizational subunits.

Functions or Positions

Are people, activities, and resources selected for analysis on the basis of function? Or, by job title or position? Scope and boundary statements defined in terms of functions or positions might indicate that the case cover, for examples:

- Teachers, but not principals or other administrators
- Labor but not management
- Full time employees, but not part time or contract workers
- Marketing, sales, and service personnel

Geographical Areas, Sites, or Locations

If the parent organization operates at multiple sites, or locations, then it will probably be necessary to clarify which are included and which are not. This statement may be presented in geographical terms, by site name, or some other appropriate identifier.

The case covers operations in the European region only.

Costs and benefits are estimated for the Chicago plant only.

The author may have to define scope and boundaries in terms of organizations, functions, geography, technology, and other categories.

The case includes Avanti Corporation's operations worldwide.

Technology

Does the case cover certain technology categories but not others? If there is any chance of confusion on that point, a scope and boundary statement should clarify that the case covers, for instance:

- Computer hardware but not software
- Vehicle engine and drive train maintenance, but not body work
- Electrical but not mechanical devices

▣ You may even state that the case that covers a fictional "typical" organization or site rather than any real one.

Other Categories

Still other kinds of scope and boundary statements may be necessary to clarify whose costs and whose benefits are covered. You may even state that the case that covers a fictional "typical" organization or site rather than any real one.

In the case report, of course, one statement can include more than one of the categories above:

Cost estimates cover the operations of the 25 service technicians, 4 managers, and 5 administrative staff at the Birmingham and Leeds offices.

Financial Metrics and Other Decision Criteria

What must the case deliver in order to accomplish its purpose? Before estimating costs and benefits, the author and case building team should identify clearly what kind of results will meet recipients' needs. If recipients will decide something, based on the results, what do they need to know, in order to make the decision? If the results are to be used for planning something (e.g., setting budgetary ceilings, or developing a business plan), what kind of information is required?

▣ The author and case building team should identify clearly what kind of results will meet recipients' needs.

A large part of that answer will be stated in terms of *financial metrics* (financial measures) that will be developed. It is not very helpful to say simply that the case will project "all costs and benefits" associated with a proposal. In order to be useful, information of certain kinds has to be extracted from the body of results. The cost and benefit cash flow numbers need to be *analyzed.*

The parallel between the case building process and report structure that we have already seen over and over, applies to financial metrics and other decision criteria as well. The case building team needs to know the information requirements, early, to be sure that the selection and quality of data meet the need. Case recipients need to know what the information targets are, early in the "Methods and Assumptions" section, in order to know where the rest of the methodology and data are leading.

When recipients first get the completed case in hand, they will probably look immediately to the "results," summarized by financial metrics such as:

- Total net cash flow for the analysis period
- Net present value (NPV) of the cash flow stream
- Payback period
- Return on investment (ROI)
- Internal rate of return (IRR)

Each of these measures something different in the overall cash flow summary. These metrics are straight from the discipline of finance; this much of business case analysis is taught and practiced everywhere. (For an introduction to these terms or a review of them, see Appendix B, "Financial Metrics." Also see "What's the Difference: Cost/Benefit vs. ROI vs. Justification vs TCO," pp. 48–49).

Other financial metrics might be equally important or even more important to your recipients. They might want to consider, for instance, such measures as:

- Projected profits
- Total cost of ownership
- Average cost per employee
- Average cost per transaction
- Average cost per "seat"

▣ Recipients probably have clear needs and expectations.

If the case supports decision making, authors and recipients need to know early just how these measures will be used. You may indicate in the report's methods section, for instance, that in order to obtain funding, capital proposals "must show a payback period of 2 years or less, and an IRR of 40% or more." Or, you might indicate that competing proposals will be judged primarily on the basis of "total cost of ownership."

At this point you may be wondering if we have things backwards: shouldn't we gather cost and benefit data first, perform analyses, and *then* decide which results are important, based on results? In reality, case results do sometimes turn up information that is unexpected and important. That kind of finding should certainly carry weight in the "Conclusions and Recommendations" at the end of the report. The important point, however, is that your recipients probably have clear needs and expectations. If you don't make these your targets for the case, you may not come back with the results they need.

How do you know which financial metrics or other decision criteria are required, if the case is to meet its purpose? The first advice, always, is to *ask* the recipients themselves specifically which kinds of information they need to see in the results. Another prudent step is to find out how similar decisions or plans were made in the past, that is, by which criteria or by which analyses.

If recipients are unhelpful, and if previous examples are unavailable, then you are on your own to choose target financial metrics. You will base this on your knowledge of what each potential metric actually says about a cash flow stream (Appendix B), the purpose statement, and the important business objectives addressed by the case subject (see pp. 64–68).

Finally, remember that case analysis may turn up business impacts that are measured, initially in non financial terms. Important non financial results may still be important decision criteria for recipients. Table 2.4 (Chapter 2, p. 28) suggests that a proposed action might lead to such things as:

◨ Non financial measures that support the purpose of the case should also be designated as target decision criteria.

- Increased market share
- Improved earnings per share
- Shorter product development time
- Winning an award for service excellence
- Improved employee morale
- Improved product reliability

You may be able to assign financial value to some of these outcomes, but it is also possible that you cannot do so in a way that is appropriate or acceptable for recipients. However, if non financial measures like these support the purpose of the case, then these, too, should be designated as target decision criteria.

Major Assumptions

Each business case includes at least one scenario, a concrete and detailed picture of one possible future. Anything having to do with the future, strictly speaking, is an assumption. And, because your scenarios need lots of details, your case will very likely require many, many assumptions. Assumptions play a central role in determining case results and in analyzing case results.

Someone might ask if it is possible to avoid assumptions all together and limit the case to "facts" that are more certain. There are at least three important reasons, however, why case authors and recipients should live comfortably with the idea that the case is a structure built on a foundation of assumptions.

- Prediction

Your case will project future financial results based on factors that can change over time: business volume, prices, salaries, the organization's cost structure and many other things. Suppose that your case anticipates purchasing fuel oil, real estate, or computer hardware several years from now. What prices do you enter in the case now for future purchases? You may use today's prices, assuming they will not change, or you may try to project future prices assuming that current price trends continue. Any way that you look into the future, there is some uncertainty, and for that reason, price data for the case have to be called assumptions.

• Simplification

Most cases also require simplifying assumptions. Cost items in one scenario might include, say, salaries for 100 clerical workers. You might be able to obtain the actual salary figure for each person involved, but for most purposes, that is not worth the trouble. A far more practical approach is to assume the company average for this job category, for all 100. If you cannot get the average for your company or organization, then you may have to assume an average salary level based on other sources, such as profession-specific salary surveys.

• Clarification

Finally, assumptions may be necessary for clarification. In one scenario, for instance, you might assume that 20% of new equipment in the proposal will be acquired by direct purchase and the remaining 80% through capital lease. There may be many other workable financing options as well, but the author has to choose one in order to complete the case.

Assumptions for the case come in many shapes and sizes. There will be background, or global assumptions that apply to all scenarios, and help set the subject and purpose statements:

Market size will continue to grow at an annual rate of 10%, for at least the next five years.

The US dollar/euro exchange rate will remain stable for the next three years, varying no more than 5% from its present value

Other assumptions may support the purpose of the case (such as choosing between implementation scenarios), by having different values in different scenarios:

Implementation will be completed in a single, three-month phase (scenario 1)

and

Implementation will be completed in three one-month phases, with a two-week interval between phases. (Scenario 2)

As author and case builder, you will create one assumption after another, Two points of advice are important here.

First, *record every assumption*. All but the smallest and simplest of cases rest on dozens and probably hundreds of assumptions. If you do not record assumptions as you create them, you will forget them. That is one certainty you can count on. Keep the notebook open or the computer running, recording each assumption as it comes up, *and* the reason for assuming what you do. When you later explain or defend your case, the discussion will focus heavily on your assumptions. It is unhelpful if you cannot remember what you assumed. It is just as unhelpful if cannot remember *why* you assumed it.

▣ Record every assumption and be sure the assumptions are written into the case report when they are important.

Second, be sure that assumptions are written into the case report, when they are important, and whenever you cannot take it for granted than any other author or recipient would make the same assumptions automatically. Some assumptions will probably appear in the introductory section ("Situation," or "Background") to clarify why some business objectives are important. All other important assumptions—those that one must know in order to make sense of the case results—should go in the "Methods and Assumptions" section, possibly in a subsection of their own, or in the sub section where you define individual scenarios (see pp. 84–86) . Other assumptions will also appear throughout the rest of the report. Assumptions that are *not* so necessary for understanding case results may not go beyond the author's private notes, or they may go into an appendix to the report.

Data Sources

Recipients will want to know how cost and benefit values are estimated, or from what sources they were taken. This information helps them judge the quality of the data and—assuming your sources are credible sources—adds to the credibility of the case as a whole. It might also help explain why different cases on the same subject have different results.

When cost and benefit data are taken from other documents, or when they were developed first for some other purpose, identify the source as a specific:

- Business case.
- Business plan.
- Feasibility study or pilot project.
- Outside consultant's estimate.
- Published industry average, benchmark, or best-in-class figure.
- Vendor proposal.
- Published price list.

Also describe the methods for assigning cost and benefit values, if they are not obvious and known to all. If cost estimates come from an "activity based costing" scheme or another costing method unique to this case, describe this briefly. On the benefits side, be especially clear on the source and rationale applied to all gains that have an arbitrarily assigned value. If assigning value to "Time savings for professional staff," for example, you might indicate that the expected time savings were estimated from workflow analysis and interviews with line organization managers, while the assigned values represent an average salary and overhead costs for people in this group.

Scenario Design

Scenario design begins by deciding which set of scenarios addresses the business case purpose.

At any point in time, there is only one past but many possible futures. Accountants and others who deal with financial history have only one reality to find, measure, and analyze. The business case author, on the other hand, has to *create* one or more possible future scenarios before anything can be measured or analyzed. How many scenarios should a case have? What does the scenario consist of, and how are costs and benefits estimated for each scenario? Those topics are the subject of the remaining case design elements in this chapter. (You may wish to review "Scenarios: The Future in Detail," pp. 25–26).

Scenario design begins by deciding which *set* of scenarios addresses the business case purpose. Ask: What questions is the case meant to answer? What will be done with the results?

The logical framework for addressing the case purpose begins by choosing scenarios to build, analyze, and compare. If the purpose is to support a "lease vs. purchase" decision, the case obviously needs a "lease" scenario and a "purchase" scenario, at a minimum. To decide which alternative is the better business decision, you will compare results of the two scenarios. If "do nothing" is also a possible alternative, you will also need a "business as usual" scenario as well. (Some people prefer to use the term "To Be" for proposal scenario and "As Is" for business as usual).

Notice that not all the cases in Table 4.2 have a business as usual scenario. When, specifically, do you need one, if "do nothing" is *not* a viable alternative? If not taking action means the company is out of

Table 4.2 Scenarios for business cases with different purposes. Most cases require one scenario for each alternative or action being considered. The case may also need a "Business as usual" scenario to provide a baseline for comparison with the an action scenario

Case Purpose	Possible Case Scenarios
Select an IT vendor.	• IBM scenario • Hewlet-Packard scenario • Dell scenario
Decide whether to lease vehicles or purchase them.	• Lease scenario • Purchase scenario
Decide whether or not to bring a product to market	• Product launch scenario • Business as usual scenario
Decide whether to continue two environmental impact programs	• Program A only scenario • Program B only scenario • Program A and B scenario • Neither program scenario
Project the impact of a new product line on the company's business plan.	• Product line scenario • Business as usual

business, or if managers, or commanders, or law require some action, then doing nothing is not an option. Nevertheless, if the objective behind the action is to improve something, or reduce something, or otherwise change something, you will probably need business as usual results in order to measure the change.

A hospital system, for instance, may use a business case to estimate improvements that should result from renovating patient rooms, operating rooms, and examination rooms. If the objectives for considering renovation are better patient care, lower operating expenses, and a more professional work environment for staff, there has to be some basis for knowing how much things *change* under the proposal scenario. Terms like "better," "lower," and "more" are relative terms that have meaning only when the expected new level is compared to a baseline. The business as usual scenario anticipates levels of patient care, operating expenses, and professional quality of the workplace if the present facilities are *not* renovated (even if not renovating is an unthinkable option).

Once you know which scenarios belong in the case, you can start defining them. This begins by identifying the unique actions, conditions, and assumptions for each scenario. These definitions can appear in the case report in subsection of Methods and Assumptions that introduces scenario design (which scenarios are in the case) and scenario definitions.

If your case only has two scenarios, "Proposal" scenario and "Business as usual" scenario, then you already have your proposal scenario subject statement in the subject statement for the case (as in the example, p. 63). The business as usual scenario is defined simply as continuing under present conditions.

▣ If the objective is to improve something, reduce something, or otherwise change something, you will probably need a business as usual scenario.

Your case will have some "global" assumptions which apply to all scenarios, as well as other assumptions unique to each scenario. All of these should also be identified here. When comparing a "lease" scenario with a "purchase" scenario for a fleet of service vehicles, important assumptions might include:

Global assumptions:

- Number of vehicles
- Vehicle model
- Average number of miles/kilometers driven per vehicle per year
- Service life of each vehicle
- Fuel costs per 1000 miles/kilometers per vehicle

Purchase scenario assumptions

- Purchase price per vehicle
- Special prices for volume purchase
- Resale, market value, or salvage value at end of service life
- Tax savings from depreciation expenses over service life

Lease scenario assumptions

- Kind of lease proposed (capital lease, operating lease, etc.) and financial implications (e.g., whether lessor or lessee claims depreciation expense)
- Term of the lease (length of time)
- Lease initiation fees and payment schedule
- End-of-lease purchase options
- Early-termination conditions of the lease

Other assumptions might be either global assumptions or scenario-specific assumptions, depending on specific conditions of the proposed lease (assumptions about maintenance costs, or insurance costs, for instance).

Defining scenarios in terms of assumptions like these enables us to build the case with only one scenario for each major decision alternative. Authors and recipients will certainly want to ask "What if?" questions about changes in assumptions: How do Purchase and Lease results compare if we take 100 vehicles? 500 vehicles? 10 vehicles? What does the comparison look like with a 3-year service life? With a 6-year service life? And so on. Sensitivity and risk analysis (see Chapter 6) enable us to address the "What if?" questions.

"Lease" and "Purchase" options are qualitatively different in many ways, so each needs its own scenario. "100 vehicles" vs. "500 vehicles" is probably not such a qualitative difference; probably all that will change in that case are the magnitudes of several figures in the assumptions.

◻ Defining scenarios in terms of assumptions enables us to build the case with only one scenario for each major decision alternative.

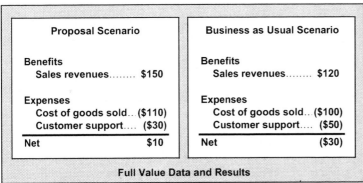

Proposal Scenario		Business as Usual Scenario		Deltas	
Benefits		**Benefits**		**Benefits**	
Sales revenues........	$150	Sales revenues........	$120	Increased sales revenues........	$30
				Support cost savings............	$20
Expenses		**Expenses**			
Cost of goods sold..	($110)	Cost of goods sold..	($100)	**Expenses**	
Customer support....	($30)	Customer support....	($50)	Increased Cost of Goods Sold.	($10)
Net	**$10**	**Net**	**($30)**	**Net**	**$40**
Full Value Data and Results				**Incremental Data and Results**	

Figure 4.1 The full value case presents a cash flow statement for each scenario, using full value data. The statement at left (Proposal Scenario) and the statement in the center (Business as Usual Scenario) are both required in order to compare one scenario with the other. The incremental cash flow statement at right presents only the deltas (differences) between the two full value scenarios. It is a mistake to mix the two kinds of data on the same cash flow statement. Figures in parentheses are negative values (cash outflows)

Data Structure

▣ The role of the "Business as usual" scenario is closely related to an important but usually ignored issue in case building: Data structure.

The role of the "business as usual" scenario is closely related to an important but usually ignored issue in case building: Data structure, or in other words the "full value vs. incremental data" issue. You will not have do deal with the practical implications of the issue (developing and analyzing data) until the business impact analysis begins (Chapter 5). However, you need to know about the issue now, when choosing scenarios for your case.

The easiest way to explain this issue, its importance, and the reason so many business case results are meaningless, is to consider a very simple example. Figure 4.1 above summarizes a case analysis for a very small and simple company that is considering improving the design and quality of its products. The business as usual scenario in the center shows projections for next year if nothing is done to improve products. The company will have sales revenues of $120. For simplicity here, assume here that sales revenues are the same as cash inflow. You can also see that expenses (cost of goods sold and customer support) will total $150, bringing a net loss of $30. That is the outlook for business as usual.

The proposal scenario cash flow statement at left shows the likely results if the product improvement proposal *is* implemented. The Marketing department projects sales of $150, Manufacturing sees an increase in cost of goods sold to $110, and Customer Service looks forward to lowered expenses, down to $30. Under the proposal scenario, the company expects a slim net gain of $10. Now, the question is, "How do we make the case for implementing the proposal?" We have two possibilities:

• The full value approach.

We present both the business as usual scenario and the proposal scenario, and then point to the differences between them. Note that all data in the case are *full value* data. For example, sales revenues in the Proposal scenario are entered as $150 because that is the full value projected.

• The incremental approach

Here, we calculate the deltas, or differences, between the same line items in the two scenarios. Proposal scenario revenues minus business as usual scenario revenues produces incremental sales revenues of $30 for the cash flow summary at right. Data in the incremental statement are always the differences between two full values.

Note that you can always calculate the incremental statement from the two full value statements. You cannot recover the full value statements from the incremental statement alone. The two full value statements contain more information.

If you grasp the ideas involved in Figure 4.1, you may be asking: "What is so confusing about this issue? Do people really trip up here and invalidate their own results?"

Just look at some of the business cases from your own organization or examine some that are available on the internet, and you will see that people stumble here in several ways:

Problem 1: Mixing Incremental and Full Value Data in the Same Scenario Cash Flow Summary.

People often err by putting full value cost figures in one line item, but incremental gains in another. Results become meaningless when incremental and full value data are mixed.

▣ People often say: "I have a projected cost savings. Is that a 'cost' or a 'benefit' item?"

Look through existing business cases from your own organization or elsewhere, and you will very likely find many instances of mixed data.

Problem 2: Confusing Plus and Minus Signs, Especially Where Cost Savings are Involved.

In Figure 4.1, customer support costs are $50 under business as usual, but only $30 under the proposal scenario. The proposal brings a cost savings on this item, but does that go into the business case as a positive or negative figure? People often say: "I have a projected cost savings. Is that a 'cost' or a 'benefit' item?"

The answer depends on which data approach we use. Under the full value approach, we see the cost savings by comparing the two negative figures in the two scenarios. Under the incremental approach we see the cost savings as a positive cash inflow. In the full value statements, *customer support* appears under expenses. In the incremental statement, *support cost savings* is a benefit.

Figure 4.1 covers only one time period, a year. What do you do in a multi-period statement, where the incremental data are positive in some periods and negative in others? It is just a personal preference, but I list the item twice: once under benefits (with "0" for every period where there is a net cash outflow), and once under costs or expenses (with a "0" for every period where there is a net cash inflow). That way, benefits are always cash inflows with positive values and costs are always cash outflows with negative values on the cash flow (see the examples on page 122).

If that sounds overly complicated, consider the alternative: a single line item entry under costs or expenses, with both positive and negative values in the same cash flow stream for that item. To many of us, that is *really* confusing: writing a positive inflow as a "negative outflow" asks recipients to deal mentally with something that is essentially a double negative.

Problem 3: Not Meeting Needs of Decision Makers Planners.

Incremental and full value data carry different messages and meet different needs. Which should you present? Of course, you can present both approaches, but we are discussing here which approach to focus on for analysis and making recommendations. Here are some factors to consider:

Incremental values may be preferred if ...

▣ Incremental and full value data carry different messages and meet different needs.

- The proposed action or acquisition is viewed primarily as an investment (i.e., in terms of ROI, payback, or IRR).
- Incremental costs and benefits are quite small relative to full value figures. If the differences between scenarios are small but important, the full value approach may "mask" the differences that need to be seen clearly.

Full values may be preferred if ...

- The business case purpose is business planning rather than decision support. If case readers need to plan budgets based on cost projections, for instance, they need full value figures.

- "Business as usual" is unthinkable. If a business as usual scenario is completely unrealistic (e.g., the company would be out of business), a business as usual baseline would have questionable value.

Third Introduction to Costs and Benefits

Many people probably think of the business case primarily as a collection of costs and benefits. That must be why so many produce something like the "double-list" case we saw from 39,000 feet in Chapter 1 (pp. 3-5), little more than a list of costs and a list of benefits. When they set out to find the cost and benefits for an action, however, many discover they have no clear sense of what really belongs in the case and what does not. On that first introduction to costs and benefits, we saw that financial math is not the central problem in case building. The central problem is determining which cost and benefit items belong in the case and what they are worth in real money.

☐ The central problem is determining which cost and benefit items belong in the case and what they are worth in real money.

Passing over the same business case terrain at 3,000 feet (Chapter 2), we met two tools for dealing with these problems, namely the cost model and the benefits rationale. (You may want to review the second introduction to costs and benefits, "Business Impacts: Costs and Benefits," pp. 27–34, before going on). Think of Chapter 4 as your third introduction to costs and benefits, this time as a ground-level walkthrough. You already know, conceptually, how the case builder approaches costs and benefits. Now it is time to focus on the practical details.

Cost Terms

The terms "cost" and "benefit" are good words for telling the outside world what we bring together in the business case. Most people understand the general meaning. The case author needs a more precise understanding of cost and benefit terminology, however, in order to know exactly what to look for, what to measure, and how to analyze results.

Remember from Chapter 2, that finding costs and benefits really begins by finding all *business impacts* from the case subject that we expect during the analysis period, under each scenario.

Business Impact: An important business consequence that follows from scenario assumptions and the specific action or conditions that the scenario represents (e.g., "Lease" scenario, or "Purchase" scenario).

The universe of possible business impacts under each scenario was summarized in Table 2.4 (p. 28). That table puts all the possible important business consequences under each scenario into three impact categories:

Business Impacts

- Direct Financial Impacts
  ◦ Cost Impacts (Source: Cost Model)
  ◦ Income Impacts (Source: Benefits Rationale)

- Contributions to Business Objectives
  (Source: Benefits Rationale)

This *Guide* first covers the impacts we identify with the cost model, and then those that come from the benefits rationale.

You already know that the most basic financial metric in the business case is *cash flow*, and that cash flow events include cash inflows and cash outflows:

Cash Flow: Cash that actually flows into or out of the company or organization.

Building the financial case is, in simplest terms, a process of identifying business impacts under each scenario, measuring impacts (often in non financial terms), and then assigning cash flow value to impacts. You will repeat the process suggested by Figure 4.2 below, over and over as you build your case. Of course, the completed business case may contain impacts we can measure in some way, but do not or cannot value in cash flow terms. However, all impacts that contribute to the financial summary ultimately need cash flow values.

A *cash outflow* is not the same thing as a *cost*. If you purchase a personal computer with a credit card, you incur a cost. Charging the item is a cost event. There is no cash flow until you actually pay the credit card bill, perhaps three weeks later or in several cash flow events over an extended time. The cost event leads to the cash flow event.

The tool that guides your search for business impacts that are cost impacts is the cost model (first introduced in Chapter 2, pp. 29-31). The cost model does not actually identify impacts, but rather, it helps identify all the *cost items* that might be impacted:

> 🔲 Building the financial case is a process of identifying business impacts, measuring impacts, and assign cash flow value to impacts.

> 🔲 A cash outflow is not the same thing as a cost.

| Identify Business Impact | → | Measure Business Impact | → | Assign Cash Flow Value |

Figure 4.2 Building the financial case, is a process of identifying business impacts under each scenario, measuring impacts (often in non financial terms), and then assigning cash flow value to them

Cost item: A spending category for something the company or organization spends money on, including assets, goods, services, and resources of all kind. Examples include staff salaries, security service fees, and the purchase of computer hardware.

> ▣ Cost items are the line items in budgets and spending plans.

Cost items are the line items in budgets and spending plans. Cost items for your business case will probably represent continuing short term expenses for such things as salaries and overhead, telephone charges, security services, travel expenses, and training costs. Depending on your case subject, you may also have cost items in the case for expensive, long-term items that enter the company's balance sheet as capital assets, such as buildings, production machinery, service vehicles, and large computer systems.

Most business cases have many, many cost items, and just a few benefit items. It is not unusual to see dozens or hundreds of cost items in the cash flow statement, while the number of benefit items is typically smaller, perhaps no more than three to five. For that reason, you will probably find that most of your case analysis time goes into the cost side of the cost/benefit picture. In a typical four- to six-week case building project, for instance, 80% or more of the project work time goes into finding cost items, identifying cost impacts, and measuring and valuing them. That work may be tedious, but if you develop and use the cost model properly, at least the path through it will be clear and straightforward.

Finally, you may wonder about the difference between the terms *cost* and *expense*. Sometimes it seems the two terms are used interchangeably, but accountants do not consider them quite the same thing. Cost is the broader and less precise term. Expenses are one kind of cost, and expense does have a clear definition:

Expense: A measure of resources that are used up and which do not go on the balance sheet as assets.

Salaries are expenses because labor is a resource that is used up. Similarly, travel expenses, the cost of electricity, and internet service fees are expenses.

In summary, some expenses are one kind of "cost," but not all costs are expenses. The cost of a new building (an asset that goes on the balance sheet) is an asset cost, not an expense.

The Cost Model I: Resource-Based Approach

How do you know that every important cost impact is included in the case? How do you know that you have excluded cost items that are not relevant to the case purpose? The cost model is a tool that provides the "rules" for deciding which cost items belong in the case and which do not.

The cost model is really nothing more than an organized list of cost items. Recall the double-list business case (Chapter 1, pp. 3–6), with an *un*organized list of cost items (*dis*organized might be a better term). It is almost impossible for anyone to look at an unorganized list of hundreds of cost items, and decide whether or not it is complete or what it means. The cost model, however, brings organization by defining the cost item *categories* that belong in the case. Once we know which cost item categories we need for the case, finding the items for each category is straightforward.

In this section we examine a typical cost model that uses a resource-based approach to identifying cost items. The alternative, an activity-based approach is introduced in the next section.

The cost model in Figure 4.3 below was introduced in Chapter 2 (p. 30). This is a resource-based cost model, which works well when the case subject is an IT acquisition (hardware or software system), or an acquisition of major assets that have a predictable life cycle (such as buildings, production machinery, laboratory test equipment, service vehicles).

The white cells of the matrix are cost categories: each cell holds a group of cost items that change together, which need to be planned and managed together. With the resource-based approach to cost modeling, cost items grouped together in cells of the matrix represent the names of resources, whose costs can be estimated over the life of the system. Usually all the cost items within a cell have common cost drivers. The upper left cell, for instance, holds all "Hardware Acquisition Cost" items. Figure 4.4 (next page), is a more detailed view of the same cost model, with suggested individual cost items.

Try to develop a cost model that divides the universe of potential

> ▣ The cost model brings organization by defining the cost item categories that belong in the case.

		System Life Cycle		
		Acquisition	Operation	Growth & Change
Resources	Hardware			
	Software			
	Personnel			
	NW &Comm			
	Facilities			

Figure 4.3 The cost model for a business case dealing with an IT system proposal. Each cell in the model holds cost line items.

Cost Model		Acquisition & Implementation Costs *Costs at acquisition or during initial implementation*	Operation Costs *Periodic or frequently occurring costs that continue 3-5 years.*	Ongoing Change & Growth Costs *These costs come with adds, moves and changes to the computing environment*
IT Resources	Hardware Costs	• Server system purchase or upgrade • PC Client system purchase • W/S client system purchase • Storage space purchase • Other peripheral HW	• HW maintenance fees • HW lease expenses	• Additional server systems • Additional client systems • Additional server CPUs • System upgrades • Storage space expansion • Other peripheral HW
	Software Costs	• OS/NOS original purchase/license • Application purchase, one-time charge • Development/migration SW purchase	• Periodic SW license fees • SW maintenance/warranty fees	• OS/NOS upgrade • Migration software purchase

	Personnel Costs: IT Staff	• Preplanning costs
		In-house or outside consultant
		• HW Installation labor
		• SW Installation labor OS, OS/NOS utilities, appl
		  – Install at Server
		  – Install at client
		• Initial NW set up
		  – Set up user accounts
		  – Directory creation labor
		  – Set up /install NW services
		  – Set up/install NW or mail server
		• SW migration labor
		• Initial training costs (professionals)
		• Professional hiring costs
			• Administrative labor
			  – Systems operators
			  – Systems programmers
			  – Applications programmers
			  – Network admin labor
			  – Storage management
			  – IT/IS management
			  – Other Admin
			• Trouble shooting
			• Continuing contract labor
			• Continuing training (professional)
				• HW reconfiguring, setup
				• OS/NOS upgrade labor
				  – Upgrade at Serve
				  – Upgrade at client
				• NW changes -Administrative costs
				  – Add/move/delete user accounts
				  – Add/move/delete a NW service
				  – Add/change a NW or mail server
				  – Assign/change security
				• Capacity planning, other change planning (in-house)
				• Capacity planning, other change planning/consulting (outside source)
				• Temporary contract labor
				• General moving labor

	Personnel Costs: Users	• Initial training costs (users) • Organizational downtime costs during install or upgrade	• User Trouble shooting, system management • User help / other user services • Continuing training (users)	• Additional user training
	NW & Comms	• NW/Comms HW (including NW server systems) • NW/comm SW • Line acquisition/hookup charges • Installation of comm wiring, cables	• Line usage charges • Satellite or other WAN charges • Wireless charges • Outside internet service providers	• NW change planning costs • Additional NW/comm HW and SW • Additional cables, site/preparation for changes
	Other Costs	• Floor space acquisition, renovation, construction • Initial site planning	• Electricity • Security costs (e.g. disaster recovery services)	• Site expansion • Site consolidation, • Site renovation

Figure 4.4 Suggested cost line items for the IT cost model of Figure 4.3.

cost items in two ways (two dimensions in the model). Here, the horizontal dimension groups cost items by "System Life Cycle" categories (Acquisition, Operation, and Growth and Change). Every IT cost item in every scenario in the case, falls into one of these categories. As we saw in Chapter 2, this model is an effective tool for finding and organizing all the cost impacts when the subject of the case is an IT acquisition, because acquisition costs are planned and managed differently from continuing operational costs, which are planned and managed differently from ongoing growth and change costs.

In the resource-based approach to cost modeling, the cost model's vertical dimension divides all costs into different resource categories. For an IT system acquisition, these might be Hardware, Software, Personnel, Networking and Communications, and "Other" costs. This division of possible cost items also makes sense, because each resource category is planned and managed differently from the others.

In brief, the resource-based approach creates two different ways of categorizing cost item impacts for the subject of the case:

- One set of cost categories covers the major kinds of life cycle events, or phases.

- One set of cost categories groups cost items by kind of resource.

This kind of cost model is a powerful tool for identifying, analyzing, and communicating all the cost impacts in your business case in at least five ways:

- The model provides a simple, visual rule showing which items belong in the case and which do not.

There may be hundreds of cost items in your business case and recipients naturally want to know how you decided what to include and exclude. You can show that cost items were selected by a simple rational system, by drawing and explaining the model framework.

- The model helps *case builders* identify every relevant cost item.

By naming cost categories, the cost model shows case builders where to look to find possible cost items. One effective way to fill in the cost line items is to use the model framework as a guide and for a "brain storming" workshop with the project team. In that kind of meeting, be sure the scope and boundary statements are clearly in view as well—so that everyone has a clear reference to whose costs, and whose benefits are relevant to the case over the analysis period.

- The model assures *recipients* that every relevant item is included and that irrelevant items are excluded.

◙ The cost model provides a simple, visual rule showing which items belong in the case and which do not.

◙ The cost model helps builders identify every relevant cost item.

With a long, unorganized list of cost items, it is difficult to judge whether or not everything relevant to the case is included. Even when the list is organized in traditional accounting categories, it is difficult to make that judgement. By organizing cost items in terms of life cycle phases and resource categories that are important for this kind of acquisition, however, that judgement is much easier to make. The judgement becomes a two-step process: First, ask whether or not all relevant cost categories are included. Once that question is settled to satisfaction, then ask if the list of resource items within each category is complete.

• The model ensures that different scenarios in the case are comparable with respect to cost coverage.

The same cost model structure should be applied to all scenarios in the case. Recall, for instance, the IT director's example from Chapter 2, in which the business case for a proposed local area network implementation had three scenarios:

Scenario 1: Large scale implementation
Scenario 2: Small scale implementation
Scenario 3: Business as usual

Each scenario was analyzed with the same cost model for that case, shown in Figure 4.4. (Chapter 5 has more detail on how that is done). Not every cost item in the model appeared in every scenario. However, applying the same cost model framework to all scenarios, to test for the presence of each cost item, ensured that cost estimates for all three scenarios were truly comparable.

• The model provides management with an effective tool for cost planning and control.

A cost model analysis provides practical management information that may be difficult to see in the cash flow statement. Recall that each cost item in the model becomes a line item in the cash flow statements. Ultimately, we have to measure the resources required for each item under each scenario, and then assign a cash flow value for each time period in the overall analysis (a major focus in Chapter 5). However, summarizing the cost item totals for each cost model category, across the whole analysis period, is informative in its own right.

Figure 4.5 (next page) shows how this analysis looks for one scenario in another IT business case for a large company. Only the cost totals for each line item category appear here in each cell, added across a five-year analysis period. In this way, the cost model has become a five-year total cost of ownership (TCO) tool for the IT systems in this scenario. This kind of summary makes some important points that might not be so easy to see in the scenario's cash flow

⊡ The same cost model structure should be applied to all scenarios in the case.

⊡ A cost model analysis provides practical management information that may be difficult to see in the cash flow statement.

statement. For example, almost 74% of the life cycle costs for this scenario come *after* acquisition. Any serious attempt at cost control has to give serious attention to planning and managing operational and change costs. Purchase price and total cost, in other words, are not the same thing. When planning IT spending or evaluating competing vendor proposals, it is natural to focus on the acquisition and operational costs of hardware and software (the four cells at the upper left in Figure 4.5). However, the cash flow estimates in these four cells account for only about 27% of the five-year costs. Staff and user costs together account for more than 48% of the total costs. Clearly, "people" costs for implementing this scenario are large and require careful management.

The Cost Model II: Activity-Based Approach

The resource-based cost model works well for analyzing major acquisitions of various kinds but it is not so effective for painting the expected cost picture when the business case subject is a project, a program, or a product launch. In these kinds of actions, the largest resource category, usually overwhelmingly, is labor. For that reason, these kinds of subjects are more effectively approached with an activity-based cost model.

Consider for instance one common kind of decision in companies that operate in highly competitive arenas, such as the automotive or consumer electronics industries. Each new product model has a relatively short life and new product design and launch are continuing activities. The challenge for product management is to maximize earnings from the product line (or product portfolio), by effectively

Life Cycle Stages $ in 1,000s

Resources	Acquisition & Implementation	Operation	Ongoing Changes & Growth	Total	% of Total
Hardware	$ 1,523	$ 605	$ 924	$ 3,052	21.8%
Software	$ 1,192	$ 545	$ 520	$ 2,257	16.1%
IT Staff	$ 120	$ 3,315	$ 1,472	$ 4,907	35.1%
Users	$ 230	$ 1,342	$ 297	$ 1,869	13.4%
NW & Comms	$ 472	$ 771	$ 110	$ 1,353	9.7%
Other Costs	$ 112	$ 189	$ 238	$ 539	3.9%
Total	$3,649	$6,767	$ 3,561	$13,977	100.0%
% of Total	26.1%	48.4%	25.5%	100.0%	

Figure 4.5. The cost model as a cost analysis tool. Each cell shows the five-year total for all cost items in the cell, from one implementation scenario. The shaded cells represent the cost categories normally considered first when evaluating IT proposals, in this case, only about 27% of the total five year cost. The marginal totals provide other useful information. Column totals show, for instance that almost 74% of the total costs come after acquisition.

□ The complete case design and all that follows depend very directly on the definition of subject, purpose, and choice of financial metrics.

managing the product life cycles of individual products. Product life cycle management centers on a never ending series of decisions, each of which calls for business case support. One such decision might have the following options:

- Develop and market product A
- Develop and market product B
- Develop and market both products
- Develop and market neither product (business as usual)

Each option deserves a business case scenario, and we need a cost model that can be applied to all scenarios. Figure 4.5 (below) shows an activity-based model this should meet this need. This kind of model has exactly the same role and strong points as the resource-based model in the previous section: it helps identify all relevant cost items, ensures comparability between scenarios, and so on. Its structure and contents are a little different, however.

The horizontal axis identifies the major product life cycle phases in this company: intelligence, development, production, support, and

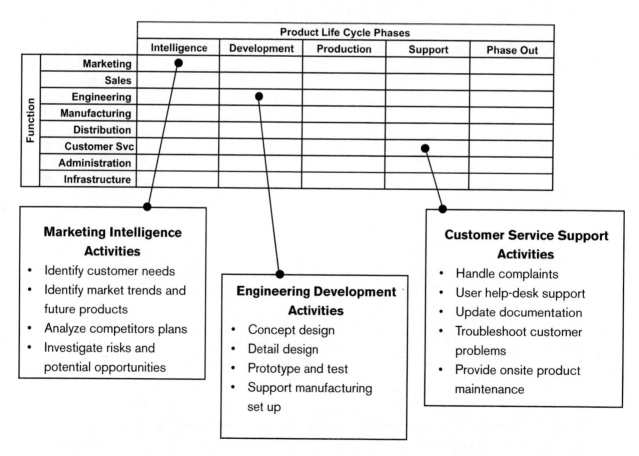

Figure 4.5 An activity-based cost model to analyze product launch scenarios. The horizontal axis represents the major phases of the product life cycle, while the vertical axis represents major functions in the company that will provide resources during product life. Individual cost items in the cells are identified as activities.

phase out. This axis is not a time line, but it does help put activities in each row in sequence.

The vertical axis is divided by functional areas: these categories come from the business case scope and boundary statements, where the case building team identified functions likely to contribute resources during product life. (For other cases, it might be more helpful to represent organizations, or even workgroups on this axis).

The figure also shows possible cost items for several of the cells. Notice especially that cost items are activities in the activity-based model. Even the acquisition or use of resources can be can be written as an activity by adding a verb (*acquire* software upgrades, *provide* vehicle maintenance). The business case author and case project team fill in the cells based on their knowledge of product development projects. They will also draw upon cross-organizational, cross-functional assistance from the core team and other sources.

If the business case subject is a project or program, finding all the activity items for the cost model is much easier if the project plan or program plan already exists. Otherwise, business case builders will find themselves engaged in project (or program) planning in order to complete the cost model.

◨ In the activity-based cost model, cost items are activities.

Introduction to Business Case Benefits

There is more to business and organizational life than costs. Businesses and other organizations usually exist in order to meet certain objectives. Yet that simple and obvious fact often gets lost in business case building. Case builders normally find the job of identifying, and estimating costs tedious but straightforward (I mentioned that probably 80% or more of your case building time will go into cost analysis). Cost analysis does sometimes lead to one kind of benefit: cost savings (or avoided costs). Finding and identifying other benefits, however, presents different kinds of challenges.

In order to make benefit analysis clear and straightforward, we need to review and introduce a few benefit-related terms. Recall again that case analysis is largely a process of finding, measuring, and valuing business impacts from the subject of the case. Remember that the universe of possible business impacts can be summarized, as it was in Table 2.4 (p. 28), this way:

Business Impacts

- Direct Financial Impacts
  ○ Cost Impacts (Source: Cost Model)
  ○ Income Impacts (Source: Benefits Rationale)

- Contributions to Business Objectives
  (Source: Benefits Rationale)

From this outline of business impact possibilities, three qualitatively different kinds of potential benefits appear:

- Cost savings or avoided costs

We know that these benefits come from the cost analysis, by comparing cost estimates under different scenarios (a proposal scenario compared to a business as usual scenario, for instance). They will show up as positive cash inflow in the incremental cash flow statement (pp. 87–90). Most people have no reservations whatsoever about including cost savings in the case results as benefits as long as the cost analysis is realistic. Cost savings are readily viewed as "hard" benefits.

- Increased income

Case scenarios might anticipate cash flow coming into the company or organization through increased sales, improved profits, or the acquisition of funding from some outside source. The only reservations people generally have about including increased income as a business case benefit comes from the known difficulty of forecasting future sales and profits and the uncertainties involved in obtaining outside funding. Increased income is often accepted as a "hard" benefit, *if* recipients have confidence in the estimation process.

▣ Benefits that come from contributions to non financial business objectives can be the highest value in the case..

- Other contributions to business objectives

This is the problem child in the benefits family. Benefits in this category are sometimes called "soft" benefits and they often present the most serious challenges to case builders and recipients. Yet, these can be and often should be the highest value benefits in the case. The benefits rationale presented in the following section is designed to provide practical steps for identifying, measuring, and valuing this kind of benefit, but it is also designed to accomplish something else: establish the legitimacy of these benefits and make their place in the business case analysis acceptable.

We met the benefits rationale in Chapter 2, in our 3,000 foot overview of the business case terrain. Now, we can prepare to meet it

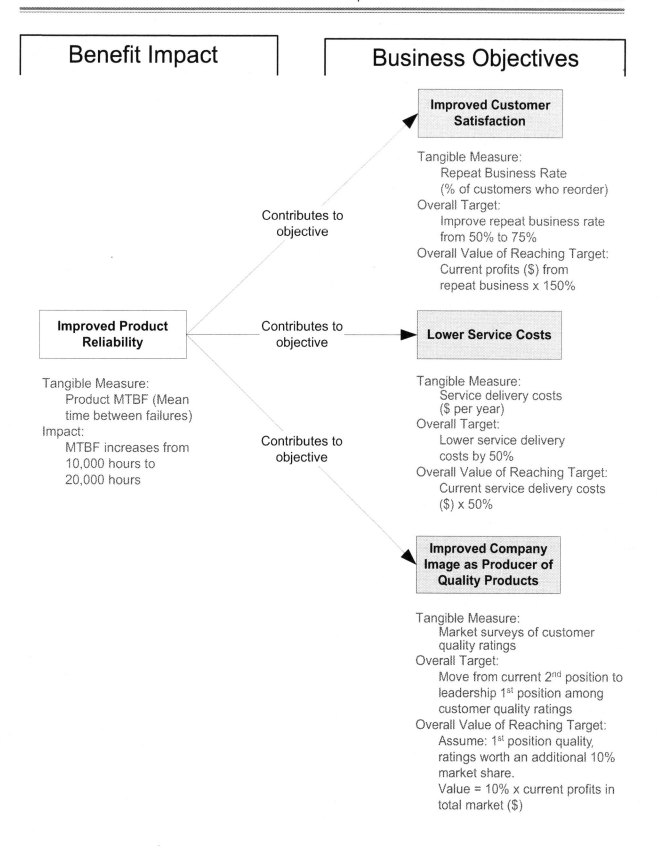

Figure 4.6 One benefit impact can contribute to several business objectives.

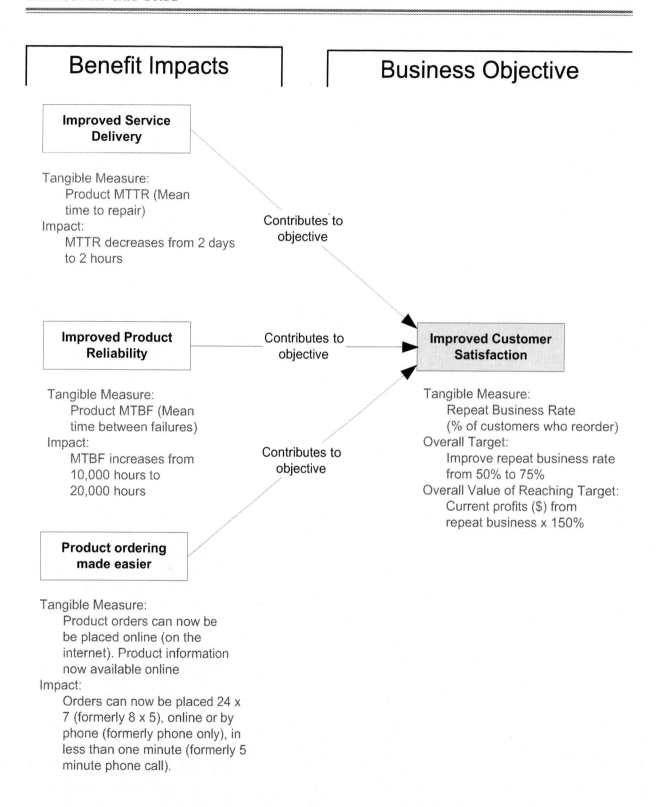

Figure 4.7 Several benefit impacts can contribute to one business objective.

at ground level by digging a little deeper into the meaning of "benefit."

This *Guide* emphasizes the basic benefits principle: benefits come from meeting business objectives. If a business impact from an action does not contribute to an objective, it is not a benefit. There is a difference between the benefit impact itself, however, and the objective. Figure 4.6 (next page) shows how one benefit impact can address several business objectives. The figure is also meant to show that we need to have tangible measures for both the impacts and the objectives. Here, for example, the business case analysis examined a proposed hardware design improvement in a mobile phone product.

Under one scenario, product reliability should be improved. In order to enter the business case, we need a tangible measure for reliability, and for that we can use "Mean Time Between Failure" (MTBF). Under the scenario's assumptions, MTBF improves from 10,000 hours to 20,000 hours.

That improvement has no financial value, however, until we connect it with at least one business objective. Figure 4.6 suggests in fact that improved reliability will support three objectives: Improved customer satisfaction, lower service costs, and improved company image as a producer of quality products. In order to apply the benefits rationale and assign cash flow value to the benefit (improved reliability), we need three kinds of information about each objective served:

- A tangible measure for the objective (what is seen or measured as evidence that the objective is reached). For the objective "improved customer satisfaction," one plausible measure is "repeat business rate."

- An overall target level on the tangible measure. Here, the company has a targeted objective to improve the repeat business rate from 50% to 75%. Measuring the repeat business rate at any time will show how progress toward the objective is going.

- The overall value of reaching the target level for the objective.

Figure 4.7 at left shows how several benefits can support a single objective. Analysis of one scenario might project several business impacts, all designed to support the objective "improved customer satisfaction." Here, it is reasonable to expect that improved service delivery, improved product reliability, and easier product ordering all contribute.

In brief, benefits are always tied to business objectives, but there need not be a one-to-one correspondence between impacts and objectives. Figure 4.8 (next page) represents the typical situation facing the benefits analyst.

A benefit impact has no financial value until it is connected with a business objective.

Figure 4.8 In most business case scenarios, there is not a one-to-one correspondence between benefits and business objectives.

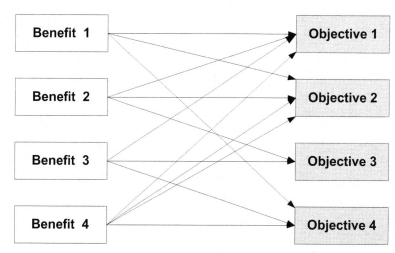

The Benefits Rationale

□ If the author develops the rationale in isolation, case credibility may suffer.

Understanding benefits terminology, we can now apply the benefits rationale that we met in Chapter 2. Remember that we have *two* objectives for doing so. One is to develop a cash flow value for the benefit, and the second is to establish the legitimacy of the benefit and the cash flow in the minds of recipients. Whenever we include benefits beyond cost savings and increased income, this latter objective needs special care.

In any situation where case author and case recipient are not the same person, the benefits rationale should be developed as a dialog between both parties. The dialog should start as early as possible in the case building process. If, instead, the author develops the rationale in isolation, and then delivers a completed case loaded with benefits that address objectives like improved customer satisfaction, or company image, case credibility may suffer. On the other hand, if authors and recipients have this dialog during the case building project, there should be no question about the legitimacy or appropriateness of such benefits.

Here, again, are first steps in the benefits rationale

- Ask: What are the important business objectives for this company or organization?

The important business objectives should be known now, since they were developed along with the subject statement and purpose statement at the start of case design. Table 3.1 (p. 66) lists many possible objectives, in these categories:

- Financial and Business Performance.
- Strategic Position and Ownership.
- Competitive Marketing.
- Operations and Functions.

- Products and Services.
- Employees and Work Environment.
- Image.
- Sales Performance.

No such categorization scheme is complete or perfect, and Table 3.1 is meant only to provide enough suggestions to get you started finding objectives that apply in your own situation. I mentioned earlier that business objectives do not classify neatly (some seem to fit in several categories).

▣ The benefits rationale works most effectively as a dialog between author and recipient, over time.

Sometimes it is hard to distinguish between a business objective and its tangible measure: Is "improved repeat business" a measure of "improved customer satisfaction"? Or, is this a situation where one objective (satisfaction) supports another objective (repeat business)? In fact, the answers to those questions depend on how the organization states or defines its objectives. The potential for confusion here is one reason why the benefits rationale works most effectively as a dialog between author and recipient, over time. It may take discussion and a little time to bring everyone to the same understanding. For now, assume we've identified an objective in "improved customer satisfaction.

- Ask: can the proposed action (business case subject) contribute to the objective?

For some actions and objectives, the answer will be "Of course it can!" That will probably be the case if the objective was the primary motivation for the action. Customer surveys, for instance, might have shown that low product reliability was a factor accounting for poor customer satisfaction. On the other hand, you may find some actions contributing to business objectives that were not at all behind the initial motivation (lower service costs, for instance). However, if you are confident you can demonstrate a connection between improved reliability and lower service costs, the answer to the question should be "yes."

▣ Your benefit will not gain much credibility if its legitimacy is tied to a business objective with low priority.

If the answer is "no," then it is time to go back and look for another objective. If the answer is "yes," carry the dialog to the next step.

- Ask: Is this business objective a targeted objective for the company? If "no," is it still an important objective?

Your benefit will not gain much credibility if its legitimacy is tied to a business objective that has low priority. The priority of different objectives should be evident in high level management statements and in places such as the annual report, press releases, and internal communications. Priorities for different objectives may also be evident in the company's current situation: if the company has reported a net loss, or if there is a cash flow shortage, or if the company is losing market share, it should be obvious which business objectives have high priority.

In non-profit organizations, objectives and priorities should be clear from mission (or charter) statements, periodic performance reports, and statements from management. The same is true for government and military organizations.

One of the clearest indicators that an objective is important, however, is the existence of a clear and well communicated *target* for the objective.

If author and recipient agree that the objective in view is important, proceed to the next step.

- Ask: What is the tangible evidence for reaching this objective?

In fact, you may discover several tangible measures of progress. Progress toward the objective "improved customer satisfaction," could be reasonably inferred from tangible measures such as the repeat business rate, the frequency and severity of customer complaints, the cost of providing customer service, the number of new customers referred by existing customers, and certainly, by customer satisfaction surveys.

You must find a credible, tangible way to measure progress toward the objective, or else the benefit must forever remain an "intangible benefit." If author and recipient agree on the evidence, then proceed.

- Ask: What is the targeted level for the objective (in terms of the tangible measure (from the previous step).

The targeted level may very well be known, for example: Improve the repeat business rate by 50%, or reduce the frequency of customer complaints by 25%.

It is very possible, however, that no such level has been established for some important objectives. They may be "targeted" in the sense that they receive a lot of attention and visibility, yet no one has put a "stake in the ground" on a tangible measure. If that is the case for a benefit and objective in this dialog, then author and recipient should propose and agree on a target. The target level should be both realistic and desirable. "Desirability" is important for the next step:

- Ask: Does reaching the target have value for the company?

If the dialog has come this far, it is unlikely that the answer will be "no." If the answer is "yes," the only questions remaining are: What is the value of reaching the target? And, how much of that value will the business case subject contribute. These last questions are taken up in Chapter 5, where we actually estimate and analyze cash flow values for all the cost and benefit impacts in the case.

> One of the clearest indicators that an objective is important is the existence of a clear and well communicated target for the objective.

Next Steps: Complete and Review Case Design

You will know that case design is completed when you have the complete set of cost items for your cost model, and when you have established the inventory of benefits. What remains is the design and execution of the analysis, the main subjects in Chapter 5.

When draft versions of the cost model and benefits inventory are completed, another meeting of the core team can be very helpful. Their job, again, is to review, adjust, and approve case design. They may very well make the final contributions, as well.

———— ❧ ————

What's the Difference?

Non Financial vs. Intangible

The business case was introduced on page 1 of this *Guide* as "...a decision support and planning tool that projects the likely financial results and *other business consequences* of an action." What are those other consequences? Are they important?

By now you should know that the case may very well contain non financial costs and benefits, and these may play an important role in the author's conclusions and recommendations. Nevertheless, once the case design is underway and the case building team is working overtime to fill the cost model and benefits inventory, with an eye to the coming financial analysis, it's easy to forget about non financial impacts that turn up. The result is a case that is less accurate and not as useful as it could be.

Remember that "non-financial" and "intangible" do not at all mean the same thing (this may be the time to review the section "Non financial Benefits Belong in the Case, pp. 44–47). As a matter of principle, case authors should try to quantify every business impact in cash flow terms, even those that are very hard to analyze or establish through the benefits rationale. After all, impacts with no assigned cash flow value contribute exactly nothing to the financial results. However, they can still contribute to conclusions and recommendations, and help make the case, if they are made tangible.

In Summary

The business case, like a scientific report needs a "methods" section describing case design and analysis methods, so that recipients can judge for themselves whether the results mean what the author says they mean. This chapter presents a ground level walkthrough of the following business case methods:

- Scope and boundary statements describe whose costs and whose benefits belong in the case, as well as the time period to be analyzed (the analysis period). Case scope and boundaries may be defined in terms of organizations, functions or positions, geographical areas, technology, or other categories.
- Financial metrics and other decision criteria describe what the case must produce in order to meet its purpose. Criteria from the world of finance include net cash flow, net present value, payback period, return on investment, and internal rate of return. Each says something different about the projected cash flow stream.
- Creating assumptions is a major part of case building, especially when creating case scenarios. Assumptions are necessary because the case deals with the future, and predictions are always assumptions. Assumptions are also necessary to simplify data requirements and to clarify exactly what the scenario describes.
- Recipients will want to know how cost and benefit values are estimated, or from what sources they were taken.
- Scenario design begins by deciding which scenarios are needed in order to address the purpose of the case. Normally just one scenario is needed for each major decision alternative. A business as usual scenario may or may not be necessary, depending on the purpose of the case.
- Data structure refers to the kind of data that enter the cash flow statement: full value data or incremental data. Each approach says something different about the case results. For the incremental approach, a business as usual scenario is necessary to serve as a baseline.
- Many case builders make the mistake of mixing incremental and full value data on the same cash flow statement. Mixing the two kinds of data can turn case results meaningless.
- Building the financial case is the process of identifying business impacts, measuring them, and then assigning financial value. Two tools that guide this process are the cost model and the benefits rationale.
- The cost model organizes the list of cost items by providing a simple system for defining cost categories. The model is then filled with cost items in each category.
- The cost model line items may be either resource categories, or activities that use resources.
- The cost model helps case builders identify every relevant cost item, assure recipients that every relevant item is included, and that different scenarios are comparable. The model also serves as a cost analysis tool in its own right.
- Business impacts are benefits only when they contribute to business objectives.
- The benefits rationale serves to establish the legitimacy of benefits for the business case. The rationale should be developed as a dialog between case author and recipient, over time, during the case building project.

Chapter 5

Analyzing Results

Chapters 3 and 4 covered case design. It is finally time to use the cost model, benefits rationale, and other design elements developed so far to produce cost and benefit estimates. These will be cash flow figures, which we analyze with financial metrics that support the case purpose.

It's Time to Do the Numbers

THE OBJECTIVE for today's hike across the business case landscape is to climb Mount Cash Flow and get the cost and benefit numbers that everyone back home is waiting for. We will also analyze them and extract information to support the purpose of the case. Before starting, however, let us be sure that everyone has packed properly for the trip.

In your backpack should be the fruits of all the case design work we did in Chapters 3 and 4. Here is the list of essentials:

- Subject statement.
- Purpose statement.
- Scope and boundary statements.
- Business objectives.
- Important global assumptions (those that apply to all scenarios).
- Scenario design (case scenarios identified and important scenario-specific assumptions).
- The cost model (cost model structure and most cost items).
- A list of benefits supported by the benefits rationale.

▣ When case design is essentially complete, we can go after the cost and benefit estimates because we know what we are looking for.

Of course all of these are to some extent "works in progress," and you will no doubt modify them before we enter the land of Conclusions and Recommendations. Now we can go after the cost and benefit estimates—the cash flow numbers—because now we know what we are looking for.

The path to Mt. Cash Flow leads through the Forest of Details, by the way, and once we are deeply into that area it is easy to lose sight of the day's objective. For that reason, I suggest we stand on this small rise, pick up the binoculars, and take a good look at where we are going. Keep the objective firmly in mind as we wrestle with the details between here and there.

The highlighted section of Table 5.1 (next page) summarizes the main content of this chapter more formally. We know by now that the table plays two roles: it is an outline of the case report and description of the case building project. Once we have most of the case design complete (Sections A and B), we can project the financial and non financial business impacts (Section C). We will analyze the financial impacts to develop the financial metrics and other decision criteria that support the case purpose.

Figure 5.1 (next page) should be familiar because we saw it in Chapter 2. This is an outline of the all-important cash flow statement that we intend to produce. This is where the cash flow estimates for each cost and benefit item appear and it is the starting point for developing financial metrics such as NPV or payback period. The "bottom line" of this statement is also the focus of attention as we perform risk and sensitivity analysis and develop conclusions and recommendations (Chapter 6).

In fact, we will have a cash flow statement like this with full value data for each scenario in the case. We may also create a statement with incremental data, representing the differences between a proposed action scenario and a business as usual scenario.

Business Case Structure

A. Introduction
Defines what the case is about (the subject) and why it is being built (the purpose). Also presents the business objectives addressed by the subject of the case.

B. Methods and Assumptions
Design elements fix the boundaries of the case (whose costs and whose benefits are examined, over what time period). Also outlines the rules for deciding what belongs in the case and what does not, along with important assumptions.

C. Business Impacts
The main business case results: financial and non financial business impacts expected in one or more scenarios.

D. Sensitivity, Risks, and Contingencies
Shows how results depend on important assumptions, as well as the likelihood that other results appear.

E. Conclusions and Recommendations
Recommends specific actions based on business objectives from Section A and the results from Sections C and D.

Table 5.1 Five major sections of the business case. Before cash flow business impacts can be valued and analyzed, case design must be nearly complete.

Figure 5.1 Structure of the business case cash flow statement. There will be one such statement for each scenario in the case.

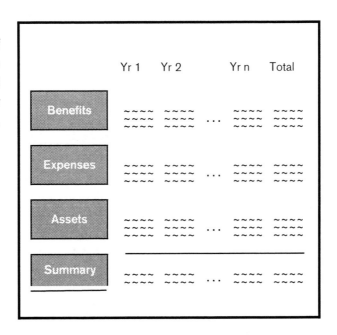

📧 Cash flow statements are the main summary vehicle for financial results in the business impacts section of the case report.

We will examine both the structure of this statement and its contents, in order to see how they address the questions that case builders set out to answer in the first place. We will also contrast the cash flow statement with an income statement and identify the one situation where the business case actually does call for income statement analysis.

In brief, cash flow statements are the main summary vehicle for projected financial results in the "Business Impacts" section of the report, outlined in Table 5.2 below. Before leaving that section, of course, we will also establish any important non financial benefits or costs that we find.

Now, in order to move from designing the case to designing the analysis, we must head into the Forest of Details.

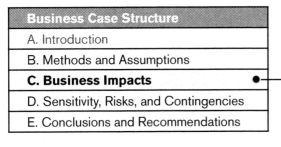

Business Case Structure
A. Introduction
B. Methods and Assumptions
C. Business Impacts
D. Sensitivity, Risks, and Contingencies
E. Conclusions and Recommendations

Table 5.2 Major blocks in the Business Impacts section

C. Business Impacts
- **Cash flow projections**
- **The dynamic financial model**
- **Financial analysis, development of financial metrics**
- **Rationale for including important non financial impacts**

The Cost and Benefit Time Line

⊡ The cost model and
the benefit inventory both
contribute line items to the
cash flow statement.

In a sense, the cash flow statement has two "parents:" the cost model and the benefit inventory (the list of benefits identified for the case). Both parents contribute line items to the cash flow statement. For the moment, think of the cash flow statement simply as a two dimensional table with row headings and column headings, like a spreadsheet.

Each row holds one line item, and the line items are grouped along the vertical dimension under major section headings such as "Benefits" or "Expenses." The horizontal dimension represents the analysis period. As you know, we will estimate the *magnitude* of cash inflow or outflow for each item and the cash flow *timing*.

Columns represents equal-length time periods that cover the analysis period. For each cost or benefit line item such as "IT Administrative Labor costs" we want to end up with cash flow estimates that have the form of Table 5.3 below. Here, each estimate covers a full year,

		Analysis Period				
Cash flow in $1,000s	**Year 1**	**Year 2**	**Year 3**	**Year 4**	**Year 5**	**Total**
IT Administrative Labor	(328.7)	(352.0)	(387.2)	(445.3)	(497.1)	(2,018.5)

Table 5.3 Cash flow estimates for one line item in the cash flow statement. The series of time periods covers the complete analysis period for the case. Parentheses indicate negative numbers (cash outflows).

but the columns could just as well represent quarters or months. In any case, the periods have to be tied to the calendar before cash flow estimates can begin.

Depending on your choice of analysis period, the "years" may or may not run from 1 January through 31 December (choosing the analysis period was covered on pp. 76–77). If your analysis period years *do* coincide with calendar years covering, say, 2003 through 2007, then column headings can be simply:

2003   2004   2005   2006   2007

If the analysis period years coincide exactly with fiscal years, and the fiscal year begins some time other than 1 January, you can still designate annual periods by naming the years:

FY	FY	FY	FY	FY
2003	2004	2005	2006	2007

If your analysis period does *not* begin with the calendar year or the fiscal year, it is a good idea to label years with their end dates. Consider a five-year analysis period running:

15 August 2003 – 14 August 2008

⊡ Authors and recipients need to understand clearly the exact calendar dates covered by each period.

The dates covered by each column could be conveyed clearly with a simple year-end note above the year numbers:

For the year ending 14 August ...
2004	2005	2006	2007	2008

Of course the same approach applies if the periods are quarters or months. Analysts and recipients may need to be told, for instance, that the periods are fiscal year quarters, not calendar year quarters:

Q1	Q2	Q3	Q4	Q1
FY 03	FY 03	FY 03	FY 03	FY 04

In all these cases, authors and recipients need to understand clearly the exact calendar dates covered by each period.

Before beginning the cost analysis, be sure you examine carefully the relationship between the horizontal axis of your cost model and the cash flow time periods. When the subject of the case is a project, program, or product life cycle, there may very well be the kind of relationship shown in Figure 5.2, below. This kind of situation raises some interesting questions for the case author.

⊡ Examine the relationship between the cost model and the cash flow time periods.

Projects, programs, and product life cycles are often planned and managed as a sequence of phases. At the bottom of the Figure 5.2 are the five product life cycle phases from the horizontal axis of a cost model we saw earlier (the model is shown on p. 98). Phases are a natural choice for defining one set of cost categories (one dimension

Figure 5.2 The relationship between one set of cost model categories (bottom) and a calendar year time line on the cash flow statement (top).

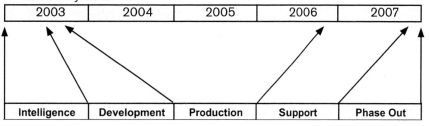

115

of the model). Development phase activities, for instance, tend to be planned and managed differently from production phase activities.

Notice that phases are *sequential* but they are not distributed evenly across the analysis period. The intelligence phase covers only six months in 2003, for instance. while the production phase extends nearly three years. long. The year 2003, in fact, includes the whole intelligence phase, the whole development phase, and even the first few months of the production phase. Yet the cash flow table is set up to cover the analysis period in five segments of one year each. You may wonder if one-year increments are too coarse for the first year. By putting all 2003 cash flow into a single column, we lose sight of the individual contributions from the intelligence phase, development phase, and early production phase. On the other hand, a cash flow statement covering five years in 20 quarters or 60 months would probably have too much detail to interest recipients or justify the extra work from the case building team. So, should we stay with the cash flow estimates on a yearly basis? Should we analyze by quarters or months? Or, should we analyze the first year by quarters and then analyze later years on an annual basis? Like so many things in business case analysis, this is a judgement call for author and analyst. As you make the call, here are some points of guidance:

▣ One dimension of the cost model can help identify exactly when cash flow events occur, but the dimension itself is not a time line.

- All time periods in a cash flow statement should be equal length. Do not mix quarterly columns and yearly columns in the same table, for instance, even if you think you can label them in some clever way to show which is which.

- If a quarterly or monthly analysis is truly desirable for one year but that year only, use a *second* cash flow statement to show that. For the current example, you would have the main cash flow statement covering annual periods:

2003   2004   2005   2006   2007

Then, a *second* cash flow statement showing cash flow for the first year by quarters:

Q1   Q2   Q3   Q4
2003   2003   2003   2003

- Remember that cost item spending by cost category can be captured and analyzed with a cost model analysis (illustrated in Figure 4.5, p. 97).

In brief, one dimension of the cost model can help identify exactly when cash flow events occur, but the dimension itself is not a time line. The relationship between cost model and calendar time may tell

116

Acquisition	Operation	Growth and Change

Figure 5.3 Horizontal axis of the cost model for an IT system life cycle. This set of cost items is even less directly tied to calendar time than the cost categories in Figure 5.2. Nevertheless, the timing of cash flow for a cost item depends partly on which of these categories the item belongs to.

🔲 Cost categories do not really describe a single sequence, but cost items in different categories do have different time dynamics.

you whether an annual view meets recipient needs, or whether smaller time periods are necessary in order to show useful information.

The difference between calendar time and cost model categories is even clearer in Figure 5.3. The figure shows one set of cost categories (one dimension) from the resource-based cost model we met in Chapter 4 (pp. 93–97). The subject of the case was an IT system life cycle, and cost items were resources such as hardware, human resources, maintenance services, and facilities. The three categories in the Figure work well as a cost model dimension because the items in each category are planned and managed differently. The categories do not really describe a single sequence, but each does have its own time dynamics. Knowing that a cost item belongs to one category or another helps the analyst anticipate the timing of cash flows.

Cash Flow Categories

From the previous section we know that the cost and benefit figures depend on the choice of analysis period and its division into equal length time segments. Cost and benefit figures also depend on the choice of line item categories for the vertical dimension of the cash flow statement. Once the cash flow statement is structured, we can finally start estimating cost and benefit cash flow.

Cash Flow: Business Case vs. Accounting Statements

The business case cash flow statement is a first cousin to cash flow statements used in financial accounting, such as a cash basis "Statement of Changes in Financial Position." Figure 5.4 (next page) compares those two kinds of statements. Both statements deal with cash flow events only. Their bottom lines do not include some of the accounting conventions from the income statement that deal with non cash flow events (depreciation expenses, for example).

There are some important differences between the cash flow cousins, however:

Figure 5.4 A standard cash flow statement as a financial accounting report (right) compared to the business case cash flow statement (below). The accounting statement looks backward across one period, while the business case statement looks forward across several periods. Note especially the different conventions for dealing with positive and negative cash flows (different use of parentheses) explained in the text.

Statement of Changes in Financial Position
For the year ending 31 December 2002
Sources of Cash
Total source items $180
Uses of Cash
Total use items $150
Net Cash Increase (Decrease) **$30**

Business Case Cash Flow Statement				
For the year ending 31 December...				
	2003	2004	2005	*Total*
Benefits				
Benefit items.......................$190	$240	$460	**$890**	
Costs and Expenses				
Cost and expense items ....$(250)	$(250)	$(280)	$(780)	
Net Cash Inflow (Outflow)................$(60)	**$(10)**	**$180**	**$110**	

▣ The business case cash flow statements allows more flexibility in structuring sections and headings than the accounting statement.

- The accounting statement normally reports historical cash flow for one period, while the business case statement looks forward across all time periods in the analysis period.

- Main headings and subsections on the accounting statement follow prescribed accounting conventions. There is more flexibility to structure sections and headings on the business case statement.

Figure 5.4 also reminds us to be careful and consistent with the way minus signs are used (or the minus sign equivalent, parentheses). Accounting statements often present both inflows and outflows as positive numbers. Notice in figure 5.4, that the cash for total source items is written as $180 (these are cash inflows) while the total for uses of cash (cash outflows) is also written without parenthesis as $150. The reader understands that "total use items" is subtracted from "total source items" to create the net $30. When the net is negative, accountants *do* write *that* with parentheses, red figures, or a minus sign.

The business case cash flow statement, however, writes every *outflow* as a negative figure. That way subtotals and overall totals are always calculated by *adding* the numbers above them. This approach, by the way is only one person's personal preference: you can of course follow the traditional accounting approach shown at the top of figure 5.4. In that case, however, be sure you clearly communicate which items and totals are added and which subtracted from each other.

Before Tax or After Tax?

Should you produce a "before tax" or "after tax" analysis? How you answer the question may impact the structure of your cash flow statement.

In government and non profit organizations that do not pay taxes on operating income, the question is usually a non-issue. The author has to address this question only when the business case deals with companies, individuals, or other organizations that *do* have to consider taxes (including a few government organizations that are mandated to do so).

You can of course do the analysis both ways and present both sets of results to recipients. However the after tax approach requires extra work and requires a more complicated cash flow statement. Before taking on the work and the complexity, it is worth asking whether or not recipients really need or want to see results after taxes.

What effect does the "tax factor" have on case results? Taxes change cash flow results in two ways. First, they attenuate (reduce the magnitude) of net gains and net losses, and second, they create tax savings from depreciation expense.

▣ Taxes reduce the magnitude of net gains and net losses. They also create tax savings from depreciation expense.

The first kind of situation operates this way. Suppose a company has an average marginal tax rate of 35% (the rate applied to incremental income or loss). If you project a net cash inflow that raises operating income by $100, there is an income tax liability:

$$
\begin{aligned}
\text{Income tax} \;&=\; \text{tax rate} * \text{operating income} \\
&=\; 35.0\% * \$100 \\
&=\; \$35
\end{aligned}
$$

The net gain after taxes is no longer $100, but something less:

$$
\begin{aligned}
\text{Net gain} \;&=\; \text{operating income} - \text{tax} \\
&=\; \$100 - \$35 \\
&=\; \$65
\end{aligned}
$$

On the other hand, if your cash flow totals show a net loss for the tax period, lowering operating gains, then the tax liability is also lower. Lower tax liability is a *tax savings*, and this is equivalent to cash inflow. Suppose in another period, the business case results for the same company project a net cash outflow, or loss, such as ($240). If this lowers operating gains for the company by $240, then the company has a tax savings. The net cash flow impact of your business case results, after taxes, becomes:

$$\begin{aligned}
\text{Net loss} \quad &= \quad \text{operating loss} * (1 - \text{tax rate}) \\
&= \quad \$240 * (65\%) \\
&= \quad \$156
\end{aligned}$$

In a nutshell, bringing taxes into the picture cuts both your gains and your losses.

The other kind of tax impact comes through depreciation expenses, but only if two conditions apply:

- Business case scenarios include the acquisition of assets that will be depreciated over several years

and

- Case analysis is an after-tax analysis

If both conditions apply to your case, then you must calculate depreciation expense for each asset for each period of the analysis period. Depreciation expenses on the income statement do not represent real cash transfers. They are an accounting convention that allows the taxpayer to lower taxes each year by spreading acquisition costs across a number of years. The tax savings from depreciation *are* real cash flow events, however. If, for instance, assets covered by the case produce $10,000 in depreciation expense one year, and if the company's marginal tax rate is 35%, the tax savings that year will be:

$$\begin{aligned}
\text{Tax savings} &= \quad \text{tax rate} * \text{depreciation expense} \\
&= \quad 35\% * \$10,000 \\
&= \quad \$3,500
\end{aligned}$$

By now you should be getting the picture: taxes complicate the case analysis. Tax consequences can be large, however, and if recipients need them to support the purpose of the case, they should be included.

Tax events can be much more complicated than the examples illustrated here. Income taxes, capital gains taxes, value-added taxes, luxury taxes, and other special kinds of taxes may apply to the consequences of actions. If your case attempts an after tax analysis, it is a good idea to recruit a tax specialist for your core team, if not for the case building project team. If you include tax consequences and you do not have expert tax advice, then by all means include a disclaimer statement letting recipients know that you have done your best to provide a rough guide to tax impacts, but that actual tax consequences could be different (see "Disclaimer," pp. 61–62). In any case, here are some factors to consider when deciding whether or not to include taxes in the analysis:

□ If your case attempts an after tax analysis, it is a good idea to recruit a tax specialist for your core team.

120

- Generally, it is a good idea to include tax effects when there are large differences in tax implications for different scenarios.

- Tax implications can be especially important when different financing options are under consideration. In a "lease vs. purchase" case, or a comparison of several lease packages, tax consequences can be important differentiators between options.

- Ask: How are other, competing proposals analyzed? If your case supports a proposal that is competing for funds with other proposals, all proposals should either include or exclude tax effects.

- Ask: Are after tax results important to recipients? If recipients include people responsible for the company's business performance, they will probably want to see before tax and after tax versions. Middle managers who are not responsible for overall company performance may prefer to see results without taxes.

▣ If your case supports a proposal that is competing for funds with other proposals, all proposals should either include or exclude tax effects.

Structuring Benefits and Costs

The business case author has more flexibility than the accountant to structure line item categories for the cash flow statement. The accountant is constrained by mandatory conventions that are meant to ensure consistent reporting practice. The business case author is not reporting to stockholders or regulatory authorities. The case author's priority should be meeting recipients' decision support or planning needs. Here is one simple cash flow structure:

```
          Cash Flow Statement
     Benefits
     Costs and Expenses
     Summary
```

This is the simplest cash flow statement structure, appropriate for cases with only a few line items. Like all structures in this section it could represent either a full value or an incremental statement.

In the full value statement, all cash inflows fall under benefits and all cash outflows fall under costs and expenses. The summary section contains the net cash flow totals, a cumulative cash flow figure for each year, and discounted cash flow figures.

In the incremental statement, cost savings may appear either under costs and expenses or under benefits (see "Data Structure," pp. 87–89). If you are going to put line items that have an incremental cost savings under costs (and not under benefits), I suggest labeling the main sections this way:

```
┌─────────────────────────────────────┐
│         Cash Flow Statement          │
│   Benefits                           │
│   Costs and Cost Savings             │
│   Summary                            │
│                                      │
└─────────────────────────────────────┘
```

This is a clear signal that two items in this incremental cash flow statement might look like this:

For the year ending 31 December…

	2003	*2004*	*2005*	**Total**
Costs and Cost Savings				
Floor space rental savings	$120	$20	$140	**$380**
Increased maintenance costs	$(50)	$(60)	$(80)	**$(190)**

The author chose to put "floor space rental savings" in the same section as "increased maintenance costs," even though one is consistently a cash inflow and the other is consistently a cash outflow. The rental savings could just as well have gone in the benefits section, but the author felt that recipients would rather see two infrastructure support items, like these, together.

□ If the author consistently uses positive numbers for inflows and negative numbers for outflows, there should be no confusion.

As long as the author consistently uses positive numbers for inflows and negative numbers (parentheses) for outflows, there should be no confusion. Getting to the bottom line summary requires only that all numbers be added; under this convention nothing is subtracted from anything else. This is also the approach in the cash flow statement for the example business case in Appendix A.

Sometimes, however, incremental analysis of a line item produces inflows in some periods and outflows in other periods. Suppose, for instance you analyze floor space rental costs and find:

	2003	*2004*	*2005*	**Total**
Incremental floor space rental	$120	$30	$(140)	**$10**

You can leave the item as a single item under costs and cost savings as shown above. However, the recommended alternative suggested on page 89 is to create two items:

	2003	2004	2005	*Total*
Benefits				
Floor space rental savings	$120	$30	$0	**$150**
Costs and Expenses				
Floor space rental increase..................	$0	$0	$(140)	**$(140)**

If this part of the Forest of Details is beginning to sound confusing, let's pause at this clearing and summarize two points:

- In the full value cash flow statement, all cost and expense Items are cash outflows. All benefits items are inflows.

- In the incremental cash flow statement, cost savings (or avoided costs) can go either under benefits or as a cost item under costs and cost savings" as long as you consistently use positive numbers for cash inflows and negative numbers for cash outflows.

▣ On the after tax cash flow statement, separate assets costs from expenses.

The above cash flow statements are appropriate for the "before tax" case. If your cash flow statement deals with the purchase of assets and tax consequences, however you may use the structure in shown earlier in Figure 2.4 and again in Figure 5.1:

> Cash Flow Statement
> Benefits
> Expenses
> Assets
> Summary

For the after tax case, asset costs should be grouped separately from expenses because asset costs produce depreciation expenses (and thus, cash flow from tax savings). The purchase of other goods and services does not produce depreciation expenses. Before tax and after tax cash flow statements are compared in more detail on pages 126 and 127.

To complete this subsection, let us look at the structure above at the next level of detail, where the subject of the case is acquisition of an IT system:

```
┌─────────────────────────────────────────────┐
│                                               │
│        Cash Flow Statement                    │
│                                               │
│   Benefits                                     │
│                                               │
│   Expenses                                     │
│           Hardware expenses                    │
│           Software expenses                    │
│           Personnel expenses–IT staff         │
│           Personnel expenses–users            │
│           Networks and communications costs    │
│           Other costs and expenses             │
│                                               │
│   Assets                                       │
│           Server systems                       │
│           Client desktop systems               │
│           Software                             │
│                                               │
│   Summary                                      │
│                                               │
└─────────────────────────────────────────────┘
```

Here, the author distinguishes between expenses, which are non capital costs, and assets, which represent the purchase of items that go onto the balance sheet as assets. Notice especially that subsections under expenses are the vertical dimension of the resource based cost model we met on pages 93–93. This is one way the cash flow statement resembles its parent, the cost model. Moreover, there is a subsection under assets for each asset category that has its own depreciation schedule (see page 127 for the detail).

🔲 The subsections under expenses are one axis of the cost model.

Benefits Categories

Finally, you may wonder if there is value in dividing the benefits section into subsections. I mentioned earlier, however, that most business cases have many dozens or hundreds of cost items but only a few benefit items. When benefit items are few in number, there may be little value in grouping them.

You may wish to group benefit items, however, if several of them clearly support one business objective (e.g., increased market share), while other benefits are directed mostly in support of another business objective (e.g., shorter product development time). Or, if your cash flow statement has all three kinds of benefit items described on page 100, the following benefits categories may be helpful for recipients:

Benefits
Contributions to Strategic Objectives
Increased Income
Cost Savings

The Complete Cash Flow Statement

The complete 5-year cash flow analysis for a proposed computer server system acquisition appears in two forms on the next two pages. Table 5.4 is the before tax analysis and Table 5.5 is an after tax analysis based on the same cost and benefit estimates.

The business case behind the statements in fact had three scenarios and five cash flow statements. The purpose of the case was to support a decision between scenarios for purchase, lease, and business as usual (no acquisition). In reaching a decision, recipients compared cash flow projections and financial metrics from two incremental analyses: purchase vs. business as usual, and lease vs. business as usual. Figure 5.4 shows the relationships among cash flow statements for this case.

Figure 5.4 Cash flow statements for a case to support a lease vs. purchase decision. The incremental cash flow statement in Tables 5.4 and 5.5 is obtained by subtracting each business as usual cash flow estimate from its counterpart in the purchase scenario.

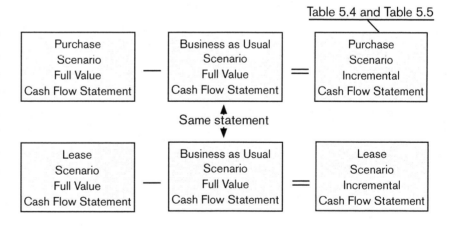

Table 5.4 and Table 5.5

The author's first step was to produce three full value statements, one for each scenario. Initially, all three statements had the same set of cost and benefit line items: this makes it possible to create the two incremental statements by subtracting each cash flow estimate in the business as usual full value statement from its counterpart in the purchase or lease full value statement. The resulting item-by-item differences are the data in the incremental cash flow statements in Tables 5.4 and 5.5 (for the purchase comparison).

Items that had zero value for all periods in the incremental statement were dropped from the final presentation. The purchase statement, for instance, omitted the item "Scheduled lease payments" on

Table. 5.4 Incremental cash flow statement for the purchase option in a lease vs. purchase analyses. In this "before tax" version, asset purchases appear in the same sections as other costs and expenses under the headings of "Hardware Costs" and "Software Costs."

Server Systems Upgrade Purchase

Summary of Financial Results and Assumptions
($ in 1,000's)

The estimated net benefit (cost) over the evaluation period is as follows:
Net Incremental cash flow: 1,537.9
Net present value 1: 1,072.9   DCF at 9.0%
Net present value 2: 854.1   DCF at 15.0%
Analysis period: Sep 2002 - Aug 2007
Analysis period length   60 Months

Incremental Cash Flow Statement

For the year ending 31 August…

	Year 0 Aug 2002	Year 1 Aug 2003	Year 2 Aug 2004	Year 3 Aug 2005	Year 4 Aug 2006	Year 5 Aug 2007	TOTAL
BENEFITS / GAINS							
Contributions to Strategic Objectives							
Productivity improvements	0.0	400.0	618.0	742.6	819.5	900.4	**3,480.6**
Customer satisfaction improved	0.0	240.0	316.8	418.2	552.0	728.6	**2,255.6**
Downtime reductions	0.0	200.0	154.5	137.9	120.2	112.6	**725.2**
Other Benefits							
Rental equipment savings	0.0	400.0	412.0	424.4	437.1	450.2	**2,123.7**
Avoided Hiring - Add'l staff	0.0	239.0	239.0	270.7	304.2	287.2	**1,340.1**
Reduced floorspace costs	0.0	12.5	12.9	13.3	13.7	14.1	**66.4**
Sale of unused equipment	320.0	0.0	0.0	0.0	0.0	0.0	**320.0**
Total Benefits/Gains	320.0	1,491.5	1,753.1	2,007.1	2,246.7	2,493.1	10,311.5
COSTS AND EXPENSES							
Hardware Costs							
Server Systems	(130.4)	0.0	0.0	(69.8)	0.0	0.0	**(200.2)**
Peripheral HW assets	(32.0)	(34.9)	(17.6)	(23.7)	(12.8)	(8.2)	**(129.2)**
PCs and workstations	(300.0)	(25.0)	(30.0)	(20.0)	(30.0)	(20.0)	**(425.0)**
HW maint cost increase	0.0	(120.5)	(120.3)	(150.7)	(150.7)	(150.7)	**(692.9)**
Additional small equip expenses	(12.8)	(57.0)	(69.0)	(33.9)	(13.1)	(13.5)	**(199.4)**
Software Costs							
Software assets	(130.0)	(60.0)	0.0	(62.2)	(41.6)	0.0	**(293.7)**
SW maintenances increases	0.0	(16.7)	(16.7)	(16.7)	(16.7)	(16.7)	**(83.5)**
End user appl's - expensed	(32.0)	(23.0)	(23.7)	(24.4)	(25.1)	0.0	**(128.2)**
Personnel Expenses							
System staffing cost increase	0.0	(320.0)	(356.2)	(396.5)	(441.3)	(491.2)	**(2,005.1)**
NW/Comms Expenses							
Line usage fee increase	0.0	(348.0)	(412.2)	(496.7)	(588.3)	(716.5)	**(2,561.7)**
Line maintenance increase	0.0	(180.2)	(180.2)	(180.2)	(180.2)	(180.2)	**(901.0)**
Other Costs and Expenses							
Electrical power increase	0.0	(6.5)	(6.5)	(6.7)	(6.7)	(7.0)	**(33.4)**
Insurance increase	0.0	(4.2)	(4.3)	(4.5)	(4.6)	(4.7)	**(22.3)**
Security increase	0.0	0.0	(268.2)	(276.3)	(260.4)	(293.1)	**(1,098.0)**
Total Impact: Costs and Exp	(637.2)	(1,196.0)	(1,504.9)	(1,762.1)	(1,771.5)	(1,901.8)	(8,773.6)
CASH FLOW SUMMARY							
Cash inflows (outflows)							
Benefit Impacts	320.0	1,491.5	1,753.1	2,007.1	2,246.7	2,493.1	10,311.5
Cost and Expense Item Impacts	(637.2)	(1,196.0)	(1,504.9)	(1,762.1)	(1,771.5)	(1,901.8)	(8,773.6)
NET CASH FLOW	(317.2)	295.5	248.2	245.0	475.2	591.3	1,537.9
Cumulative Net CF	(317.2)	(21.7)	226.5	471.5	946.7	1,537.9	1,537.9
Discounted Cash Flow							
At 9.0 %	(317.2)	271.1	208.9	189.2	336.6	384.3	**1,072.9**
At 15.0 %	(317.2)	256.9	187.7	161.1	271.7	294.0	**854.1**

◨ A Year 0 column is optional. It holds cash flow events that come immediately at the start of the analysis period.

that basis. That item *did* appear in the final presentation of the lease scenario statement, of course.

Notice that this case covers a 5-year analysis period but the author included *six* annual columns, starting with Year 0. A Year 0 column is optional: it refers to cash flow events that come immediately at the

Server Systems Upgrade Purchase

Summary of Financial Results and Assumptions

($ in 1,000's)

Table 5.5 The "after tax" version of the incremental cash flow statement shown in Figure 5.4 When tax impacts are included, asset purchases are presented in a section of their own, so that depreciation expenses and their tax consequences can be summarized clearly.

The estimated net benefit (cost) over the evaluation period is as follows:
After tax net incremtntal cash   972.2
Net present value 1:   625.7   DCF at 9.0%
Net present value 2:   462.7   DCF at 15.0%
Analysis period: Sep 2002 - Aug 2007
Analysis period length   60 Months

Incremental Cash Flow Statement

For the year ending 31 August…

	Year 0 Aug 2002	Year 1 Aug 2003	Year 2 Aug 2004	Year 3 Aug 2005	Year 4 Aug 2006	Year 5 Aug 2007	TOTAL
BENEFITS / GAINS							
Contributions to Strategic Objectives							
Productivity improvements	0.0	400.0	618.0	742.6	819.5	900.4	**3,480.6**
Customer satisfaction improved	0.0	240.0	316.8	418.2	552.0	728.6	**2,255.6**
Downtime reductions	0.0	200.0	154.5	137.9	120.2	112.6	**725.2**
Other Benefits							
Rental equipment savings	0.0	400.0	412.0	424.4	437.1	450.2	**2,123.7**
Avoided Hiring - Add'l staff	0.0	239.0	239.0	270.7	304.2	287.2	**1,340.1**
Reduced floorspace costs	0.0	12.5	12.9	13.3	13.7	14.1	**66.4**
Sale of unused equipment	320.0	0.0	0.0	0.0	0.0	0.0	**320.0**
Total Benefits/Gains	**320.0**	**1,491.5**	**1,753.1**	**2,007.1**	**2,246.7**	**2,493.1**	**10,311.5**
OPERATING EXPENSE ITEMS							
Hardware Expenses							
HW maint cost increase	0.0	(120.5)	(120.3)	(150.7)	(150.7)	(150.7)	**(692.9)**
Additional small equip expenses	(12.8)	(57.0)	(69.0)	(33.9)	(13.1)	(13.5)	**(199.4)**
Software Expenses							
SW maintenances increases	0.0	(16.7)	(16.7)	(16.7)	(16.7)	(16.7)	**(83.5)**
End user appl's - expensed	(32.0)	(23.0)	(23.7)	(24.4)	(25.1)	0.0	**(128.2)**
Personnel Expenses							
System staffing cost increases	0.0	(320.0)	(356.2)	(396.5)	(441.3)	(491.2)	**(2,005.1)**
NW/Comms Expenses							
Line usage fees increase	0.0	(348.0)	(412.2)	(496.7)	(588.3)	(716.5)	**(2,561.7)**
Line maintenance increase	0.0	(180.2)	(180.2)	(180.2)	(180.2)	(180.2)	**(901.0)**
Other Expenses							
Electrical power increase	0.0	(6.5)	(6.5)	(6.7)	(6.7)	(7.0)	**(33.4)**
Insurance increase	0.0	(4.2)	(4.3)	(4.5)	(4.6)	(4.7)	**(22.3)**
Security increase	0.0	0.0	(268.2)	(276.3)	(260.4)	(293.1)	**(1,098.0)**
Total Impact: Op Exp Items	**(44.8)**	**(1,076.1)**	**(1,457.3)**	**(1,586.5)**	**(1,687.1)**	**(1,873.6)**	**(7,725.5)**
ASSETS PURCHASED							
Cash inflows (outflows)							
GROUP 1: Server Systems							
Server Systems	(130.4)	0.0	0.0	(69.8)	0.0	0.0	**(200.2)**
Peripheral HW assets	(32.0)	(34.9)	(17.6)	(23.7)	(12.8)	(8.2)	**(129.2)**
Group 1 Total Assets:	(162.4)	(34.9)	(17.6)	(93.4)	(12.8)	(8.2)	**(329.3)**
Group1 Depreciation Expense	0.0	(39.5)	(67.5)	(74.1)	(78.7)	(65.3)	**(325.1)**
GROUP 2: Software							
Software assets	(130.0)	(60.0)	0.0	(62.2)	(41.6)	0.0	**(293.7)**
Group 2 Total Assets:	(130.0)	(60.0)	0.0	(62.2)	(41.6)	0.0	**(293.7)**
Group2 Depreciation Expense	0.0	(38.0)	(38.0)	(48.0)	(54.0)	(54.0)	**(232.0)**
GROUP 3: PC's and W/S							
PCs and workstations	(300.0)	(25.0)	(30.0)	(20.0)	(30.0)	(20.0)	**(425.0)**
Group 3 Total Assets:	(300.0)	(25.0)	(30.0)	(20.0)	(30.0)	(20.0)	**(425.0)**
Group3 Depreciation Expense	0.0	(65.0)	(110.0)	(76.0)	(55.6)	(58.3)	**(364.9)**
Total Asset Costs:	**(592.4)**	**(119.9)**	**(47.6)**	**(175.6)**	**(84.4)**	**(28.2)**	**(1,048.1)**
Total Depreciation Expenses:	0.0	(142.5)	(215.5)	(198.1)	(188.3)	(177.6)	**(922.0)**
Est Tax Savings on Deprec	0.0	48.4	73.3	67.4	64.0	60.4	**313.5**
CASH FLOW SUMMARY							
Cash inflows (outflows)							
Benefit Impacts	320.0	1,491.5	1,753.1	2,007.1	2,246.7	2,493.1	**10,311.5**
Expense Item Impacts	(44.8)	(1,076.1)	(1,457.3)	(1,586.5)	(1,687.1)	(1,873.6)	**(7,725.5)**
Net Operating Inflow(Outflow)	275.2	415.4	295.8	420.6	559.6	619.4	**2,586.0**
Tax Savings (Tax)							
on Inflow/Outflow	(93.6)	(141.2)	(100.6)	(143.0)	(190.3)	(210.6)	**(879.2)**
Asset Purchase	(592.4)	(119.9)	(47.6)	(175.6)	(84.4)	(28.2)	**(1,048.1)**
Tax Savings from all							
Depreciation Expense	0.0	48.4	73.3	67.4	64.0	60.4	**313.5**
NET CASH FLOW	**(410.8)**	**202.7**	**220.9**	**169.3**	**348.9**	**441.0**	**972.2**
Cumulative Net CF	(410.8)	(208.1)	12.8	182.2	531.1	972.2	**972.2**
Discounted Cash Flow							
At 9.0 %	(410.8)	185.9	186.0	130.8	247.2	286.6	**625.7**
At 15.0 %	(410.8)	176.2	167.1	111.3	199.5	219.3	**462.7**

start of the analysis period (if there is no year 0, the immediate events go into year 1). Year 0 is used when the immediate events are large enough to be interesting in their own right.

I should also mention that some recipients may ask to see historical costs and benefits included as well (cash flow events occurring *before* the analysis period). Historical costs and benefits can go together in Year 0, but using these figures is is not normally considered good financial practice. Historical *costs*, for example, are called *sunk costs*, meaning they are irretrievably gone. Sunk costs should carry no weight in making decisions for the future. They are "water under the bridge." If clients or managers ask for historical cash flow, be sure they know they are asking you to "bend the rules." The business case is understood to represent *future* consequences of an action.

> ▣ Taxes complicate the financial math and they also reduce the overall size of operating gains and losses.

Comparing Tables 5.4 and 5.5 you can also see that taxes do indeed complicate the picture. In the before tax statement of Table 5.4, asset costs go under the same sub headings as other costs and expenses. In the after tax version, Table 5.5, assets appear in a section of their own. Assets that receive the same depreciation treatment are listed together in asset groups. Depreciation expenses for each asset group are calculated for each year of the analysis period. These depreciation expenses do not enter the net cash flow totals directly, but they do they contribute to the tax savings cash flow summarized just above the "Net Cash Flow" line in the Summary section.

Taxes complicate the financial math and they also reduce the overall size of operating gains and losses. Compare the summary boxes at the top of each statement. The overall net cash flow is $1,537,900 before taxes, and $972,000 after taxes (tax calculations assume an average 34% marginal tax rate on income).

Cash Flow or Income Statement?

The cash flow statement differs from the income statement in several important ways that we have mentioned already:

- The income statement bottom line reflects depreciation expenses as well as indirect costs and allocated costs. These are not usually cash flow events and they do not contribute directly to the cash flow statement bottom line.
- Sales revenues and most costs on the income statement do not necessarily coincide in time with the cash flow events they cause. Sales revenues may be claimed when the customer signs the purchase contract, for instance, but cash payments may not flow into the company for weeks or months.

- The income statement reports historical performance for the company or some part of it. The business case projects future cash flow from a single action.

This *Guide* presents the cash flow statement as the appropriate summary vehicle for the business case because that statement connects a proposed action with its consequences very directly. The income statement does not describe the consequences of action as clearly as the cash flow statement. Nevertheless, case builders in business are often asked by managers and review committees to produce an income statement with the business case (they may call it by its other name, a profit and loss, or "P&L," statement). If you are in this position, try to help the requesting party understand the reasons that cash flow is preferred for the business case report (diplomatically, of course).

For contrast with cash flow structures in the previous sections, here is a typical income statement for a manufacturing company

⊡ A business case designed to predict product profits is the one kind of case that may incorporate income statement line items and income statement math.

Income Statement for Grande Company
For the year ended 31 December 2002

Net sales revenues		$2,100
Cost of goods sold		$1,390
Gross margin		$710
Operating expenses		
Selling	$85	
General and administrative	$110	
Depreciation expense	$100	
Research and development	$120	$415
Net operating margin		$295
Financial expenses		$35
Net income before tax		$260
Income tax (at 40%)		$104
Net income after tax		$156

Income statements vary from company to company and the format differs widely between, say, a manufacturing company and a financial services company. Nevertheless, income statements are not cash flow statements.

The one kind of case that appropriately includes income statement line items and income statement math is the case explicitly designed to predict product profits (or profits from a product line, or a marketing program). In the profit-predicting business case, you will calculate expected profits using many of the income statement cost categories.

	Analysis Period					
Cash flow in $1,000s	Year 1	Year 2	Year 3	Year 4	Year 5	Total
IT Administrative Labor						

Table 5.6 A cost item waiting for cash flow estimates.

However, when doing so, take care to use the actual cost of goods sold, the actual selling expenses, and other actual expenses *for that product*. Do not blindly use a given percentage of sales or percentage of some other figure, unless you know that it really describes the costs for that product (see pp. 144-145).

Estimating Costs

At this point you should know from the cost model which cost items belong in the case. From designing the cash flow statement, you know which calendar time periods require cash flow estimates. For each cost item, therefore, we have something like Table 5.6. The task now is to fill in the empty cells in with cash flow estimates.

Recall that the resource-based cost model identifies the names of cost items directly in terms of *resources*, such IT administrative labor, floorspace rental, or server system purchase (pp. 93–97). In the activity-based cost model, cost items are *activities* such as "identify customer needs," concept design," or "handle complaints" (pp. 97–98).

□ Costs come from using resources.

Either way, costs come from using resources, whether we start with the activity or with the resource directly. Either way, we have to complete the last two steps of the sequence we saw in Figure 4.2, repeated below as Figure 5.5.

Measuring cost impact and assigning cash flow value is essentially a process of identifying then making three sets of assumptions:

Figure 5.3 When a cost item is identified and the cash flow statement is designed, the next steps are to measure the business impact and assign cash flow value.

1. Assumptions: Which resources are used for this cost line item?
2. Assumptions: What drives resource usage?
3. What assumptions must we make in order to assign value to resource usage?

Notice that we *identify* assumptions before we *make* assumptions. Another way to ask these questions is to use the word "information" instead of assumptions: what *information* must we have in order to estimate resource usage? When we have the inventory of information needs, then we have the data requirements shopping list for the cost side of the business case.

On the topic of cost estimation, this *Guide* cannot be dogmatic or complete. Many of the business case templates or guidelines available within organizations or on the internet are really guides to estimating specific kinds of costs and benefits. Once you have the case designed, you should seek out this kind of help. In any case, every cost item requires different approaches to estimation, and the best approach for projecting any item will depend on such things as the:

- Amount of money involved. Large amounts obviously deserve more research and more thorough analysis than trivial amounts.
- Degree of uncertainty in making the estimate.
- Degree of certainty required by recipients.
- Factors unique to the cost item.
- Time and resources available to the case building team.

All these factors can influence your approach to assigning cash flow values to cost items. Your own financial specialists should be an excellent source of advice on "costing" (ideally, there is a financial specialist on your core team). Since you have so many choices in this area, the best we can do here is illustrate several extremes.

Estimating Costs: Quick and Simple

The task now is to fill in the missing cost figures in Table 5.6, using the process in Figure 5.3 (both on the previous page). In fact, we need cost figures for a proposal scenario and for a business as usual scenario. Sometimes, resource usage under case scenarios is predictable as a simple change from current usage. To decide whether or not we can use the "quick and simple" approach, ask first *how* this cost item supports the business objectives behind the case. Assume that we learn the following:

- The case subject is a proposed computer system upgrade.
- The business objectives are to increase transaction capacity, decrease system response time, and improve the quality of information available to users.

🔲 Identify assumptions before making assumptions.

- The resource (IT administrative labor) is dedicated 100% to meeting transaction processing needs, maintaining system performance, and ensuring that users have access to information they need.

With the cost item role clarified this way, we can now ask the "big three" questions about assumptions.

Question: What resources does this cost item use?
Answer:
- IT staff labor and overhead.
- Travel resources (transportation, lodging, and meals).

Question: What drives resource usage?
Answer:
- Number of users.
- Transaction volume.
- Travel requirements.

Question: What else must we know in order to assign cash value?
Answer:
- Current costs for IT administrative labor and travel.
- Expected changes in labor and travel cost rates.
- Expected changes in number of users and transaction volume.

So, what is the estimate for next year? We have identified assumptions. Now, let us *make* the assumptions. We assume that:

- The current year's costs for this item are $290,100 (including salaries, overhead, and travel).
- Year 1 salaries will average 3% higher than this year's salaries.
- The user base will remain constant through year 1.
- Travel requirements and travel cost rates will remain constant through year 1.
- Transaction volume will increase by 10% in year 1 under the proposal scenario.

Leaving out the factors that do not change anything under these assumptions (travel requirements and user base), estimated year 1 cash flow under the proposal scenario is:

Proposal scenario

Year 1 = Current Cost * Salary growth rate * Transaction growth rate
  = $290,100 * 1.03 * 1.10
  = $328,683

Ask:
- What resources does the cost item use?
- What drives resource usage?
- What else must we know in order to assign cost values?

This estimated cash outflow will go into the proposal scenario cash flow statement with parentheses as ($328,683).

Now consider the business as usual scenario. What is the cash flow estimate for Year 1? We have to determine which assumptions are different under business as usual. Assume there is only one:

- Transaction volume will remain constant through the end of year 1 under business as usual.

We can use the same formula for calculating business as usual Year 1 cash flow, by setting the growth factor for transaction rate to 1.00 (i.e., no growth):

Business as usual scenario

Year 1 = Current Cost $*$ Salary growth rate $*$ Transaction growth rate

$\quad\quad$ = $290,100 $*$ 1.03 $*$ 1.00

$\quad\quad$ = $298,803

This cash outflow also goes on the full value cash flow statement as a negative number, that is, ($290,803). Finally, if we are building an incremental cash flow statement, the year 1 incremental cash flow for IT administrative labor is:

Incremental cash flow

Year 1 = Proposal cash flow – Business as usual cash flow

$\quad\quad$ = ($328,683)– ($298,803)

$\quad\quad$ = ($29,880)

The case building team for this example was comfortable with the "quick and easy" approach. Notice the logic behind this approach: Simply apply growth factors to the current resource usage and its cost. Other situations may call for a more rigorous cash flow estimate, however (see the section after the next).

After making similar estimates for each year in the analysis period, *be sure to document every assumption and the calculation formula* for this item. You will need these assumptions and the formula later, for the sensitivity and risk analysis (Chapter 6), you will need them during the rest of the case building project as assumptions change, and you will need them to fully establish credibility for the case when it is delivered.

Looking back through this section you can see how the necessary documentation for one simple line item could easily require twenty lines or more. If you have, say, 100 cost items in the case, documenting assumptions and formulas becomes a non-trivial task. It is still an essential task, however. You can be certain that you will not remember everything.

▣ After making estimates for each year in the analysis period, be sure to document every assumption and the calculation formula for this item.

Estimating Costs: Spotlight on the Core Team

Some cost estimates will have so little uncertainty that there is almost no need for modeling or listing assumptions. Vendor price quotes for equipment to be delivered in two months, for instance, probably fit this category. Prices for equipment to be delivered three years from now would be less certain. For some cost items like the labor cost example, above, we may or may not be so certain.

The quick and simple approach actually relied on some unstated assumptions. Assuming that year 1 costs can be projected by simply "growing" current costs also assumes that other factors are constant between now and the end of year 1, such as the number of people required at each job level. Is that appropriate? Or, should the author and case building team dig a little deeper into these assumptions?

Questions like these are best answered by people who know the current operation first hand, who can judge credibly what will change under each scenario. The core team can play a valuable role in modeling cash flow estimates this way if the team includes experienced people from all the major areas impacted by the business case subject (the core team was introduced on pp. 19–23). Managers of line organizations and support organizations, for instance, should be the best judges of what the various scenarios imply in terms of resource usage and operational changes in their own areas.

Estimating Costs: All the Assumptions

Based on their understanding of the action scenarios and the current operating environment, the author and core team may decide that a more thorough analysis is called for in order to bring all the assumptions into view.

We will still ask the same questions about resources that we used in the quick and simple approach, but we need to dig a little deeper into the answers. Staying with the example item, "IT administrative labor," we ask again *how* this cost item supports the business objectives behind the case. This time, assume the situation is a little more complicated:

- The business case subject is a proposed computer server system upgrade. The server systems support transaction processing for the customer database.

- The business objectives are to increase transaction capacity, decrease system response time, and improve the quality of information available to users, for all activities involving the customer database.

The core team can play a valuable role in modeling cash flow estimates.

• The item (IT administrative labor) is dedicated partly to meeting customer database needs and partly to providing IT support for design engineering (which is outside the scope of this case).

Question: What resources does this cost item use?
Answer:
• IT staff labor and overhead.
• Travel resources (transportation, lodging, and meals).

Question: What drives resource usage?
Answer:
• Number of users.
• Transaction volume.
• Number of system problems per day.
• Number of trips required to remote sites.
• Distance of remote sites visited.

Question: What else must we know in order to assign cash value?
Answer:
• Salary and overhead costs for IT administrative labor:
  ○ Average current annual salary for each job level.
  ○ Number of people in each job level.
  ○ Percentage time dedicated to customer database, per individual in each job level.
  ○ Expected changes in salaries over the analysis period.
  ○ Expected changes in overhead costs over the analysis period.
  ○ Average current annual salary for each job level.
• Travel resources, current situation.
  ○ Number of trips required per person at each job level.
  ○ Average transportation cost per trip.
  ○ Average travel time per trip, per person.
  ○ Average work time per trip at remote site.
  ○ Average lodging cost per night.
  ○ Average number of nights lodging per trip.
  ○ Average meal expenses per day per person.
• Expected changes in resource drivers *under each scenario*.
  ○ Expected number of users per year.
    (Or the current user base and its expected growth rate).
  ○ Current number of systems problems per day and expected changes curing the analysis period
  ○ Expected transaction volume (or rate) per year (or the current volume and its expected growth rate).
  ○ Expected changes in travel demands over the analysis period.
  ○ Expected changes in geographical locations visited during the analysis period.

Ask:
• What resources does the cost item use?
• What drives resource usage?
• What else must we know in order to assign cost values?

You can perhaps appreciate more fully now why I estimate that something like 80% or more of your case building time will go into the "cost" side of the analysis. However, do not despair at the apparent complexity you see developing here. The way forward through this kind of cost modeling is tedious but straightforward.

First, notice that cost estimates for complex cost items like this one are often made up of several distinct components. Here, the item "IT administrative labor" has two components:

IT administrative labor cost $=$ salary and overhead $+$ travel expenses

Remember that another analyst might have chosen to list travel expenses as a separate line item. Or, another analyst might have added another component:

IT administrative labor cost $=$ salary and overhead
$+$ travel expenses
$+$ training expenses

▣ To estimate cash flow items for complex cost items, take the additive components one by one.

A	B	C	D	E	F	G
Position	Number of FTE*	FTE* growth rate this scenario	Percent to customer database	Current average annual salary	Avg salary growth per year	Overhead rate
IT Management	4	0.0%	60.0%	60,000	5.0%	30.0%
Systems Operators	10	10.0%	60.0%	31,000	4.0%	25.0%
Systems Programmers	6	10.0%	80.0%	36,500	4.0%	25.0%
Applications Programmers	8	5.0%	80.0%	32,000	4.0%	25.0%
Network administrators	4	0.0%	0.0%	30,000	4.0%	25.0%
User Help Desk	3	0.0%	50.0%	27,675	4.0%	25.0%
Storage and Backup	2	10.0%	90.0%	28,312	4.0%	25.0%

* FTE = "Full Time Equivalent" employee

Table 5.6 Capturing the assumptions for estimating salary and overhead costs in table form. Some of these will change value from scenario to scenario, most likely columns B and C, having to do with the number of full time equivalent employees.

To estimate cash flow for cost items like this, take the additive components one by one. Start with the salary and overhead component, for example. Often you can summarize the assumptions for the calculation as shown in Table 5.6 (previous page). Values in the cells represent assumptions for one scenario.

Some of these values would probably change under other scenarios. Assumptions having to do with the number of full time employees dedicating labor to customer database services (columns B and C, for instance), would very likely differ under other scenarios.

Table 5.7, below, shows the salary and overhead figures determined by Table 5.6. In this case, the cash flow estimate for each job position (each row of Table 5.7) for each year, is calculated as shown below. Capital letters refer to the values in columns of Table 5.6.

Salary and over head for year n
$$= B * (1 + C)^n * D * E * (1 + F)^n * (1 + G)^n$$

We still have to add the travel component for this line item before we can fill in cash flow estimates in Table 5.6 back on page 130. However, this book is not intended as a guide to modeling individual cash flow items, and we will not get out of the Forest of Details before sunset if we carry every example to its full elaboration. These examples are meant only to show the general approach. When you have complex line item estimates like this, you will have to work them out, one by one, drawing on the insight and expertise around the table at case building project meetings, as well as the contributions of core team members.

▣ If your case deals with a project, program, or product life cycle, it is likely that an activity based cost model is appropriate.

Position	Year 1	Year 2	Year 3	Year 4	Year 5	Total
IT Management	196,560	206,388	216,707	227,543	238,920	1,086,118
Systems Operators	265,980	304,281	348,098	398,224	455,568	1,772,150
Systems Programmers	250,536	286,613	327,885	375,101	429,116	1,669,251
Applications Programmers	279,552	305,271	333,356	364,024	397,515	1,679,718
Network administrators	0	0	0	0	0	0
User Help Desk	53,966	56,125	58,370	60,705	63,133	292,299
Storage and Backup	72,875	83,369	95,374	109,108	124,820	485,546
Total IT Admin Salaries and Overhead	1,119,469	1,242,047	1,379,790	1,534,705	1,709,071	6,985,082

Table 5.7 Estimated salary and overhead estimates for IT administration, based on information in Table 5.6.

Estimating Costs: Activities as Cost Items

The examples above used a cost item from a resource-based cost model. The subject of that business case was a computer system upgrade. If your case deals with a project, program, or product life cycle, however, it is much more likely that an activity based cost model will be appropriate (the two kinds of cost models were introduced and compared on pp. 93–99).

Consider an example from Figure 4.5 (p. 98). This is a cost model for a case designed to help choose between some product development options:

- Develop and market product A.
- Develop and market product B.
- Develop and market both products.
- Develop and market neither product (business as usual).

The columns of this model are product life cycle phases such as "Intelligence" and "Development." The rows are organized as rows are organizational functions such as "Marketing" and "Engineering." In the cost model cell "Marketing Intelligence," the activities listed are:

- Identify customer needs.
- Identify market trends and future products.
- Analyze competitors plans.
- Investigate risks and potential opportunities.

In order to estimate cash flow for cost items from an activity-based cost model, we can proceed in much the same way we did with the cost item from a resource-based model. The process is basically centered on finding and making assumptions. Take the first activity item as an example: Identify customer needs.

Case builders will probably discover over and over as they go through the cost model item by item, that many of the activity items they put into the model are really made up of several sub activities. The first step in analyzing an activity as a cost item, then, is to determine if the item really has component activities.

"Identify customer needs" might include component activities:

- Conduct customer survey.
- Acquire and analyze market research data.
- Review and analyze customer feedback.
- Review commentary from industry analysts.
- Identify relevant technology trends, product trends.
- Review what is known of competitor's product strategies.

Once you have the cost item activity reduced to a list of its most basic sub activities, you can then analyze each sub activity in practi-

> □ The first step in analyzing an activity as a cost item is to determine if the item really has component activities.

> □ Cost items from activity-based models tend to consist overwhelmingly of labor items.

cally the same way we analyzed the resource-based cost item. Cost items from activity-based models, however, tend to consist overwhelmingly of labor. In any case, we ask the same "big three" questions about assumptions for this item. Start with the sub activity "Conduct customer survey."

Question: What resources does this cost item use?
Answer:
- Market research staff labor
- Communications resources (to recruit respondents, distribute surveys, collect responses) .

Question: What drives resource usage?
Answer:

- Complexity and quantity of information required.
- Number of customers to be surveyed

Question: What else must we know in order to assign cash value?
Answer:
- Current costs for market research staff labor and overhead.
- Number of people at each job level.
- Average salary and overhead at each job level.
  - ○ Average overhead rate for each job level.
  - ○ Average salary increase expected over analysis period.
  - ○ Labor hours or days required for designing survey.
  - ○ Labor hours or days required for pre-testing or validating survey.
  - ○ Labor hours or days required for recruiting participants.
  - ○ Labor costs required for collecting survey.
  - ○ Labor hours required for survey analysis.
- Number of surveys to be distributed.
- Average distribution cost per customer surveyed.
- Communications costs for distributing surveys.

🔲 Once you have the assumptions for each sub activity, then you have the inventory of data requirements for the cost analysis.

Once you have the list of assumptions for each sub activity then you have the inventory of information needs or data requirements, at least for the "cost" side of the analysis. When you or your staff do the research and return with the best available estimates for all the above assumptions, for each scenario, you have what you need to make a straightforward cash flow estimate. In this case, we determined earlier that the intelligence phase falls entirely within year 1 of the analysis period (Figure 5.2, p. 115). For this item, therefore, all cash flow estimates fall in year 1.

Estimating Costs: General Comments

To summarize this section on estimating costs, consider again some of the main points we have just covered:

- Costs come from using resources;. This is true whether you start with a cost item from a resource-based cost model or an activity based cost model.
- Identify the set of assumptions you need for each cost item, before making individual assumptions.
- Identify assumptions that help estimate of resource usage for the line item during each time segment of the analysis period, under each scenario.
- Record and document every assumption for every cost item. You will need them for further analysis, for making adjustments to the analysis, and for establishing credibility with recipients. You will not remember them if you do not record them.

Concerning the last bullet, "Record every assumption," you may be doing some back-of-the-envelope math, thinking perhaps: OK, if we have 120 items in the cost model and 3 scenarios, and if we average 20 assumptions per cost item, that works out to 120 * 3 * 20 = 7,200 assumptions to research and record! And that means 120 complex costing models to create!

Yes, the math is correct and those numbers are typical, but there is some good news to consider as well: Many of your assumptions will be global assumptions, applying to all or many items in all scenarios (probably average salary for each job level, for instance). Other assumptions will apply to all items in a single scenario. In brief, given the numbers above, no case imaginable would have 7,200 *unique* assumptions. Furthermore, the cost calculations for many items will be very similar. Once you have modeled labor cost for one item, for example, labor cost for another item may be nearly identical except for a minor difference in assumptions.

> Many assumptions will be global assumptions, applying to all or many items in all scenarios. Other assumptions will apply to all items in a single scenario.

Estimating Benefits

From your knowledge of the business objectives behind the subject of the case, you should now have a have a rough list of likely benefit impacts (you may wish to review "Introduction to Business Case Benefits," pp. 99–106).

As you know by now, business cases typically have relatively few benefit items, even when there are hundreds of cost items. The first time you analyze business impacts under each scenario, you may initially find several dozen candidate benefits. Testing each of them through the benefits rationale (pp. 104–106) is likely to shorten the list considerably.

By way of review, remember:

- A business benefit is a business impact that contributes to a business objective. If the impact does not contribute to an objective, it is not a benefit for the business case.

- The benefit and the objective are not necessarily the same thing. Improved product reliability (the business impact) may contribute to improved customer satisfaction (the business objective). The same benefit may also contribute to other objectives, such as lower service costs.

Now it is time to assign cash flow values for each benefit item—insofar as possible. In fact, each of the three classes of benefits introduced in Chapter 4 (p. 100) calls for a different approach.

Estimating Benefits: Cost Savings and Avoided Costs

Cost savings are both benefits and a business objectives for almost everyone. In profit making companies, cost savings go "straight to the bottom line." Cost savings, that is, usually contribute their full value directly to profits (increased revenues, on the other hand do not). If one proposed scenario implies an expected $200,000 savings in research and development expenses, then profits will increase by $200,000.

Non-profit and government organizations are not concerned with profits but they are concerned with budgets, and some are concerned with paying their own way (the postal service in many countries, for instance). Most try to make the best use of the funding they receive (educational or military organizations, for example). Money saved in one area is money to apply to high priority items elsewhere.

In a nutshell, cost savings are a valuable, targeted business objective for almost everyone.

As you know by now, cost savings for the business case really come from the cost analysis rather than from a separate benefit analysis. The word "savings" (or "reduction") implies a comparison: cost figures represent savings only when compared to an alternative. In other words, you must have at least two scenarios in the case in order to find cost savings. Of course one of these can be a business as usual scenario.

Suppose, for instance, that cash flow estimates for the cost item "Floorspace rental" turn out as shown in the first two rows of Table 5.8 (next page). The proposal scenario and the business as usual scenario figures are full value cash flow estimates. Remember that the

---

▣ A business benefit is a business impact that contributes to a business objective.

▣ Cost savings are both benefits and business objectives for almost everyone.

author can point out the cost advantage under the proposal scenario in either of two ways:

- Present two full value cash flow statements, one for each scenario. "Floorspace rental" is an item under costs and expenses in both statements. The author points to the differences between these two cost lines to show the proposal advantage.

- Create an incremental cash flow statement, where each estimate represents the proposal value minus the business as usual value. Because every cost value in a full value cash flow statement is a cash outflow, we subtract one negative number from another (as indicated by parentheses). In year 1 of the Table 5.8 example, subtracting negative 300 from a negative 260 yields a *positive* 40. The positive value means this item is a cash inflow for the incremental cash flow statement. That is how cost savings turn into benefits.

> 🔲 Do not apply cost savings math blindly. To do so risks seriously overstating benefits.

As we saw earlier, the incremental item "Floorspace rental savings" does not have to go under costs and expenses on the incremental cash flow statement. It can go under benefits, if the author wishes.

One final word about cost savings developed this way: do not apply the math we have just demonstrated blindly. To do so risks seriously overstating benefits. When a cost savings like this appears, the author has to ask: does the calculation represent real value?

The risk is highest when cost savings are calculated for labor savings. In the IT director's business case presented back in Chapter 2, for

Table 5.8 Cost savings are apparent only when two scenarios are compared in the cost analysis. The incremental cash flow summary (bottom) is one way of making the comparison.

Cash flow in $1,000s

PROPOSAL SCENARIO	Year 1	Year 2	Year 3	Year 4	Year 5	Total
Floorspace rental	(260)	(260)	(290)	(290)	(320)	(1,420)

BUSINESS AS USUAL SCENARIO						
Floorspace rental	(300)	(300)	(350)	(350)	(400)	(1,700)

INCREMENTAL CASH FLOW						
Floorspace Rental Savings	40	40	60	60	80	280

instance, analysis showed that loan officers and sales people in bank branches would save an average of one hour per day under one proposal scenario, compared to business as usual. To estimate the cash flow value for one year, he applied the "time-equals-money" formula that is used widely in business case analysis:

Benefit = (time saved) * (the cost of labor)

Here were the raw data (the assumptions) for this calculation:

Number of loan officers and sales people nationwide: 1,040
Average annual salary plus overhead: $45,000
Time saved: One hour per workday = 12.5% of work time saved

Benefit = (1,040) * ($45,000) * (12.5%)
       = $5,850,000

When applying the time-equals-money formula, ask whether or not the time savings really turn into productivity or other value.

Is that value credible? Will the bank actually see the savings? The answer is "yes" only if the author shows convincingly that time savings turn into productivity at the value calculated. In the director's case, he argued plausibly that loan officers and sales people *would* use their extra hour a day to process more loan applications and sell more financial services.

Other times, however, the time-equals-money formula stands on a weak foundation. The classic example is the new PC operating system upgrade that saves users 60 minutes a month compared to the old operating system (presumably from a few less reboots). That works out to roughly 0.6% of work time. For a PC user who costs the company, say, $60,000 a year in salary and overhead, the formula says the benefit is $375 per year—enough to pay for the upgrade with change left over. Multiply similar savings in a company with 20,000 computer users and the apparent benefit grows even larger. But is it a "real" benefit that deserves a line in the business case cash flow statement? Only if users turn their extra 0.6% of time (about 3 minutes a day) into added productivity. It would be difficult to argue that point plausibly in most organizations.

When your analysis shows that cost savings under a proposed scenario are real, most case recipients have little problem accepting them as legitimate benefits. Cost savings are what some people have in mind when they say "hard benefits."

Estimating Benefits: Increased Income

The business case approach is often applied in profit making companies to support product development and marketing decisions. Should product A or product B be developed? Should the marketing program be implemented world wide? Or, just in selected regions? The primary financial metrics that answer questions like these are projected sales and projected income under different proposals.

Non profit and government organizations also make decisions designed to improve their income. Decisions about fund raising drives and funding proposals are often supported with business case analysis.

Increased income is usually an acceptable business case benefit if the author satisfies recipients that the projections are unbiased and that uncertainty has been reduced to a minimum. Increased income also qualifies as a "hard benefit" for many people, because the estimation techniques are straightforward and because the measure of the benefit is tangible cash. Forecasting sales or other income is a topic beyond the scope of this book, but if your business case anticipates using increased income as a benefit, here are some points to keep in mind.

Forecasting sales or profits for products not yet on the market is a complex and subtle art that should be practiced by people who specialize in making such predictions. The forecaster—whether based in marketing, sales, or product management—must make assumptions about many things that come with a high level of uncertainty, including market size, market growth, market share, market share growth, unit sales, pricing, technology trends, economic trends, competitors actions, changing customer demands, and many other things. The conditions underlying such assumptions are constantly changing.

Sales forecasts, moreover, are not cash flow benefit forecasts. Increased sales usually bring increased costs for producing, selling, delivering and servicing the products. Expected profits are not quite the same thing as expected cash flow value, either. The profit calculation often reflects indirect costs, allocated costs, and depreciation expense that are not true cash flow that follows from the product sale.

You may use projected sales and the income statement structure to calculate expected cash flow benefits for a profit-producing product, but do so with caution. Insofar as possible, try to use the actual cost of sales, cost of selling, distribution costs, and so on, for that product. Avoid allocated or indirect costs that do not change directly with product sales. Decision makers are better served if they see what the product is actually expected to bring into the company (cash flow benefit) rather than what the product will contribute to the company's reported income.

▣ Projected increased income is usually an acceptable business case benefit if the author can satisfy recipients that the projections are unbiased and that everything has been done to reduce uncertainty to a minimum.

Estimating Benefits: Contributions to Other Business Objectives

We know by now that business cases often include large and important benefits that do not appear initially as cost savings or increased income. This kind of benefit was introduced in Chapter 2, with some examples from Table 2.4 (p. 28):

Contributions to Business Objectives

Example

- Sales / marketing objectives.....Increase market share
- Financial objectives ....Improve earnings per share
- Operational objectives.............Shorten product development time
- Image objectives.....................Win award for service excellence
- Internal objectives ....Improve employee morale
- Product / service objectives .....Improve product reliability
- Other business objectives ....Establish strategic alliance

If an action contributes to an important, targeted objective, and if the business impact is measurable in some tangible way, it belongs in the case. We will try our best to assign financial value to all such benefits because non financial benefits contribute exactly nothing to the financial results.

When critics point to a benefit item and call it a "soft benefit," it is usually a benefit in this class. However, if you use the benefits rationale with your recipients to establish the legitimacy of an item in your benefits inventory, the only remaining question should be: what's it worth? By the time you sit down to estimate cash values, you should be confident that you and your recipients have established the following for each benefit:

- The impact contributes to at least one business objective.
- The objective is a targeted or obviously important objective.
- Progress toward the objective can be measured with tangible evidence. There is a target level identified for this measure.
- Reaching the target for the objective has value for the organization or company.

If an action contributes to an important, targeted objective, and if the business impact is measurable in some tangible way, it belongs in the case.

The challenge now for each potential benefit is to find the value in monetary terms. Before moving on, however, we have to point out that there is no "one size fits all" method for answering the "what's it worth?" question. We can illustrate several approaches that work very well in different circumstances, and in the final analysis, you may actually have your choice of several methods for a given benefit. If this paragraph makes you uneasy about going forward, then please review the four bullets above this paragraph and reassure yourself that you stand on very solid ground.

We can approach the question "what's it worth?" by asking two more questions:

Question A:
What is the value of reaching the target for the objective?
Question B:
How much of that value should be credited to this benefit in each time segment of the analysis period?

If we have numerical for both questions, the math is easy:

Benefit value = Answer A * Answer B

If reaching the target level for the objective is valued AT $3,500,000, for Year 1, and if the proposal scenario gets 25% of the credit for reaching the target, the Year 1 benefit is $3,500,000 * 25% = $875,000.

Once we establish that the benefit is real and legitimate, all we have to do is to establish a legitimate *value*. To do this we will examine questions A and B separately.

Estimating Benefits: Finding the Target Objective Value

Financial Objectives

The value of reaching the target for financial objectives is usually easy to establish:

Our target is to save $1,000,000 in production costs over the next year.

Our objective for the next 3 years is to reach best-in-class operating margin for this industry, which is 20%.

These statements are easily translated into cash flow value. The $1,000,000 cost savings has an incremental cash flow value of $1,000,000. The incremental cash flow value of reaching a 20% operating margin is also a straightforward calculation if we know the current operating margin, current sales and projected sales, and current and expected profit ratios (profits as a percentage of sales).

Marketing and Sales Objectives

Marketing and sales objectives also have a value that usually translates directly into financial terms:

The target market share for next year is 50%.

We intend to maintain a sales growth rate of 10% for the next five years.

The value of reaching these targets requires knowledge of such things as current market share, current market size, and market growth rate, but those factors can usually be estimated credibly.

Operational Objectives

The value of reaching targets becomes more complex, however, when we move to operational objectives.

Our objective is to reduce new product development time from 18 months to 12 months over the next two years.

For many such objectives, reaching the target has two qualitatively different value components. The first component is a cost savings. Shorter development time means less time for designing, engineering, testing, manufacturing set up, and other development work. If you know resource usage and costs for an 18 month development time, you can probably estimate the proposal scenario 12 month resource needs and costs. (Note, however, that you cannot automatically assume that all *phases* in the process will have the same 33% reduction).

The second value component may be more subjective or less certain, but it can also be larger and more important than cost savings. Companies in highly competitive industries such as consumer products, aerospace, and automotive place a value on shorter development time as a competitive weapon. Getting to market first often means winning market share. Getting to market early usually means a longer product life cycle and more lifetime sales. Those advantages have a value of their own that can be larger than the cost savings from shorter development time.

▣ Target levels for operational objectives may have two qualitatively different components. One is cost savings, and the second comes from such things as increased competitiveness or longer product lifecycles.

Image Objectives

Image objectives are important to businesses, to non-profit organizations, to government agencies, to military organizations—just about everyone.

Our objective at this studio is to win an Oscar for "Best film of the year."

Our objective is to become recognized as the industry leader in customer satisfaction.

This school district will be recognized as the leader in academic excellence in this city.

If "image" sound a little "soft" for the business case, remember that achieving a target "image" objective usually translates immediately into support for *other* objectives. Those other objectives may have very clear financial value. It is likely that:

- Branches of military service convert improved image directly into less recruiting expense, better quality volunteers, and success in obtaining funding.
- Product selling companies gain market share and customer loyalty from improved image.
- Educational institutions recruit and retain more talented faculty and students with improved image.
- Fund raising for non-profit organizations is more successful when they have a good image.

These "other" objectives, by the way, ma	y be the best tangible evidence that the image objective is achieved. In brief, when a benefit impact contributes to an image objective, ask the next questions: *Why* does the organization want an improved image? What changes when image improves? What is *that* worth?

Strategies for Difficult Objectives

Remember that this step—finding the value of reaching a target—is still part of the benefits rationale. That means that legitimacy and credibility are established most effectively through dialog between author and recipient *during* the case building process. You may have to "try out" several different methods to find the most agreeable value for successfully reaching the target. Here are several suggestions.

- Ask: What is the cost or other tangible effect of *not* reaching the target?

  The answer will probably stated in negative terms: lost customers, lost funding, lost market share, or extra cost and expense. If you know the cost of not reaching the target, then you also know the value of reaching the target.

◙ Reaching strategic objectives has a very high value.

- Look for other tangible measures that should be impacted by reaching the target. Suppose the focus is an organizational objective, to "improve employee morale," and the target is to raise the average satisfaction rating on internal surveys by 50%. Look for *other* obvious indicators of improved morale that should be easier to quantify in financial terms. Improved employee morale should lead to less absenteeism, less employee turnover, and more productivity. How much will these things change if the target satisfaction rating is achieved? If possible, look for other environments for comparison (other companies or organizations perhaps, or even your own organization in better times).

- Ask: What would the company or organization simply pay on the open market to achieve the objective? That is, ask recipients, senior management, or subject matter experts to estimate the worth of the objective directly.

Estimating Benefits: How Much Does this Benefit Contribute?

◙ Most benefits will deserve something less than 100% of the credit for reaching the target.

Reaching the target for strategic objectives usually has a very high value. Strategic objectives are what management says *must* be done if the organization is to survive and grow. The value in dollars, euro, pounds, yen, or other currency will be substantial.

If you establish the cause and effect linkage between your proposed impact and a target objective with agreed value, then only one question remains: How much of that value should be credited to this benefit? When the objective is a *strategic* objective, even a small percentage of a big number is a big number.

In all but the simplest situations, it is very unlikely that one benefit will be entirely responsible for reaching the target for a strategic objective. Lower service costs (an objective) probably result from several factors besides improved product reliability (a benefit impact). This means that benefits often deserve something less than 100% of the credit for reaching the target.

Assigning a percentage credit to a benefit will in most cases call for subjective judgement. Remember that this step is also part of the benefits rationale and the results are most acceptable when developed in dialog with recipients during the case building process. Not many recipients will (a) agree that the benefit contributes to the objective, (b) agree that the target has large value, but then (c) say that the benefit deserves no financial credit for getting there.

Here are some points to discuss with your recipient as you make that judgement together:

- If the target is unreachable without the benefit, then the benefit deserves a large share of the value, arguably 50% or more.

- Ask: What is the next best way of reaching the target level without this benefit? What would that cost? What percentage of the overall target value is that?

  For example, the objective in a manufacturing company is to reduce new product time to market from 18 months to 12 months. The estimated value of reaching that target is large: $50,000,000 per year, based on lower development costs, improved competitive position, and longer product life cycles (see the previous section, above). Assume that a new engineering design system is expected to contribute substantially to that goal by increasing designer productivity. What percentage of the target value should go to the design system productivity? Suppose that the *next best* way to reach the 12 month target is to hire 50 more professionals at an annual cost of $100,000 each. The total cost of the second best solution is thus $5,000,000 per year, or 10% of the value of reaching the target.

- If you can establish a direct link between the tangible measure for the benefit and the tangible measure of the objective, you may be able to estimate the benefit value directly. For example:
  ○ Benefit: Improved product reliability.
  ○ Benefit measure: Mean time between failure (mt bf).
  ○ Benefit Impact: mt bf increased from 10,000 hours to 20,000 hours.
  It is likely that the frequency of service activities due to product failure (and thus the cost) can be calculated directly.

- You may have to select a percentage contribution that is entirely subjective. Most people will view this approach as valid if you keep the estimate conservative and if you are very firmly grounded in the other steps of the benefits rationale.

Financial Analysis: Putting it All Together

Remember that we are in the "Business Impacts" section of the case report. Here, we let the "numbers do the talking." In the next chap-

	For the year ending 31 August...						
	Year 0 Aug 2002	Year 1 Aug 2003	Year 2 Aug 2004	Year 3 Aug 2005	Year 4 Aug 2006	Year 5 Aug 2007	TOTAL
CASH FLOW SUMMARY							
Cash inflows (outflows)							
Benefit Impacts	320.0	1,491.5	1,753.1	2,007.1	2,246.7	2,493.1	10,311.5
Cost and Expense Item Impacts	(637.2)	(1,196.0)	(1,504.9)	(1,762.1)	(1,771.5)	(1,901.8)	(8,773.6)
NET CASH FLOW	**(317.2)**	**295.5**	**248.2**	**245.0**	**475.2**	**591.3**	**1,537.9**
Cumulative Net CF	(317.2)	(21.7)	226.5	471.5	946.7	1,537.9	1,537.9
Discounted Cash Flow							
At 9.0 %	(317.2)	271.1	208.9	189.2	336.6	384.3	1,072.9
At 15.0 %	(317.2)	256.9	187.7	161.1	271.7	294.0	854.1

Table 5.9 The cash flow statement summary section. The NET CASH FLOW line is the starting point for most analyses.

ter we will push the analysis process further, examining sensitivity of the results to different assumptions and the risks of obtaining other results. For this section of the report, however, we will stick with the messages coming from a few basic financial metrics.

When you have cash flow estimates for every cost and benefit on the cash flow statement, the "bottom line" is ready for preliminary analysis. We have seen a complete cash flow statement in Tables 5.4 and 5.5 (pp. 126 and 127). Now, we turn to the summary section at the bottom, to have a first look at financial metrics that support the case purpose.

Figure 5.9 (previous page) is the before tax version of the statement we saw earlier. Notice how the Net Cash Flow line is developed simply by adding the cash inflows and outflows in each column.

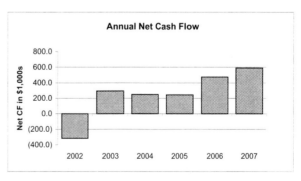

Figure 5.4 Annual net cash flow from the incremental cash flow summary in Table 5.9. Graphing the net cash flow for each time segment in the analysis period shows recipients the pattern of results across time.

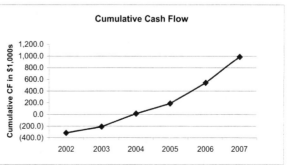

Figure 5.5 Cumulative net cash flow from Table 5.9. The cumulative graph shows when the total inflows equal the total outflows (payback), and it shows how the overall return on this investment builds over time.

Net and Cumulative Cash Flow

Cash flow is the most basic financial metric for the case and recipients will naturally want to see the magnitude and timing of cash flow totals, as summarized in the Net Cash Flow line. The five-year net is estimated at $1,537,900, but recipients will also examine the timing of cash flow in individual year columns.

Cumulative net cash flow for each period is calculated by adding the cash flow value for the period to the values of all previous periods. The cumulative net cash flow is also very interesting because it helps identify the point in time when the cumulative inflows become larger than cumulative outflows. The net and cumulative cash flow lines are also communicated effectively with graphs, such as Figures 5.4 and 5.5 (previous page).

Discounted Cash Flow

The Cash Flow Summary section is also the best place to summarize discounted cash flow, the source of the net present value financial metric (for more on NPV and other financial metrics, see Appendix B, "Financial Metrics").

In this case, the author performed discounted analysis at two different discount rates, 9.0% and 15.0% (note that this example shows end of year discounting, but mid-year discounting could have been used just as well).

In Chapter 6 we return to the Net Cash Flow line to extract more financial metrics and begin sensitivity and risk analysis.

Non Financial Benefits

Potential benefits seem to have a high mortality rate going through the benefits rationale. You may start the benefits rationale with 20 or 30 candidates, and then discover that many overlap or contribute to each other. Improved customer satisfaction, increased repeat business may sound like two different benefits, but you have to ask: where does the value in customer satisfaction come from? If it comes from repeat business, be sure not to count the same value twice.

Other benefits candidates sound desirable at first but simply cannot be connected to tangible evidence that they contribute to reaching business objectives.

Still other benefit candidates will survive well into the benefits rationale: everyone will agree that the benefits are tangible and they contribute to important business objectives, *but*, you cannot reach agreement on appropriate financial value. As a matter of principle, you should not avoid trying to assign financial value to a benefit

> ▣ As a matter of principle, you should not avoid trying to assign financial value to a benefit simply because it is hard to quantify.

simply because it is hard to quantify in monetary terms (but do avoid assigning financial value if the benefit is uncertain). Despite your best efforts, however, not every important benefit will get a financial value. Those non financial benefits still belong in the case.

This may be a good time to review pp. 44–47 ("Non Financial Benefits Belong in the Case"). Here, again are the main recommendations from that section:

1. Be sure the expected impact is recorded.

Identify the impact immediately after the cash flow statement and its analysis in the "Business Impacts" section, in the Executive Summary, and in Conclusions and Recommendations.

2. Make the impact tangible.

Even if the impact is not valued in financial terms, describe its effects in ways that can be observed and verified.

3. Compare the impact directly to the financial impacts of the case, but in non financial terms.

We will see how this is done in the next Chapter.

Next Steps: Get Ready to Build the Dynamic Financial Model

We will shortly perform sensitivity and risk analysis on the complete set of assumptions and cash flow estimates. For that, we must build a dynamic financial model (introduced on in Chapter 2, pp. 37–39). The *Guide* has emphasized over and over the importance of recording all assumptions and formulas. Now is the ideal time to organize the total list of assumptions into groups: global assumptions that apply to all scenarios, scenario specific assumptions, and other assumptions that apply only to specific line items. It is also a good time to review the formulas developed for cash flow estimates: you will soon be putting these into spreadsheet cells, linked to your assumptions.

Precise vs. Vague Understanding

Everyone talks about the business case but few people have a precise understanding of what they should get when they ask for one. In this respect, you may have to clarify the concepts we have covered about the essential nature of the business case, many times over with colleagues, mangers, and people who work for. Those around you will probably need help on the following points (which should be review for you by now).

- Costs and benefits do not exist until the case is designed. They are not defined until the subject, purpose, scope and boundaries, cost model, and benefits rationale are established.
- Cash flow, not income, is the basic metric for measuring financial consequences of a proposed action.
- Benefits come from meeting business objectives. If a business impact does not contribute to a business objective, it is not a benefit. Understanding business objectives is the first step in understanding benefits for the case.
- Numbers alone do not make the case. The author and case building team have to communicate the methods by which results were developed.
- Incremental and full value data should never be mixed in the same cash flow statement. Doing so invalidates results.
- There may be hundreds of cost items in the case, but they should come from an easy-to-explain cost model that provides a system for deciding what belongs in the case and what does not.
- Business benefits can include much more than cost savings or increased sales. Contributions to business objectives of many kinds legitimately enter the case as benefits.

In Summary

This chapter began the implementation of design tools created earlier. The objective was to create a complete cash flow statement for each case scenario, filled with cost and benefit estimates and to begin analyzing them.

- Once we have most of the case design complete we can project the financial and non financial business impacts (Section c).
- The horizontal dimension of the cash flow statement represents the analysis period. The case estimates not only the *magnitude* of cash inflow or outflow for each line item, but also the cash flow *timing*.
- Authors and recipients must understand clearly the exact calendar dates covered by each period on the cash flow statement.
- One dimension of the cost model can help identify exactly when cash flow events occur, but the dimension itself is not a time line.
- The business case cash flow statement is similar to cash flow statements used in financial accounting, such as a cash basis "Statement of Changes in Financial Position."
- In the after tax business case, taxes reduce the magnitude of net gains and net losses. Taxes also create tax savings from depreciation expense.
- A business case designed to predict product profits is the one kind of case that may incorporate income statement line items and income statement math.
- Costs come from using resources, whether we start by analyzing the resource directly, or with an activity that uses resources.
- Measuring cost impact and assigning value is essentially a process of identifying, then making, three sets of assumptions:

    1. Assumptions: Which resources are used for this cost line item?
    2. Assumptions: What drives resource usage?
    3. What assumptions must we make in order to assign value to resource usage?

- Cost estimates for complex cost items are often made up of several distinct components.
- Cost items from activity-based models tend to consist overwhelmingly of labor.
- A business benefit is a business impact that contributes to a business objective.
- Cost savings are both benefits and a business objective for almost everyone.
- Increased income is usually an acceptable business case benefit if the author can satisfy recipients that the projections are unbiased and that everything has been done to minimize uncertainty.
- If an action contributes to an important, targeted objective, and if the business impact is measurable in some tangible way, it belongs in the case.
- Not every important benefit will get a financial value. Those non financial benefits still belong in the case.

Chapter 6

Packaging, Presenting, and Using the Case

The final legs of our trek across the business case landscape are designed to bring out all the information that is latent in the material developed so far. The author builds a dynamic financial model to serve as a basis for sensitivity and risk analysis. The dynamic model also produces results for preparing and packaging the case report. The final section of the report will include conclusions and recommendations that link financial and non financial results to the purpose of the case.

Making Sense of the Results

Yesterday we came down from Mount Cash Flow with a lot of information (Chapter 5). That body of material now needs analysis, interpretation, and packaging, before presentation to recipients.

Here is what we determined while on the mountain:

- The number of cash flow statements for the case (full value statements and incremental statements).
- The structure of cash flow statements (section headings, time line, and tax consequences if appropriate).
- Assumptions underlying cash flow estimates.
- Formulas or models for making cost and benefit cash flow estimates.
- Cash flow estimates for many (if not all) cost and benefit line items.
- A list of important non financial benefits under case scenarios.

☐ Results are very tentative at this point.

If we *do* have cash flow estimates for all cost and benefit items at this point, we can project a net cash flow result for each scenario. We may also have some preliminary financial metrics, such as the net present value. All of this is still very tentative at this point, however.

The final legs of our trek across the business case landscape are designed to bring out all the information that is latent in the material we have developed so far. It is now time to put the results into practical, usable form.

We will complete the analysis of cash flow projections for the fourth major section of the case report (Section D. in Tables 6.1 and 6.2, next two pages). Sensitivity analysis will show us which assumptions are most important in controlling results. Risk analysis will show us the likelihood of realizing other outcomes besides the central predicted figures. Finally, we will assess the importance of some non financial results by comparing them to financial results.

With all of these results in hand, we can move into the land of Conclusions and Recommendations (Section E. in Tables 6.1 and 6.2), and provide the best available information to support recipients who are making decisions or planning.

A Time for Silence

I have stressed the value of open communication throughout this *Guide*, but I need to point out that there is also a time in the case building process when it is prudent to maintain silence with the outside world (everyone beyond the case building team and the core team). That time is now, after developing the assumptions, calculations, and preliminary cash flow estimates, but before building a dynamic financial model, before analyzing sensitivities and risks, and before thinking carefully through conclusions and recommendations. Preliminary results will almost certainly change before the final report

Table 6.1 Five major sections of the business case. The final steps in business case analysis include sensitivity and risk analysis (Section D), and development of conclusions and recommendations based on all the preceding design considerations and results (Section E).

Business Case Structure

A. Introduction
Defines what the case is about (the subject) and why it is being built (the purpose). Also presents the business objectives addressed by the subject of the case.

B. Methods and Assumptions
Design elements fix the boundaries of the case (whose costs and whose benefits are examined, over what time period). Also outlines the rules for deciding what belongs in the case and what does not, along with important assumptions.

C. Business Impacts
The main business case results: financial and non financial business impacts expected in one or more scenarios.

D. **Sensitivity, Risks, and Contingencies**
Shows how results depend on important assumptions, as well as the likelihood that other results appear.

E. **Conclusions and Recommendations**
Recommends specific actions based on business objectives from Section A and the results from Sections C and D.

Table 6.2 Major blocks in the final two sections of the business case report.

Business Case Structure
A. Introduction
B. Methods and Assumptions
C. Business Impacts
D. Sensitivity, Risks, and Contingencies
E. Conclusions and Recommendations

D. Sensitivity, Risks, and Contingencies

- Sensitivity analysis:
  Which assumptions are important in determining results?
- Risk analysis:
  How likely are the projected results?
  · How likely are other results?
  Which factors must be watched?
- Contingency analysis:
  Which factors must be managed?

E. Conclusions and Recommendations

- Results rationale:
  Linking case results to case subject and purpose
- Choice of scenario(s) for action
- Strategy and tactics for optimizing results

🔲 It is counterproductive to set expectations by announcing preliminary results now and then delivering final results that are different.

is submitted. It is counterproductive to set expectations by announcing preliminary results now and then delivering final results that are different.

In the late 1990s, I worked with the IT Director at a large commercial bank on the business case example highlighted throughout Chapter 2. The Director and his staff were the project team and some of the bank's very senior managers were on the core team. Late in the case-building process, however, the President of the bank himself made a surprise visit to the case building project room (the President was not a core team member). "How is the business case analysis going?" he wanted to know. "What are you projecting?"

A completely candid answer would have been something like this: "Well, at this point we think the proposal will either bring a loss of about $120 million or else a gain of about $150 million. It could be either way." And that was—to risk using a redundant phrase—the honest truth. Several very critical assumptions still needed research and checking. Depending on these assumptions, case results could have been very negative or very positive. But to convey that reality to the President or other recipients would not have inspired confidence in the case. Instead, I had to tell him (diplomatically, of course) that "we still need to validate a few key assumptions before we can make a preliminary prediction." "Yes," he pressed on, "but just tell me *roughly* what you are projecting." The IT director and I respectfully

159

declined to provide numbers, and instead offered to give the President a private briefing as soon as we did have preliminary projections we could present.

People outside your project team or core team who have a strong interest in the business case results may want to "look over your shoulder" as you complete the final analyses and packaging. Open communication is desirable during case design and when making initial cash flow estimates for cost and benefit items. Communication is necessary for establishing case credibility and acceptability for results. The benefits rationale, especially, depends on dialog between author and recipients. Preliminary case analyses, however, should have very limited exposure. Remember that overall results are still volatile at this point. People like the bank President no doubt understand *in principle* that assumptions determine results, and that everything is still subject to modification. However, numbers or other specific outcomes, once announced, have a way of being remembered as concrete predictions.

◨ Specific outcomes, once announced, have a way of being remembered as concrete predictions.

A Single Spreadsheet System

The most practical approach to completing the analysis, packaging, and presentation of case results begins by bringing all the financial information together into a single spreadsheet system, or model. By "single system," I mean a spreadsheet file, or files, in which a data point or formula anywhere in the system can use formulas or data anywhere else in the system.

Spreadsheet System : Full Value Analysis

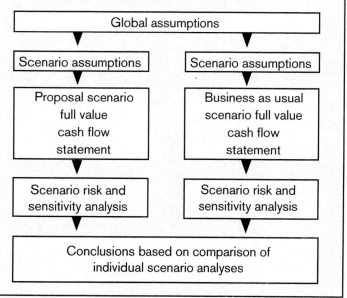

Figure 6.1 Components of the complete spreadsheet system for a two-scenario case analyzing full value data. Arrows show lines of information flow. Conclusions and recommendations are based on a comparison of the individual analyses for each scenario.

Cash flow statements like the examples in Chapter 5 are certainly part of the complete spreadsheet system (Tables 5.4 and 5.5, pp. 126 and 127), but the system has other components as well. In fact, we want to bring *everything* that contributes to cash flow estimates into the system, insofar as possible. Figures 6.1 (previous page) and 6.2 (below) suggest the major components of the full system.

Ideally, cost and benefit estimates in the cash flow statements are created by formulas that are driven by assumptions. In the section below, "The Dynamic Financial Model," we look more closely at the way assumptions create cash flow estimates for individual items. For now, however, focus on the overall structure of the system, and how that addresses the purpose of the case.

⊡ The most fundamental structural issue has to do with the distinction between full value and incremental data analysis.

Figures 6.1 and 6.2 illustrate the most fundamental structural issue: are we going to analyze and present full value data or incremental data? (You may wish to review the distinction between full value cash flow statements and incremental statements in the section "Data Structure," pp. 87–90). Remember these points from Chapter 4:

Spreadsheet System : Incremental Analysis

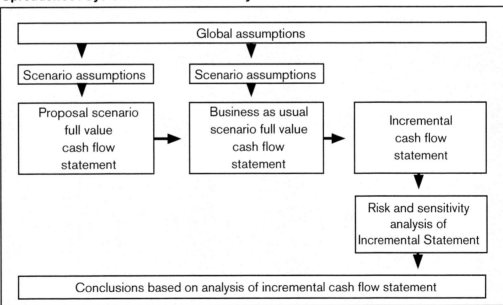

Figure 6.2 Components of the complete spreadsheet system for a two-scenario case analyzing incremental data (the differences between proposal and business as usual scenarios). Arrows show lines of information flow. Conclusions and recommendations are based on analysis of the incremental cash flow statement.

- The incremental analysis may be preferred if the case purpose is to choose between alternative investment options or to make a "go/no–go" decision. The incremental analysis shows where the options differ, or what changes if we choose to act.

- The full value analysis is usually preferred if the case purpose is to support business planning or budgeting. Recipients need to know the full values of expected cash flows.

In brief, the case author has to decide which approach to focus on for making recommendations and conclusions in the case report, in order to structure the spreadsheet system. The author could, of course present and discuss both full value *and* incremental results and analyses, although doing so may risk confusing recipients. If I am going to focus on incremental analysis in a case report, I prefer to publish incremental cash flow statement in the main body of the report and put the full value statements in an appendix.

Spreadsheet Skills and Spreadsheet Errors

Building a typical business case spreadsheet system does not call for "rocket science" or the skills of a professional programmer. It does require what I would call intermediate level spreadsheet skills. You should be able to build the spreadsheet system if you can do the following:

- Assign names to cells and ranges of cells, and then use the names elsewhere in a formula.
- Write formulas with references to cells and ranges on other pages (worksheets) of the same spreadsheet file (workbook).
- Write and understand formulas with multiple terms and exponents.

No matter who creates the spreadsheet system, make it a requirement that all spreadsheet formulas be checked and re-checked.

If these skills are beyond your limits, then you will need to recruit someone with more spreadsheet experience for the case building team.

No matter who actually creates the spreadsheet system, make it a requirement that all spreadsheet formulas be checked and re-checked. Errors in spreadsheet programming can be extremely insidious: once implanted they may never be detected. Programmers who work in source languages like C++ or Visual Basic make mistakes all of the time as well, but most of these "bugs" reveal themselves by crashing the program, causing unexpected events, or producing absurd results. An incorrect spreadsheet formula can perform smoothly with no hint of a problem.

Consider, for instance the following Microsoft Excel example. Assume we are estimating a cost line item, "Salaries and Overhead"

Table of Assumptions		
Assumption	Assumed Value	Assigned Name
Average annual salary	50,000	Base_Salary
Salary salary growth rate	5.0%	Salary_Growth
Overhead rate	30.0%	OH_Rate
Overhead growth rate	5.0%	OH_Growth
Number of employees	5	Number

Table 6.3 Important assumptions for estimating a cost line item, "Salaries and Overhead." In a business case spreadsheet system, each "Assumed Value" cell is assigned the name to its right.

for Years 1, 2, and 3 of the analysis period. The assumptions for making the estimate appear in Table 6.3 above. Notice that each assumption has an assigned a name that can be used in formulas. Assume that five employees have an annual salary of $50,000 each. Assume also that overhead expenses are 30.0% of salary. If that is all there is to the calculation, each year's estimated cost is (in Microsoft Excel format):

Salaries and Overhead
   =   Number * Base_Salary * (1 + OH_Rate)

An overhead rate of 30.0% is applied by multiplying the base salary by 130% (that is, 1+ OH_Rate). Now, factor in one more assumption: salaries are expected to grow by 5% a year. This means that each year's salaries will be different. Adding the salary growth rate to the equation produces these formulas:

Salaries and Overhead for Year 1
   = Number * Base_Salary * (1 + Salary_Growth)^1 * (1 + OH_Rate)
Salaries and Overhead for Year 2
   = Number * Base_Salary * (1 + Salary_Growth)^2 * (1 + OH_Rate)
Salaries and Overhead for Year 3
   = Number * Base_Salary * (1 + Salary_Growth)^3 * (1 + OH_Rate)

The salary growth rate is applied twice for year 2, and 3 times for year 3 (the exponents accomplish the repeated applications of the growth rate). So far so good. Now, however, add in the final assumption. The case building team has good reason to assume that the overhead rate itself is actually growing by 5.0% each year. See if you can tell whether example "A" or example "B" is correct by simply examining the numbers in Table 6.4 (next page) .

Table 6.4 Two possible sets of estimates for "Salaries and Overhead" based on the assumptions in Table 6.3. One set is incorrect, but most people would not notice the error by simply examining the figures.

Example A	Year 1	Year 2	Year 3
Salaries and Overhead	345,188	366,788	389,913

Example B	Year 1	Year 2	Year 3
Salaries and Overhead	358,313	395,040	435,531

If you are still not sure which example is correct and which is not, see if you can tell by examining the Year 2 formulas:

Example A: Salaries and Overhead for Year 2
= Number * Base_Salary * (1+Salary_Growth)^2 *
(1+ OH_Rate * (1+OH_Growth)^2)

Example B: Salaries and Overhead for Year 2
= Number * Base_Salary * (1+Salary_Growth)^2 *
(1+ OH_Rate) * (1+OH_Growth)^2

▣ The spreadsheet produces numbers without complaining, even when programming errors are present…if the author or someone else on the case building team does not detect errors, it is unlikely that anyone else will find them, either.

There is a programming mistake in one of the examples. Will you notice such mistakes if you simply review spreadsheet figures or casually look through spreadsheet formulas? It is easy to overlook them, especially if you are the spreadsheet creator proofing your own work. The spreadsheet produces numbers without complaining no matter which formula is used. In fact, Example A is correct. The overhead *growth* rate is applied to the overhead rate as it should be. For these assumptions, one rate grows by another rate. In Example B, the overhead growth rate is applied incorrectly to the base salary, along with OH_Rate and Salary_Growth.

If the spreadsheet author or someone else on the case building team does not detect such errors, it is unlikely that anyone else will find them, either.

The Dynamic Financial Model

There is no single correct way to implement the spreadsheet systems that are shown schematically in Figures 6.1 and 6.2 (pp. 160–161). The layout and appearance of your system will reflect stylistic and structural choices of the case building team, especially the person who actually builds the spreadsheet. Again, the best this *Guide* can do is suggest some example approaches that work.

Our immediate objective is to build a system that supports sensitivity and risk analysis and for that we need a truly dynamic model (the dynamic system, or model was introduced in Chapter 2, pp.

37–39). In a dynamic financial model, all of the estimated inflows and outflows in the cash flow statements are created by formulas and assumptions, not by direct entry of the figures. Changing an assumption automatically changes all data and results that depend on that assumption.

Notice also that a good dynamic model, or system, has value that extends well beyond sensitivity and risk analysis. The spreadsheet system you are developing can be a valuable tool in its own right when delivered along with the case report. Parts of the spreadsheet model are published in the case report, but the system itself should also serve as:

▣ A good dynamic model, or system has value that extends well beyond sensitivity and risk analysis.

- The vehicle for further testing of assumptions and establishing case credibility.
- A tool for managing and controlling costs, benefits, risks, and contingencies throughout the analysis period.
- An example or template for those who build similar cases. Ideally, however, spreadsheet system will be built as a completely dynamic financial model.

Spreadsheet Implementation: General Principles

The dynamic model will be well exercised during the final stages of case analysis and it should also serve management and control needs during the analysis period. The model, in other words, should be something more than a tool to be used once and discarded. For that reason, the spreadsheet system should designed so that it can be easily understood and used by others besides its creator.

Several design principles contribute to its usability by everyone on the case building team and beyond: consistent, helpful formatting, abundant notation, and a structure that is logical and understandable

Consistent, Helpful Formatting

The spreadsheet creator knows which cells are for data entry and which cells are supposed to be left alone. The distinction may not be so clear to other users. When working with an unfamiliar spreadsheet, it is easy to enter data mistakenly into a cell that holds a formula for deriving results—thereby eliminating the formula in the process. You can help prevent that kind of problem by using a color scheme such as the following throughout the spreadsheet system:

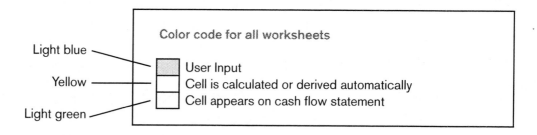

Light blue — User Input
Yellow — Cell is calculated or derived automatically
Light green — Cell appears on cash flow statement

Color code for all worksheets

Under this scheme, all user input goes into blue cells. Yellow cells hold values that are derived from assumptions and user input elsewhere in the spreadsheet. When green cells appear in worksheet pages, users know they hold results that also appear on a cash flow statement. Of course you can use any other formatting system you wish; what is important is that users know immediately where they are supposed to enter data and where the ultimate results come from.

Another step that helps prevent accidently overwriting formulas and other content is to lock all cells that are not meant for user input.

> What is important is that users know immediately where they are supposed to enter data and where the ultimate results come from.

Abundant Notation

Be sure that the spreadsheet itself explains clearly and completely what users are supposed to input. Here, for example, is an input item asking the user to supply two different discount rates for calculating net present value:

11 DCF Rate 1   8.0%
DCF Rate 2   15.0%

The spreadsheet author may know what a DCF rate is, and why it is in the model, but other users may not. It is more helpful to present the input with a little more notation, such as shown below. The item label is more complete. The small red triangle indicates that a pop-up cell comment is available for users who want still more explanation

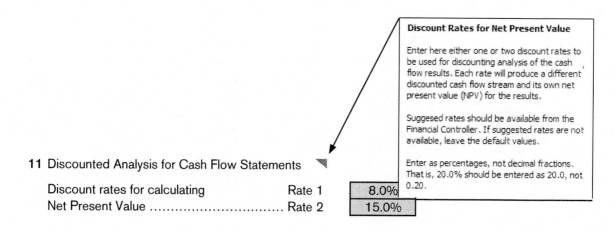

Discount Rates for Net Present Value

Enter here either one or two discount rates to be used for discounting analysis of the cash flow results. Each rate will produce a different discounted cash flow stream and its own net present value (NPV) for the results.

Suggested rates should be available from the Financial Controller. If suggested rates are not available, leave the default values.

Enter as percentages, not decimal fractions. That is, 20.0% should be entered as 20.0, not 0.20.

11 Discounted Analysis for Cash Flow Statements

Discount rates for calculating   Rate 1   8.0%
Net Present Value .... Rate 2   15.0%

(This is an Excel example. Lotus 1-2-3 uses a small red dot to indicate that a cell note is available).

Logical Structure

▣ Ordinarily, users should not have to make direct entries or changes to cash flow statements, graphs, or supplementary analyses.

Your financial system *could* be implemented entirely on one spreadsheet page (one worksheet). Both Microsoft Excel and Lotus 1-2-3 provide 65,536 rows and 256 columns per worksheet, more than enough space, even for very complex financial models. The single-page system is not recommended, however, unless the entire system is very, very simple. Different kinds of information may require different column widths and row heights—formatting that may not work for elements elsewhere in the same rows or columns. Worksheets that cover huge areas are also very difficult to navigate. Instead, the recommended approach is to build the entire system within a single spreadsheet workbook (single spreadsheet file), using different worksheet pages for different kinds of information.

Figure 6.3, for instance, shows the page structure of a typical two-scenario business case system. Notice that the pages are divided into two groups: those calling for user input and those that derive results. Ordinarily, users should not have to make direct entries or changes to the cash flow statements, graphs, or supplementary analyses (except, perhaps, to format these pages for publication). Below are some brief descriptions of the kinds of items that might go on each kind of page.

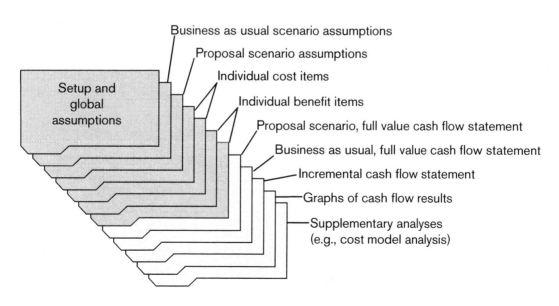

Figure 6.3 Page structure for a typical two-scenario business case, implemented in a single spreadsheet file (workbook). Sheets in blue call for user input. Sheets in yellow derive results from input on the blue sheets.

Set Up and Assumptions Pages

You can save a lot of spreadsheet labor by using set up items to provide headings for use throughout the system. Figure 6.4, for example, is a snapshot of a page with several set up items. All of the blue fields are for user input, and all have been assigned names by the author. The names can be referenced easily from other pages. Here, the organization name, business case subject, and currency symbol provide headings for other input pages, cash flow statements, graphs, and tables.

▣ Set up items can save a lot of spreadsheet labor by providing headings for use throughout the system.

In this system the analysis period is designated by choosing a length and a start date (items 3 and 4). The small table within item 4 fills in automatically, showing the user a complete list of time segments for analysis. This table also provides column headings through out the system, for cash flow estimates and cash flow summary columns.

This first pages of the workbook are also a good place to identify and enter global assumptions: values that contribute to many cost and benefit estimates, in all scenarios. Figure 6.5 has some examples from one such page. Every user input cell has an assigned name so that it can be referenced in formulas throughout the system.

Set up the business case by identifying the sponsoring organization, the analysis period, and a currency symbol

1 Sponsoring Organiztion.......... Marine Division, Acme Diesel Corporation

2 Business Case Subject.......... Proposed upgrade of design engineering software and hardware

3 Analysis period years............. 5

4 Analysis period start date .... 15 August 2002

Analysis period summary:

Length of analysis period: 5 Yrs
(60 Months)

	Begins	Ends
Year 1	15-Aug-02	14-Aug-03
Year 2	15-Aug-03	14-Aug-04
Year 3	15-Aug-04	14-Aug-05
Year 4	15-Aug-05	14-Aug-06
Year 5	15-Aug-06	14-Aug-07

5 Currency symbol (e.g., , $, ¥, £, etc.) .... $

Figure 6.4 Sample items for setting up the financial system. The information entered here will appear throughout the spreadsheet system to provide titles and headings.

Figure 6.5 Examples of possible global assumptions. They are called "global" because they apply to cost and benefit line items in all scenarios.

Financial performance
Items 6-10 can be found on the most recent income statement

6	The company's most recent annual net sales..............	$ 565,023,400
7	The company's's costs of goods sold (CGS)..............	$ 325,793,100
8	Research and development costs (R&D)...................	$ 14,575,000
9	Selling, General, and Administrative (SG&A)..............	$ 95,310,900
10	Operating Margin before taxes...............................	$ 129,344,400

Financial Practice

11 Discounted Analysis for Cash Flow Statements

Discount rates for calculating — Rate 1: 8.0%
Net Present Value ....Rate 2: 15.0%

Discounting convention: At year end or at year mid point?
Enter E for "End of Year" or M for "Mid-year".................................. E

Engineering Salaries

12 Average annual engineering salary plus overhead .... $ 55,000

13 Average annual engineering salary increase, per year.......... 3.0%
This rate will be applied to all salary and labor costs after year 1.

⊡ If each scenario's assumptions appear together on a page of their own, this set of pages provides a clear summary of the differences between scenarios.

⊡ Each cost and benefit item is a small model in its own right, drawing on three kinds of assumptions (global, scenario, and item-specific).

For this case, the income statement items in Figure 6.5 (items 6–10) contribute to cost and benefit estimates on later pages. The business case subject, a proposed upgrade of design engineering hardware and software, is meant to reduce research and development costs (R&D). In order to "scale" or estimate the size of the reduction in later calculations, analysts must know the *current* level of R&D spending. Whenever the current R&D figure is needed, the name of blue cell in item 8 is used. Similarly, engineering salaries and salary increases contribute to many of the cost items to be estimated later. This author decided that one average salary assumption for all engineering staff is sufficient for the purpose of this case, and that number appears here. That assumption may be used by dozens of labor calculations on the cost page.

I suggest keeping scenario-specific assumptions on pages separate from the global assumptions. If each scenario's assumptions appear together on a page of their own, the set of scenario pages provides a clear summary of the differences between scenarios.

Cost and Benefit Item Worksheets

Cost and benefit figures in the dynamic financial model come from formulas, not from direct entry of the cash flow numbers through the keyboard. Each cost and benefit item is in fact a small model in its own right, drawing on three kinds of assumptions (global, scenario, and item-specific). The cash flow statements themselves are not the best place to bring together the assumptions and formulas that make up all the estimates, however.

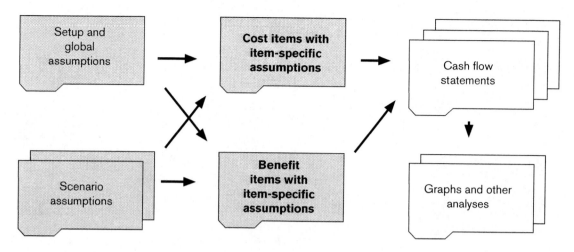

Figure 6.6 The cost and benefit item worksheets (center) provide space for bringing together different assumptions and for modeling cash flow estimates. Arrows indicate information flow.

Instead of trying to build all these models on the cash flow statement pages, is much easier and less risky to use separate pages for developing the individual cost and benefit estimates, and then transfer the "bottom line" results directly to the cash flow statement. In Figures 6.1 and 6.2 (pp. 160–161), we see two ways to build the *logical structure* of the analysis. Figure 6.3 (p. 167) is one way to show the structure of a spreadsheet implementation that supports those analyses. Figure 6.6 above is the same set of spreadsheet pages, arranged to emphasize the cost and benefit item worksheets and their position in the information flow.

⊡ Worksheets for individual cost and benefit items provide the space to bring together assumptions and write formulas that estimate cash flow.

Cost Item Estimates

Looking first to cost estimates, remember that the ideal cost estimate is based on three kinds of assumptions: global assumptions, scenario assumptions, and item-sepecific assumptions. The cost items page is the place to develop item-specific assumptions and combine them with the other assumptions.

Figure 6.7 next page shows one approach to estimating cost items in a dynamic model. This example is part of a worksheet for "individual cost items" in a business case for a consumer products company. The subject of the case is a proposed new product service offering, and the purpose of the case is to help management decide among several different implementation plans. There were in fact three scenarios in the case (one for each implementation plan), and Figure 6.6 has a few items from the "Scenario B" cost item sheet. The system also had similar worksheets for scenarios B and C.

What is important now is not the formulas (which you cannot see in the figure), but rather the general approach to creating a workspace for each cost item, and then summarizing results for the cash flow

Service Product Unit Costs Proposal Scenario B: 100% cost responsibility	Item Assumptions	Hourly Labor	Fraction This Senario	Year 1 31-Dec 2002		Year 2 31-Dec 2003		Year 3 31-Dec 2004		TOTAL		
Figures in $				Hrs	Ext Cost	Hrs	Ext Cost	Hrs	Ext Cost	Hrs	Row Total	Item Total
1 Develop negotiation strategy for partners		68	100.0%	100	6,800	0	0	0	0	100	6,800	
Occurs once in the Develop Capability phase												
Line Item Total					6,800		0		0			6,800
2 Produce test process for certification		NA	100.0%	NA	400,000	NA	80,000	NA	80,000	NA	560,000	
Contracted on a flat-fee basis. Flat Fee for Year 1	400,000											
Flat Fee for Year 2	80,000											
Flat Fee for Year 3	80,000											
Line Item Total					400,000		80,000		80,000			560,000
3 Establish training capability		68	100.0%	100	6,800	0	0	0	0	100	6,800	
No impact of partnering												
Cost occurs once in Develop Capability phase												
Training equipment costs					2,400		0		0		2,400	
Assumed days/trip domestic travel	1											
Assumed number of trips domestic travel	1											
Travel expenses					1,000		0		0		1,000	
Line Item Total:					10,200		0		0			10,200
4 Delivery of support services		68	100.0%	3,520	239,360	3,520	246,541	3,520	253,937	10,560	739,838	
Cost occurs every year												
Number of people	2											
Hours per person / Year	1,760											
Assume: no significant travel												
Line Item Total:					239,360		246,541		253,937			739,838
5 Follow-up audit of sites		68	100.0%	0	0	256	17,930	256	18,468	512	36,398	
Cost occurs each year starting Year 2												
Labor hours per audit	32											
Number of partners audited per year	4											
Days per partner	3											
Number of audits per partner per year	2											
Travel costs					0		11,200		11,200		22,400	
Assume 1 trip per audit												
Line Item Total:					0		29,130		29,668			58,798

Figure 6.7 Five items on a cost item worksheet. Blue cells are for item-specific user input, yellow cells contain derived values, and green cells hold results that appear on the cash flow statements.

statement. Over the years I have found this kind of structure works well for modeling a wide variety of cost items.

There are five cost items in Figure 6.7 needing cash flow estimates for each year of a three year analysis period. The column headings at upper right cover the same periods as the cash flow statements. Each cost item has its own distinct work area, essentially a yellow rectangle. Notice that the color scheme mentioned earlier (p. 166) is applied consistently. Blue cells call for user input, yellow cells hold derived results, and green cells hold values that appear in the cash flow statement. Line item names appear on the cash flow statements exactly

Cash Flow Summary		Scenario B: 100% Cost responsibility			
Projected results for the year ending ...		Year 1 31-Dec 2002	Year 2 31-Dec 2003	Year 3 31-Dec 2004	TOTAL
Figures in $					
1 Develop negotiation strategy for partners		(6,800)	0	0	(6,800)
2 Produce test process for certification		(400,000)	(80,000)	(80,000)	(560,000)
3 Establish training capability		(10,200)	0	0	(10,200)
4 Delivery of support services		(239,360)	(246,541)	(253,937)	(739,838)
5 Follow-up audit of sites		0	(29,130)	(29,668)	(58,798)

Figure 6.8 Extract from the scenario B cash flow statement, showing five cost line items from Figure 6.7. Green cells in Figure 6.6 correspond to the figures in the cash flow statement.

as entered or updated in the blue cells here. Table 6.8 (below) shows how the same items appear in the cash flow statement.

Cost item 1 is the simplest in this example. Item 1 uses the hourly labor rate (a global assumption) and one scenario assumption, namely that the service product unit will bear 100% of the costs for this item. In the figure of course, you cannot see the formula but you should be able to see where the $6,800 value in the year 1 green cell comes from. The global and scenario assumptions were entered on other pages into cells with assigned names. On this page, formulas refer to these assumptions by using their names. For item 1, the user simply enters the number of hours estimated per year for this activity. For this example case, the cost activity is entirely completed in year 1. The formula behind the $6,800 year 1 value is simply:

= Year_1_Hours * Hourly_Rate * PSU_Cost_Fraction

Each factor in the formula is a named cell, either from this page (Year_1_Hours) or from other pages (Hourly_Rate and PSU_Cost_Fraction).

The second cost item in Figure 6.7 is also very simple: there is a flat fee to be paid to outside contractors for each year of the analysis period. The intent is to keep as many item-specific assumptions as possible in the column labeled "Item Assumptions" at left. You can see how the three figures in blue cells at left transfer directly to item totals for each year (green cells).

The third cost activity item includes a labor cost, an equipment cost, and travel costs:

- The labor costs (all in year 1) depend on the same global labor rate assumption, the scenario assumption (100% cost responsibility), and user-entered labor estimates for this item.
- The equipment costs are simply a user-entered item-specific assumption.
- The travel component also uses a combination of global assumptions from another sheet (cost per travel day and transportation cost per trip), and item-specific assumptions (Days per trip and number of trips).

The fourth and fifth items apply the same kind of approach, showing that cost item can have multiple components, and the estimated cost of each can depend on global, scenario, and item-specific assumptions.

The green cells for yearly cash flow totals also have names, which allows the cash flow statements to access them directly as shown in the cash flow statement extract of Figure 6.7. Notice, by the way, that

Formulas refer to assumptions by using names assigned to cells on the assumption pages.

cost items become *cash outflows* in the full value cash flow statement, as indicated by parentheses.

Benefit Estimates

Recall from Chapters 4 and 5 that your business case may include several kinds of benefits:

- Cost savings or avoided costs
- Increased income
- Other contributions to business objectives

Cost Savings or Avoided Costs

▣ Cost savings and avoided costs appear only on incremental cash flow statements.

Remember also that cost savings or avoided costs appear only on the incremental cash flow statements. Cost savings cannot appear on the full value cash flow statements because all cost items there are cash outflows. Cost savings appear on the incremental cash flow statement when, for instance, business as usual cost estimates are subtracted from proposal estimates. We saw how this worked in Figure 5.8, which is presented again, below, as Figure 6.5

Increased Income and Contributions to Other Business Objectives

Benefit items other than cost savings will probably require worksheet space for modeling, just as most cost items do. The example in Figure 6.9 (next page) is one way to model one such item.

In this case, a proposed design system (the subject of the case) is expected to help shorten new product design and development time from 24 weeks (business as usual) to 16 weeks (proposal scenario). It

Table 6.5 Cost savings are apparent only when two scenarios are compared in the cost analysis. The proposal and business as usual estimates (top and middle) appear on full value cash flow statements. Cost savings appear only in items on the incremental statement (bottom).

Cash flow in $1,000s						
	←		Analysis Period		→	
PROPOSAL SCENARIO	Year 1	Year 2	Year 3	Year 4	Year 5	Total
Floorspace rental	(260)	(260)	(290)	(290)	(320)	(1,420)

BUSINESS AS USUAL SCENARIO						
Floorspace rental	(300)	(300)	(350)	(350)	(400)	(1,700)

INCREMENTAL CASH FLOW						
Floorspace Rental Savings	40	40	60	60	80	280

will also help shorten manufacturing set up and production from the current 8 weeks to 4 weeks. These reductions appear as a benefit in the proposal scenario cash flow statement and the incremental cash flow statement as well. The example illustrates several important points to keep in mind while modeling benefits in the spreadsheet system:

- Benefit modeling can be handled like cost modeling, that is, through a process of writing formulas that use global assumptions, scenario assumptions, and item-specific assumptions.

- The primary item-specific assumptions for this and many other benefits represent the final two steps of the benefits rationale: the value of reaching a target objective, and the percentage of that value credited to the benefit impact. In this example, the values of targets are in yellow cells, meaning they are either global or scenario assumptions from other pages (under the color conventions used here). The percentage credit for the proposed system is an item-specific assumption for each scenario.

---

1   Benefit: Shorter overall design and production times
   contributes to competitive advantage and increased operating margin

Current design time is 24 week(s)
The target time is 16 week(s)
The estimated annual value of increased margins and competitive
advantage from reaching the target is .... €   120,000,000
- What percentage of this value should be credited
  to the proposed system?................................. 50.0%
  Result: Projected benefit................................ €   60,000,000

Current production time is 8 weeks
The target time is 4 weeks
The estimated value of increased sales or competitive advantage from
reaching the target is .... €   34,000,000
- What percentage of this target should be credited
  to the proposed system?............................ 50.0%
  Result: Projected benefit................................ €   17,000,000

Summary: the full annual value of benefit 1 is .... €   77,000,000

Estimated benefit: Overall design and production process improvements

	Year 1 ending 14 Aug 2004	Year 2 ending 14 Aug 2005	Year 3 ending 14 Aug 2006	Year 4 ending 14 Aug 2007	**Total**
Ramp up	40.0%	80.0%	100.0%	100.0%	
€	30,800,000	61,600,000	77,000,000	77,000,000	246,400,000

Figure 6.9 Example item from a benefit worksheet. The example illustrates important points describes in the text about implementing benefit estimates into the spreadsheet system .

- Most benefits do not arrive at full value immediately. Most have a ramp up, or learning curve period, as estimated here in the "Ramp up" cells, just above the total yearly estimates. Here, the author estimates that benefits would average 40% of the maximum annual level during year 1 and 90% of maximum in year 2.

- This benefit impact has two components (shorter design time and shorter production time), which the author chose to model separately within the same overall item.

- Two different ways to measure the value of reaching the target are in view, namely, increased margins and improved competitive advantage. The author chose to combine the estimated value of both measures, however, in order to avoid the possibility of double counting (the value of improved competitive advantage, for instance, comes partly through increased margins).

- All benefit items including this one need separate treatment under each scenario. Figure 6.9 represents the proposed design system scenario. Under business as usual, there may or may not be reductions in design and production times, depending on other efforts that management takes. Each benefit item, like each cost item, should appear in the full value cash flow statement for each scenario. If the business as usual values turn out to be "0," then the benefit values will be the same on the proposal full value statement and on the incremental statement.

▣ Most benefits do not arrive at full value immediately. Most have a ramp up, learning curve period.

Cash Flow Statements

Cash flow statements and spreadsheet pages with graphs and other analyses should not require direct user input. These pages should take cost and benefit estimates and other information from other pages. Users should not have to make any entries on these pages once the spreadsheet author has created them (expect, possibly, to format them for publishing).

For many recipients, these pages are the case's "reason for being." You will probably publish them in the case report and many recipients will turn to them immediately after reading the Executive Summary. For them, the "results" begin with the cash flow statements.

▣ For many recipients, the "results" begin with the cash flow statements.

Table 6.6 (next page) is the incremental cash flow statement that we met earlier as Table 5.4 in the previous chapter. This time, however, we will look a little more closely at the sources of its components and its analysis within the dynamic financial model. In Table 6.6, yellow color identifies text, assumptions, and values that come directly from other pages in the spreadsheet system:

Server Systems Upgrade Purchase

Summary of Financial Results and Assumptions
($ in 1,000's)

The estimated net benefit (cost) over the evaluation period is as follows:		
Net Incremental cash flow:	1,537.9	
Net present value 1:	1,072.9	DCF at 9.0%
Net present value 2:	854.1	DCF at 15.0%
Analysis period: Sep 2002 - Aug 2007		
Analysis period length	60 Months	

Incremental Cash Flow Statement

For the year ending 31 August...

	Year 0 Aug 2002	Year 1 Aug 2003	Year 2 Aug 2004	Year 3 Aug 2005	Year 4 Aug 2006	Year 5 Aug 2007	TOTAL
BENEFITS / GAINS							
Contributions to Strategic Objectives							
Productivity improvements	0.0	400.0	618.0	742.6	819.5	900.4	**3,480.6**
Customer satisfaction improved	0.0	240.0	316.8	418.2	552.0	728.6	**2,255.6**
Downtime reductions	0.0	200.0	154.5	137.9	120.2	112.6	**725.2**
Other Benefits							
Rental equipment savings	0.0	400.0	412.0	424.4	437.1	450.2	**2,123.7**
Avoided Hiring - Add'l staff	0.0	239.0	239.0	270.7	304.2	287.2	**1,340.1**
Reduced floorspace costs	0.0	12.5	12.9	13.3	13.7	14.1	**66.4**
Sale of unused equipment	320.0	0.0	0.0	0.0	0.0	0.0	**320.0**
Total Benefits/Gains	**320.0**	**1,491.5**	**1,753.1**	**2,007.1**	**2,246.7**	**2,493.1**	**10,311.5**
COSTS AND EXPENSES							
Hardware Costs							
Server Systems	(130.4)	0.0	0.0	(69.8)	0.0	0.0	**(200.2)**
Peripheral HW assets	(32.0)	(34.9)	(17.6)	(23.7)	(12.8)	(8.2)	**(129.2)**
PCs and workstations	(300.0)	(25.0)	(30.0)	(20.0)	(30.0)	(20.0)	**(425.0)**
HW maint cost increase	0.0	(120.5)	(120.3)	(150.7)	(150.7)	(150.7)	**(692.9)**
Additional small equip expenses	(12.8)	(57.0)	(69.0)	(33.9)	(13.1)	(13.5)	**(199.4)**
Software Costs							
Software assets	(130.0)	(60.0)	0.0	(62.2)	(41.6)	0.0	**(293.7)**
SW maintenances increases	0.0	(16.7)	(16.7)	(16.7)	(16.7)	(16.7)	**(83.5)**
End user appl's - expensed	(32.0)	(23.0)	(23.7)	(24.4)	(25.1)	0.0	**(128.2)**
Personnel Expenses							
System staffing cost increase	0.0	(320.0)	(356.2)	(396.5)	(441.3)	(491.2)	**(2,005.1)**
NW/Comms Expenses							
Line usage fee increase	0.0	(348.0)	(412.2)	(496.7)	(588.3)	(716.5)	**(2,561.7)**
Line maintenance increase	0.0	(180.2)	(180.2)	(180.2)	(180.2)	(180.2)	**(901.0)**
Other Costs and Expenses							
Electrical power increase	0.0	(6.5)	(6.5)	(6.7)	(6.7)	(7.0)	**(33.4)**
Insurance increase	0.0	(4.2)	(4.3)	(4.5)	(4.6)	(4.7)	**(22.3)**
Security increase	0.0	0.0	(268.2)	(276.3)	(260.4)	(293.1)	**(1,098.0)**
Total Impact: Costs and Exp	**(637.2)**	**(1,196.0)**	**(1,504.9)**	**(1,762.1)**	**(1,771.5)**	**(1,901.8)**	**(8,773.6)**
CASH FLOW SUMMARY							
Cash inflows (outflows)							
Benefit Impacts	320.0	1,491.5	1,753.1	2,007.1	2,246.7	2,493.1	**10,311.5**
Cost and Expense Item Impacts	(637.2)	(1,196.0)	(1,504.9)	(1,762.1)	(1,771.5)	(1,901.8)	**(8,773.6)**
NET CASH FLOW	**(317.2)**	**295.5**	**248.2**	**245.0**	**475.2**	**591.3**	**1,537.9**
Cumulative Net CF	(317.2)	(21.7)	226.5	471.5	946.7	1,537.9	**1,537.9**
Discounted Cash Flow							
At 9.0 %	(317.2)	271.1	208.9	189.2	336.6	384.3	**1,072.9**
At 15.0 %	(317.2)	256.9	187.7	161.1	271.7	294.0	**854.1**

- The title (at top), the analysis period, dates for column headings, and discounted cash flow rates are all taken from a set up and global assumptions page.

- Each cost and benefit item has a name taken directly from either a cost item worksheet or a benefit item worksheet page. If the user chooses to edit or change item names, the changes appear on the cash flow statement, as well.

- The individual incremental cash flow estimates for each item are the difference between full value cash estimates on a "purchase" scenario statement and a "business as usual" statement.

The full set of five cash flow statements for this case was illustrated in Figure 5.4 (p. 125). In terms of spreadsheet implementation, the three cash flow statements involved in the incremental statement of Table 6.6 are shown below in Figure 6.10.

In brief, every yellow spreadsheet cell in Table 6.6 holds the assigned name of a cell on another page. The totals at the bottom of each section, and the Summary section mathematics are performed here, on the cash flow statement page. The summary box at top takes the net cash flow and net present value figures from the Summary section at bottom.

Financial Metrics: The Primary Results

Cash flow statements like Table 6.6 represent the most likely predicted results under one scenario. Figures in the table are the primary results of the case. After scanning the table, however, recipients will immediately want to see summaries and analyses that bring out the full meaning of the projected cash flow picture. In Chapter 5 we designed the cash flow statements and took a quick look at preliminary totals for cash flow and discounted cash flow (pp. 150–152). Now that we have the cash flow structure built into the spreadsheet system, we can add the calculations that produce financial metrics automatically, as well.

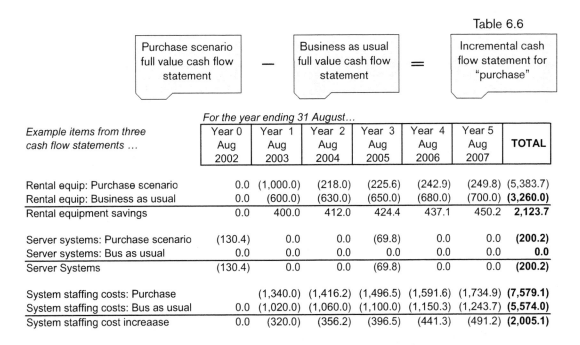

Table 6.6

Example items from three cash flow statements ...	Year 0 Aug 2002	Year 1 Aug 2003	Year 2 Aug 2004	Year 3 Aug 2005	Year 4 Aug 2006	Year 5 Aug 2007	TOTAL
Rental equip: Purchase scenario	0.0	(1,000.0)	(218.0)	(225.6)	(242.9)	(249.8)	(5,383.7)
Rental equip: Business as usual	0.0	(600.0)	(630.0)	(650.0)	(680.0)	(700.0)	**(3,260.0)**
Rental equipment savings	0.0	400.0	412.0	424.4	437.1	450.2	**2,123.7**
Server systems: Purchase scenario	(130.4)	0.0	0.0	(69.8)	0.0	0.0	**(200.2)**
Server systems: Bus as usual	0.0	0.0	0.0	0.0	0.0	0.0	**0.0**
Server Systems	(130.4)	0.0	0.0	(69.8)	0.0	0.0	**(200.2)**
System staffing costs: Purchase		(1,340.0)	(1,416.2)	(1,496.5)	(1,591.6)	(1,734.9)	**(7,579.1)**
System staffing costs: Bus as usual	0.0	(1,020.0)	(1,060.0)	(1,100.0)	(1,150.3)	(1,243.7)	**(5,574.0)**
System staffing cost increaase	0.0	(320.0)	(356.2)	(396.5)	(441.3)	(491.2)	**(2,005.1)**

For the year ending 31 August...

Figure 6.10 The three worksheet pages involved in producing cash flow estimates for the incremental cash flow statement of table 6.6. Example calculations show how line item figures on the incremental cash flow statement are derived from line items on full value statements.

Net Cash Flow

☑ Be sure that all important financial metrics are produced automatically by the system.

When the case report is delivered, recipients probably look immediately for the predicted net cash flow. This is the case's bottom line: the net inflow or outflow predicted for each segment of the analysis period. It is the most fundamental answer to the question "What does the proposed action mean to us in real money?" Net cash flow provides the answer in dollars, euro, yen, pounds, or other currency that most interests recipients. When two or more proposal scenarios compete for support, the one with the higher net cash flow is considered the better decision (other things being equal).

As you know, net cash flow is also the starting point for subsequent analyses, including cumulative cash flow, discounted cash flow (net present value), return on investment, payback period, and internal rate of return.

The bottom lines of the cash flow statement are the natural place to summarize simple cash flow totals and create the Net Cash Flow

	For the year ending 31 August...						
BEFORE TAX	Year 0 Aug 2002	Year 1 Aug 2003	Year 2 Aug 2004	Year 3 Aug 2005	Year 4 Aug 2006	Year 5 Aug 2007	**TOTAL**
CASH FLOW SUMMARY							
Benefit Impacts	320.0	1,491.5	1,753.1	2,007.1	2,246.7	2,493.1	**10,311.5**
Cost and Expense Item Impacts	(637.2)	(1,196.0)	(1,504.9)	(1,762.1)	(1,771.5)	(1,901.8)	**(8,773.6)**
NET CASH FLOW	**(317.2)**	**295.5**	**248.2**	**245.0**	**475.2**	**591.3**	**1,537.9**
Cumulative Net CF	(317.2)	(21.7)	226.5	471.5	946.7	1,537.9	**1,537.9**
Discounted Cash Flow							
At 9.0 %	(317.2)	271.1	208.9	189.2	336.6	384.3	**1,072.9**
At 15.0 %	(317.2)	256.9	187.7	161.1	271.7	294.0	**854.1**

AFTER TAX							
CASH FLOW SUMMARY							
Cash inflows (outflows)							
Benefit Impacts	320.0	1,491.5	1,753.1	2,007.1	2,246.7	2,493.1	**10,311.5**
Expense Item Impacts	(44.8)	(1,076.1)	(1,457.3)	(1,586.5)	(1,687.1)	(1,873.6)	**(7,725.5)**
Net Operating Inflow(Outflow)	275.2	415.4	295.8	420.6	559.6	619.4	**2,586.0**
Tax Savings (Tax)							
on Inflow/Outflow	(93.6)	(141.2)	(100.6)	(143.0)	(190.3)	(210.6)	**(879.2)**
Asset Purchase	(592.4)	(119.9)	(47.6)	(175.6)	(84.4)	(28.2)	**(1,048.1)**
Tax Savings from all							
Depreciation Expense	0.0	48.4	73.3	67.4	64.0	60.4	**313.5**
NET CASH FLOW	**(410.8)**	**202.7**	**220.9**	**169.3**	**348.9**	**441.0**	**972.2**
Cumulative Net CF	(410.8)	(208.1)	12.8	182.2	531.1	972.2	**972.2**
Discounted Cash Flow							
At 9.0 %	(410.8)	185.9	186.0	130.8	247.2	286.6	**625.7**
At 15.0 %	(410.8)	176.2	167.1	111.3	199.5	219.3	**462.7**

Table 6.6 Before tax and after tax versions of the cash flow statement summary section. Financial analysis begins with the NET CASH FLOW line. This is the basis for the first view of cash flow timing, for the net cash flow total, cumulative totals, and discounted cash flow analysis.

▣ Net cash flow is the most fundamental answer to the question "What does the proposed action mean to us in real money?"

stream. The summary section from Table 6.6 is repeated here, in Table 6.7. As you recall, this is a "before tax," or "no tax" statement. Table 6.7 also has the Summary section for the "after tax" version of the same analysis (we saw the full after tax cash flow statement in Table 5.5, p. 127).

I believe these examples demonstrate the value of using negative numbers (parentheses) for all outflows and positive numbers for all inflows on the statement. That way there is no chance of confusion over which lines should be added and which lines should be subtracted. Under this convention, lines are always *added*.

Using Microsoft Excel, you can easily create the Net Cash Flow figures on the before tax summary by adding Benefit Impacts" and "Cost and Expense Item Impacts." The easiest (and clearest, and safest) way to do this is to select the entire set of benefit figures and assign a name to the whole range, such as "BenefitTotals." Similarly, select the entire Cost and Expense Item Impacts row, and assign that range a name like "CostTotals." Then, the yearly Net Cash Flow figure in each column can use the same formula:

$$= BenefitTotals + CostTotals$$

Excel will use the figures in each column for the Net Cash Flow in that column. The before tax cash flow statement in Table 6.6 presents the following net cash flow figures:

For the year ending 31 August...   *$ in 1,000s*

	Year 0	Year 1	Year 2	Year 3	Year 4	Year 5	
	2002	2003	2004	2005	2006	2007	Total
NET CASH FLOW	(317.2)	295.5	248.2	245.0	475.2	591.3	1,537.9

If you are not creating an "after tax" analysis, you can skip the following notes and go directly to the next subsection "Cumulative Net Cash Flow."

On the after tax statements, the derivation of Net Cash Flow is slightly more complex. First, using named ranges as above, you can create a "Net Operating Inflow (Outflow) for each column as follows:

▣ On the after tax statements, the derivation of Net Cash Flow is slightly more complex.

$$= \text{BenefitTotals} + \text{ExpenseTotals}$$

On the after tax summary, income tax consequences apply to operating income (operating inflow), not to the overall cash flow. Operating income represents the combination of inflows and operating expenses; it does not reflect the cost of asset purchases. The tax impact on net operating inflow (income) is calculated by multiplying a tax rate by operating income, for each period:

Tax Savings (Tax) on Inflow/Outflow
$$= \text{Tax rate} * \text{Net operating Inflow (Outflow)} * (-1)$$

(The example in Table 6.6 uses an average tax on operating income of 34.0%). Notice the (–1) at the end of the equation, which turns a net outflow (loss) into a tax savings (inflow). When you have an operating inflow, the (–1) creates a tax liability (outflow). Tax savings or tax on operating inflow/outflow is the *first* tax impact to calculate.

After deriving the tax impact on operating income, then add in the actual asset purchase costs as shown in Table 6.6. Remember, this is a cash flow statement, not an income statement, so assets take their full value in the year they are purchased.

Then, finally, take the *second* tax impact, the tax savings from depreciation expenses over the analysis period. For this you will need the tax rate, again, and the total depreciation expenses for the year. However, you do not see the estimated depreciation expenses themselves in the summary section of Table 6.6. Instead, the depreciation expenses are estimated in the "Assets" section of the cash flow statement. You may wish to review Table 5.5 in Chapter 5, (p. 127) to see that depreciation expense appears for each year of each asset group, and that a "Total Depreciation Expense" row summarizes depreciation expenses for all groups.

Calculating depreciation expenses for the Assets section can be a challenging programming task. For each asset group, you will need the depreciation schedule and the value of assets acquired each year of the analysis period. The challenge comes in carrying each year's assets through the remaining years of depreciable life. In year 4 of the analysis period, for instance, some assets may be in the first year of depreciation, some in the second year, some in the third, and others in their fourth. The programming challenge becomes even more formidable when analysis period years are not the same as fiscal years or tax years. When doing an after tax analysis, it is advisable to have an accountant or financial specialist validate your depreciation calculations.

In any case, when you know the total depreciation expense for each period, the tax savings from depreciation becomes:

▣ When doing an after tax analysis, it is advisable to have an accountant or financial specialist validate your depreciation calculations.

Tax savings from Depreciation Expense

= Tax Rate * Depreciation expense * (−1)

Now, finally, you are ready to calculate the after tax Net Cash Flow line:

Net Cash flow = Net Operating Inflow(Outflow)

+ Tax Savings (Tax) on Inflow/Outflow

+ Asset Purchase

+ Tax Savings from Depreciation Expense

The before tax net cash flow was $1,537,900 for five years. As you can see, the after tax version of the same cost and benefit estimates produces a lower net gain:

For the year ending 31 August...						*$ in 1,000s*
Year 0	Year 1	Year 2	Year 3	Year 4	Year 5	
2002	2003	2004	2005	2006	2007	Total
NET CASH FLOW............(410.8)	**202.7**	**220.9**	**169.3**	**348.9**	**441.0**	**972.2**

You may wish to review the section "Before Tax or After Tax (pp. 119–121), which illustrates why taxes generally reduce both gains and losses. (Note, however, that in the after tax version of this example, the Year 0 figure of $410,800 is a *larger* outflow than the Year 0 before tax figure of $317,000. That is because Year 0 in the after tax version shows a *net operating inflow* of $275,000 before the large asset purchase is factored in; the large operating inflow creates a tax liability of $93,600 in Year 1, which the before tax version does not have. This is another demonstration of how taxes complicate the cash flow picture.)

Cumulative Net Cash Flow

After net cash flow, the most basic financial metric for your projected results is the cumulative cash flow stream, which appears directly under the Net Cash Flow line in Table 6.6). The cumulative figure for each period shows the net of all inflows and inflows, through the end of that period. If the cumulative value is negative, the total outflows exceed total inflows at the end of that period. If the cumulative figure is positive, the net for the whole analysis period is positive through the current segment.

Some people graph the cumulative cash flow figures and call the result a "Return on Investment Curve" (highlighting the point made several places in this book, that ROI means different things to different people.)

To see how cumulative cash flow is calculated, consider again the before tax cash flow summary lines from Table 6.6:

For the year ending 31 August...						$ in 1,000s
Year 0	Year 1	Year 2	Year 3	Year 4	Year 5	
2002	2003	2004	2005	2006	2007	Total
NET CASH FLOW (317.2)	295.5	248.2	245.0	475.2	591.3	1,537.9
Cumulative Net CF (317.2)	(21.7)	226.5	471.5	946.7	1,537.9	

The Cumulative figures above show why the "return on investment" view is popular and how it give a rough idea of time required for the action to pay for itself. Clearly, the net returns from the subject of the case are negative at the end of Year 1 but they become positive sometime in Year 2 (see "Payback Period," below, to calculate just when payback occurs).

Programming cumulative net cash flow into the cash flow statement is easy, once you have the net cash flow line. Here, however, you will have to name each Net Cash Flow entry separately: you cannot simply name the whole row "NetCashFlow" or something similar, because cumulative calculation requires a value from outside the current column. Instead, name the Net Cash flow Figures something like:

Yr0NetCF   Yr1NetCF   Yr2NetCF   Yr3NetCF   Yr4NetCF   Yr5NetCF

Also name cells for the *cumulative* cash flow figures something like:

Yr0CumCF Yr1CumCF Yr2CumCF Yr3CumCF Yr4CumCF Yr5CumCF

□ When two or more proposal scenarios compete for support, the scenario with the higher net present value is considered the better decision (other things being equal).

Using those names:

Yr0CumCF = Yr0NetCF
Yr1CumCF = Yr0CumCF + Yr1NetCF
Yr2CumCF = Yr1CumCF + Yr2NetCF
Yr3CumCF = Yr2CumCF + Yr3NetCF
Yr4CumCF = Yr3CumCF + Yr4NetCF
Yr5CumCF = Yr4CumCF + Yr5NetCF

Discounted Cash Flow: Net Present Value

Recipients trained in finance will almost certainly ask to see the projected cash flow stream for each scenario on a discounted basis as well as non discounted basis (for a brief introduction to discounted cash flow analysis, see Appendix B, pp. 238–241). Those who ask for discounted cash flow, or net present value," will appreciate seeing them on the cash flow statement, just below the Net Cash Flow and Cumulative cash flow lines. Discounted cash flow figures are presented in the same currency units as the original net cash flow stream (dollars, euro, yen, pounds, for example). When two or more proposal scenarios compete for support, the scenario with the higher net present value is considered the better decision (other things being equal).

In order to build the discounting calculation into your spreadsheet, you will need to determine whether your financial specialists practice end-of-year discounting or mid-year discounting. The end-of-year approach treats all cash flow events as if they occur on the last day of the year. The mid-year-approach treats all of the year's cash flow events as arriving, not surprisingly, at mid-year. If you cannot find out which approach is preferred in your organization, use end-of-year discounting. That is the most commonly used approach.

⊡ Discounting calculations require and interest rate and a decision to discount either at mid-year or year end.

The discounting calculation also requires an interest rate for each discounted cash flow stream that you produce. Discounting interest rates, however, are subject to change from time to time and it is better to treat them like global assumptions. If the Financial Controller wants to see to two discounted cash flow streams, one at an annual rate of 9.0% and another at 15.0%, like the examples in Table 6.6, then it is helpful to have two user-entry cells ready for them on the global assumptions page. These cells can be given names like DCF_Rate_1 and DCF_Rate_2.

Here, for example, are the net cash flow stream and one discounted cash flow stream from the before tax example we have been following:

For the year ending 31 August...							$ in 1,000s
	Year 0	Year 1	Year 2	Year 3	Year 4	Year 5	
	2002	2003	2004	2005	2006	2007	Total
NET CASH FLOW............	(317.2)	295.5	248.2	245.0	475.2	591.3	1,537.9
Discounted CF at 9%.....	(317.2)	271.1	208.9	189.2	336.6	384.3	1,072.9

The discounted cash flow total is the net present value (NPV) of the cash flow stream. Below are some example Excel formulas for implementing discounting, as described in Appendix B. The formulas assume that you have:

- Entered 9.0% in a cell named DCF_Rate_1.
- Assigned names to net cash flow cells, such as Yr1NetCF, Yr2NetCF, and so on.
- Assigned names to discounted cash flow cells such as Yr1DCF_1, Yr2DCF_1, etc.
- Chosen end-of-year discounting.

$$Yr0DCF\_1 = Yr0NetCF / (1 + DCF\_Rate\_1)^0$$
$$Yr1DCF\_1 = Yr1NetCF / (1 + DCF\_Rate\_1)^1$$
$$Yr2DCF\_1 = Yr2NetCF / (1 + DCF\_Rate\_1)^2$$
$$Yr3DCF\_1 = Yr3NetCF / (1 + DCF\_Rate\_1)^3$$
$$Yr4DCF\_1 = Yr4NetCF / (1 + DCF\_Rate\_1)^4$$
$$Yr5DCF\_1 = Yr5NetCF / (1 + DCF\_Rate\_1)^5$$

Notice that Year 0 cash flow is immediate cash flow for which present value and future value are the same. The "0" exponent of the year 0 discounting formula ensures that Yr0DCF_1 is the same as Yr0NetCF.

If you are asked to provide mid-year discounting instead of end-of-year discounting, the formula for Year 1 treats the entire cash flow for that year as though it comes at 0.5 years. The total cash flow for Year 2 is discounted as though it all comes at 1.5 years. Here are the Excel formulas for mid-year discounting:

$$Yr0DCF\_1 = Yr0NetCF / (1 + DCF\_Rate\_1)^0$$
$$Yr1DCF\_1 = Yr1NetCF / (1 + DCF\_Rate\_1)^{0.5}$$
$$Yr2DCF\_1 = Yr2NetCF / (1 + DCF\_Rate\_1)^{1.5}$$
$$Yr3DCF\_1 = Yr3NetCF / (1 + DCF\_Rate\_1)^{2.5}$$
$$Yr4DCF\_1 = Yr4NetCF / (1 + DCF\_Rate\_1)^{3.5}$$
$$Yr5DCF\_1 = Yr5NetCF / (1 + DCF\_Rate\_1)^{4.5}$$

Mid-year discounting is less severe than end of year discounting because the mid points of future years are closer to the present than their end points. In any case, the job of most case builders is not to weigh the pros and cons of mid-year vs. end of year discounting. The job of most case builders is to *find out* which approach your recipients expect or which is your organization's policy. The same advice holds for selecting an interest rate or rates for discounting: your organization very likely has a prescribed or recommended rate for discounted cash flow.

Payback Period

Payback period is a financial metric that answers the question: how long does it take for the action (or investment, or purchase) to pay for itself? Payback period is measured in *time*, usually decimal years. If you report that a proposed marketing program has a payback period of 1.5 years, you are estimating that program costs will be covered by program gains in a year and a half. When two or more proposal scenarios compete for support, the one with the shorter payback period is considered the better decision (other things being equal).

▣ When two or more proposal scenarios compete for support, the one with the shorter payback period is considered the better decision (other things being equal).

Payback period is a simple and appealing metric to many people because it is readily understood, and because it makes sense that an investment that pays for itself sooner is a better choice than one that pays for itself later.

Payback period for the business case is in fact a rough estimate. You cannot know the exact payback point in time unless you have access to daily cash flow data. When the smallest time segment in view is one year, the payback calculation assumes that each year's net cash flow is distributed evenly across the year. The timing of the payback event is projected by interpolation, as shown below. If the cash flow within individual years is very uneven, and if recipients need to know more precisely when real payback occurs, then the analysis period should be analyzed in terms of quarters or months instead of years.

The payback period estimate is derived from the Net Cash Flow and Cumulative Cash Flow streams in the cash flow statement:

For the year ending 31 August...						$ in 1,000s	
	Year 0	Year 1	Year 2	Year 3	Year 4	Year 5	
	2002	2003	2004	2005	2006	2007	Total
NET CASH FLOW............	(317.2)	295.5	248.2	245.0	475.2	591.3	1,537.9
Cumulative Net CF..........	(317.2)	(21.7)	226.5	471.5	946.7	1,537.9	

Before trying to build a payback formula into your spreadsheet, be sure you understand how to calculate the metric manually. Look first at the cumulative stream. You can see that the net result is negative through the end of Year 1 and positive at the end of Year 2. Payback must occur within Year 2. But when? Since we have no information about the timing of cash flow events within year 2, we have to use interpolation to estimate the timing of the payback even within Year 2. Figure 6.11 (next page) illustrates the components of this calculation. Year 1 is 1.0 years long, of course.

Referring to the figure, payback occurs when the cumulative cash flow line (blue line) cross the "0" Cumulative Cash Flow line. That is,

$$Payback = 1.0 + C$$

What fraction of Year 2 is covered by time segment "C"? From the geometry of the diagram we could (but will not) prove that:

$$\frac{|A|}{|B|} = \frac{C}{1.0}$$

A is the absolute value of Cumulative Cash Flow at the end of Year 1, 21.7, and B is the Net Cash Flow for Year 2, which is 248.2. The payback calculation is thus:

Payback period for the business case is in fact a rough estimate, unless you have access to daily cash flow data.

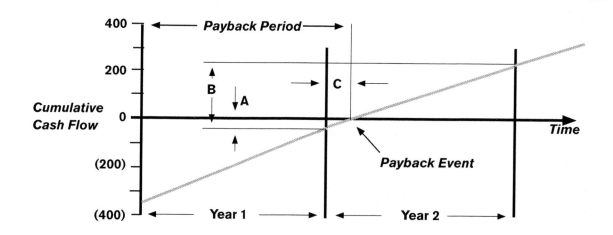

Figure 6.11 Finding the payback period by interpolation. Letters refer to components of the calculation described in the text.

$$\begin{aligned} \text{Payback} &= 1.0 + (21.7 / 248.2) \\ &= 1.09 \text{ years} \end{aligned}$$

According to this analysis, the proposed action "pays for itself" in 1.09 years.

It is easy to understand the payback concept. Most people readily follow the reasoning behind Figure 6.11. Putting the payback into spreadsheet formula form is more difficult. If you want to add the Payback metric to the spreadsheet (say, in the summary box like the one at the top of Table 6.6), here is one Excel formula that computes payback for analysis periods up to five years:

```
= IF(AND(Yr0CumCF >0, Yr1CumCF>0),0,
    IF(Yr1CumCF>0,ABS(Yr0CumCF)/Yr1NetCF,
    IF(Yr2CumCF>0,1+ABS(Yr1CumCF)/Yr2NetCF,
    IF(Yr3CumCF>0,2+ABS(Yr2CumCF)/Yr3NetCF,
    IF(Yr4CumCF>0,3+ABS(Yr3CumCF)/Yr4NetCF,
    IF(Yr5CumCF>0,4+ABS(Yr4CumCF)/Yr5NetCF,"N/A"))))))
```

The cell that holds that formula will show the payback period in years (all lines above are part of the same formula). The formula assumes that Net Cash Flow figures for each year have these names:

Yr0NetCF Yr1NetCF Yr2NetCF Yr3NetCF Yr4NetCF Yr5NetCF

It also assumes that *cumulative* cash flow figures have these names:

Yr0CumCF Yr1CumCF Yr2CumtCF Yr3CumCF Yr4CumCF Yr5CumCF

Of course you should not use such formulas blindly. If you follow the spreadsheet logic, however, you should be able to see how the formula implements the "manual" payback calculation above it. If the cumulative values in both Year 0 and Year 1 are positive, there is "0" payback time. If not, the formula checks each cell in the cumulative cash flow stream, looking for the first positive cumulative value starting with Year 1. If the cumulative values for all years are negative, the formula returns "N/A."

Internal Rate of Return

If your business case recipients want to see the internal rate of return (IRR) for the cash flow, that is easy to implement in Microsoft Excel or Lotus 1-2-3.

The IRR is expressed as a percentage. It is the interest rate that produces a net present value of 0 for the cash flow stream (Appendix B, pp. 243–245 briefly explains the source and some uses of the IRR). Some organizations use an IRR figure as a "hurdle rate:" proposals must project an IRR above the hurdle figure in order to receive funding. When two or more scenarios compete for support, the one with the higher IRR is considered the better decision (other things being equal).

In Excel, you will need to provide the IRR function with range of cells that holds the cash flow stream as well as an initial "guess" at the IRR value. (Microsoft suggests using 0.10 for the guess, but it does not really matter very much what value you choose, because it is only a starting point for repetitive iterations that search for the true IRR). When using the IRR function, I prefer to give one name to the whole cash flow stream, even if individual cells already have names. In the example we have been following, the range of cells in yellow (the cash flow stream) could be given the name NetCashFlow:

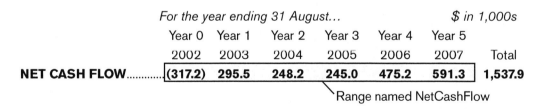

The margin note: The spreadsheet IRR function requires at least one positive and one negative value in the cash flow stream. Otherwise it returns an error message.

For the year ending 31 August...						$ in 1,000s
Year 0	Year 1	Year 2	Year 3	Year 4	Year 5	
2002	2003	2004	2005	2006	2007	Total
NET CASH FLOW (317.2)	295.5	248.2	245.0	475.2	591.3	1,537.9

Range named NetCashFlow

The internal rate of return will appear in a cell with the formula:

= IRR(NetCashFlow,0.10)

Note, however that the spreadsheet IRR function requires at least one positive and one negative value in the stream, in order to calculate. Otherwise, it returns an error message.

Return on Investment

The phrase "return on investment" (ROI) is familiar to most people in business. The idea that investment decisions can be evaluated by comparing investment returns to investment costs has a certain self evident validity and appeal. This *Guide* stresses, however, that ROI calculations should be used with caution (see pp. 24, 48–49, and 239–240). There are several different ROI metrics in common use, and, when someone asks for an ROI figure, it is always a good idea to be sure that everyone involved means the same thing. Some people have in mind the size of the financial return itself, over cost ("Our return on this investment is $100,000 more than the cost."). Others, as mentioned, have in mind the cumulative cash flow curve, which shows the net return over time, again in currency units. Still others have in mind a financial metric, expressed as a percentage.

There are several "standard" ROI metrics in use, and this Guide recommends using "Simple" ROI:

⊡ When some asks for an ROI figure, it is always a good idea to be sure that everyone involved means the same thing.

Simple ROI = (Gains - Investment Costs) / Investment Costs

Programming a simple ratio calculation for your spreadsheet system is easy *if* you know which costs and which benefits (gains) to use. Because you need to deal with costs and benefits separately, these figures cannot be taken from the Net Cash Flow summary line. On the incremental cash flow statement, such as Table 6.6, for instance,

Total Benefits/Gains = $10,311,500
Total Costs and Expenses = $8,773,600
Simple ROI = (10,311,500 – 8,773,600) / 8,773,600
         = 0.175 = 17.5%

You can designate a single cell in the spreadsheet to hold the ROI figure if you first name the appropriate cells something like Gains and IncrementalCosts. In Excel, the ROI ratio will appear in the cell with:

= (Gains–IncrementalCosts)/IncrementalCosts

In case you are getting confused by the term "incremental" in these ROI calculations, a word about that word may be helpful. The cost total in the example comes from an incremental cash flow analysis: "Total costs" already represent the incremental cost above business as usual for the action or investment. The gains, however, still need to have incremental costs subtracted from them for the ratio numerator. This is because we sill need the size of the incremental gain, *above the incremental cost.*

Cost Analysis

It is very likely that recipients will also want to see cost information independent of the benefit summaries. This is especially important when the business case results support budgetary planing or resource planning. Cost information is also especially important for the decision support case, when recipients are choosing among several options and it is agreed that benefits are more or less the same for all options, and the real decision issues are cost issues.

📖 Cost analysis is especially when the business case results support budgetary planting or resource planning.

Depending on recipient needs, you may extract certain cost totals from each cash flow statement, such as:

Total net cost for the analysis period

Total expenses

Total asset purchases

Total by cost model column, row, or cell, e.g.,

   Total development phase costs

   Total operational costs

Cost summaries based on the cost model structure, in fact, can provide information that is not so easy to see in the cash flow statements. Figure 6.12 below is one such analysis that we saw in Chapter 4 (as Figure 4.5). Each cell of the matrix holds the total analysis period costs, for all line items in the cell. The time line disappears from view in this approach, but in exchange, we can easily compare cost magnitudes, by cell, by row, or by column. The shaded cells in Figure 6.12, for instance, represent hardware and software acquisition and operation costs for an IT upgrade scenario. Decision makers naturally think first about those costs in those categories when making vendor choices, or go/no go decisions, but in fact those four cells only

Resources	Life Cycle Stages			$ in 1000s	
	Acquisition & Implementation	Operation	Ongoing Changes & Growth	Total	% of Total
Hardware	$ 1,523	$ 605	$ 924	$ 3,052	21.8%
Software	$ 1,192	$ 545	$ 520	$ 2,257	16.1%
IT Staff	$ 120	$3,315	$ 1,472	$ 4,907	35.1%
Users	$ 230	$1,342	$ 297	$ 1,869	13.4%
NW & Comms	$ 472	$ 771	$ 110	$ 1,353	9.7%
Other Costs	$ 112	$ 189	$ 238	$ 539	3.9%
Total	$3,649	$6,767	$ 3,561	$13,977	100.0%
% of Total	26.1%	48.4%	25.5%	100.0%	

Figure 6.12. The cost model as a cost analysis tool. Each cell shows the five-year total for all cost items in the cell, from one implementation scenario. Marginal totals and percentages show immediately which are the largest cost categories.

account for about 27% of the total analysis period costs. The person-nel consequences of the decision weigh more heavily, accounting for about 38.5% of the total cost (it staff + user costs).

Figure 6.12 below shows similar approach to cost analysis, using the cost model from a product life cycle scenario. Here, the model framework is presented twice: once with the cost totals them-selves (top), and again with the same cell totals and marginal totals expressed as percentages of the Grand Total (bottom). Looking at the bottom figure, for instance, planners and managers can see immedi-ately that three cost categories are considerably larger than the others (Marketing and Sales costs during Production, Engineering costs during Development, and Manufacturing costs during Production). Cost items in those cells are the natural focus for cost cutting or cost control measures.

I suggest putting cost analyses of this kind on a worksheet page of their own, following the cash flow statements. They are not difficult to program: Every cost line item on the cash flow statement comes from one cell or another of the cost model. Cells in the upper panel of Figure 6.12 contain formulas adding all the analysis period totals for the items in their cells, taken from the cash flow statement. Mar-ginal totals and percentages are then calculated from these. Like other parts of the dynamic financial model, the tables update themselves when users change assumptions.

€ in 1,000s		Product Life Cycle Phases				
		Development	Production	Support	Phase Out	Total
Function	Mkting & Sales	€ 451.1	€ 2,500.7	€ 275.2	€ 0.0	€ 3,227.0
	Engineering	€ 1,907.3	€ 342.8	€ 501.6	€ 125.2	€ 2,876.9
	Manufacturing	€ 34.5	€ 1,945.1	€ 54.0	€ 8.5	€ 2,042.1
	Distribution	€ 14.2	€ 629.4	€ 113.9	€ 5.0	€ 762.5
	Customer Svc	€ 28.4	€ 1,246.7	€ 1,132.0	€ 102.8	€ 2,509.9
	Total	€ 2,435.5	€ 6,664.7	€ 2,076.7	€ 241.5	€ 11,418.4

% of Grand Total		Product Life Cycle Phases				
		Development	Production	Support	Phase Out	Total
Function	Mkting & Sales	4.0%	21.9%	2.4%	0.0%	28.3%
	Engineering	16.7%	3.0%	4.4%	1.1%	25.2%
	Manufacturing	0.3%	17.0%	0.5%	0.1%	17.9%
	Distribution	0.1%	5.5%	1.0%	0.0%	6.7%
	Customer Svc	0.2%	10.9%	9.9%	0.9%	22.0%
	Total	21.3%	58.4%	18.2%	2.1%	100.0%

Figure 6.12. Cost analysis from a product life cycle business case. The cost model is presented once with cell and marginal totals (top), and then again with each value expressed as a percentage of the grand total. Analyzing costs this way can reveal spending patterns that are not apparent from the cash flow statement.

"Cost per" Metrics

A final class of financial metrics that is sometimes useful to decision makers and planners is the "cost per" metric, such as:

Cost per user	Cost per seat
Cost per transaction	Cost per message
Cost per order	Cost per customer
Cost per day	Cost per year
Cost per mile/kilometer	Cost per vehicle
and so on...	

> 🔲 "Cost per" metrics are averages. They can be misleading when total cost includes both fixed and variable components.

The list of possibilities could continue indefinitely. You can of course program these metrics to appear automatically in summary boxes on the cash flow statements or on separate spreadsheet pages. Costs figures will be drawn from the relevant line item totals on the cash flow statements, while units (users, transactions, orders, etc.) should be available as named cells on the pages for assumptions.

Using "cost per" metrics, however, calls for a few points of cautionary guidance, which you should pass along to recipients in the "Conclusions and Recommendations" section of the case report.

- "Cost per" metrics are *averages* (more precisely, each is the arithmetic mean of a set of values). If the annual telephone cost is $100,000, and if the company has 820 telephones, the "cost per telephone" is $100,000 / 820, or about $122 per phone per year. From the cost per phone figure itself, however, you cannot tell whether all phones have about the same cost, or whether 10% of the phones account for 90% of the costs.

- "Cost per" metrics can be misleading when the total cost includes both fixed and variable components. A fixed cost is constant no matter how many units are involved (or else it changes only in large increments with large changes in units). A variable cost changes with every unit added or removed. If the fixed component of the total is large, do not be misled by the illusion that increasing the units (transactions, users, etc.) increases the cost total by the "cost per" amount.

Graphs

Graphical images of cash flow results really add no new information to the results: the figures in cash flow statements and summary tables of financial metrics can be read precisely, whereas the recipient's eye usually gets only a rough numerical estimate from inspecting a graph.

Graphs add visual appeal to the report. They also provide easy-to-follow feedback on the effects of changing assumptions.

Nevertheless, graphs add visual appeal to the case report, and they convey a sense of the cash flow timing more readily than figures alone. Graphed results from different scenarios are easier to compare immediately than tabled numbers. And, if your graphs are part of the complete dynamic spreadsheet system, they provide easy-to-follow feedback on the effects of changing assumptions during sensitivity analysis (see the following section, "Sensitivity and Risk Analysis."

The three best candidates for graphing in the case report are: net cash flow, cumulative cash flow, and discounted cash flow. The examples in Figure 6.13 below were built within Excel on pages immediately following the cash flow statements that provided the data for graphing. From there, they can readily be taken of publication in the case report. Note that net cash flow figures for each period are more appropriately shown as bar graphs. Cumulative cash flow may be either a bar graph or line graph. The line graph is permissible with the cumulative chart, because plotted points can be thought of as part of a continuous function (cumulative payback as a function of time).

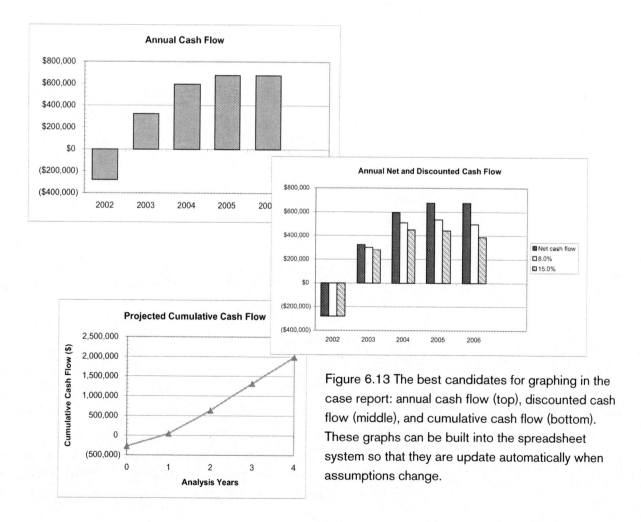

Figure 6.13 The best candidates for graphing in the case report: annual cash flow (top), discounted cash flow (middle), and cumulative cash flow (bottom). These graphs can be built into the spreadsheet system so that they are update automatically when assumptions change.

Sensitivity and Risk Analysis

Cash flow statements, financial metrics, and graphs are the visible results of the case. The visible results, however, are a structure standing on a foundation built of *assumptions*. Recipients will naturally want to know how firm that foundation is, and what happens to predicted results if some of the assumptions change.

The results may predict a net gain worth $10,425,310 over the next five years if a proposed program is launched. The net cash flow total and other financial metrics represent the author's projections of the most likely outcome. Everyone knows, however, that the real result will not be $10,425,310 *exactly*. It will almost certainly be something more or something less. But, will the real outcome be a lot more? A lot less? Or, just a little more or a little less? Authors must prepare to answer such questions because recipients need the answers in order to use the results with confidence. *Risk analysis* addresses questions like these.

▣ Recipients will naturally want to know what happens if assumptions change.

Recipients will also want to know which assumptions are most important in determining results: some assumptions may refer to factors that can be managed, so as to improve the overall results. Other important assumptions may involve factors that cannot be controlled but which can be watched closely throughout the analysis period: when these factors change, we can expect results to change. Which factors have to be managed carefully in order to achieve predicted results? Which factors have to be watched carefully? Sensitivity analysis provides answers to these questions.

In this section, we will exercise the dynamic financial model in order to ask sensitivity questions and risk questions. Before doing so, however, we will put the model through one last review and sanity check.

GIGO

Business case analysis, including the sensitivity and risk analysis we are about to undertake, are essentially *statistical* activities. Predicted results stand upon on a multitude of averages and assumptions about probabilities, for instance. Before starting the final rounds of analysis, therefore, it is important to remember the well-known truth about the statistics: "What comes out is no better than what goes in." The same idea is sometimes called the GIGO principle, for "Garbage in, garbage out."

In other words, case results are no better than the material they are made from. And, what are the results made from? Case results are built from assumptions and from the modeling system developed in the preceding section. Very shortly we will deal with the assumptions, one by one, but consider now one question about the dynamic financial model itself: Does the spreadsheet system behave realistically?

When programming the financial system, it is easy to let unrealistic behavior creep into the spreadsheet model. This is especially likely with respect to *relationships* among assumptions. Imagine, for instance, that some of the cost and benefit estimates depend on quantitative assumptions about;

- Market share %
- Market size in $
- Projected sales revenues in $

The spreadsheet author may have treated these items as independent assumptions, when it is clear they are not: Projected sales revenues certainly depend on market share and market size, at least partially. If the assumptions are treated as completely independent, then it is possible to increase market share and increase market size while reducing sales revenues—an impossibility in the real world (if market size is defined in dollars or other currency). In that case, the model should derive assumed sales revenues completely from the other two assumptions:

Sales revenues in $ = Market share % ∗ Market size in $

If market size is defined in terms of unit sales, however, another assumption can enter the picture: average unit price:

Sales revenues in $
= Market share ∗ Market size in unit sales ∗ Average unit price

Assumed sales revenues in either case depend on other assumptions, and that dependence should be reflected in spreadsheet behavior.

Other common assumptions would very likely be correlated to some degree in the real world, for instance:

- Annual inflation rate
- Annual salary increase rate

The two are not perfectly correlated, but they should probably not behave with complete independence in the model, either. Yes, it is possible with a company that is doing poorly to have inflation go up while salaries decrease, for example. But generally, we would expect inflation rate and salary increase rates to have some degree of positive correlation. The model's behavior will not reflect relationship between assumptions if they are treated as completely independent user

> It is easy to let unrealistic behavior creep into the model, especially with respect to relationships among assumptions.

entries. One way to build in the partial correlation is to derive salary increase rate from two other assumptions:

Salary increase rate = inflation rate + additional salary increment

In this way, salary increase rates would always be influenced by inflation rate, but still have room for independent changes.

The specific examples above may or may not be realistic in different situations—that is a matter for the author to judge, In any case, however, the author and case building team should examine the full set of assumptions built into the spreadsheet model, looking carefully for assumptions that are really derived from other assumptions, or correlated with other assumptions. The spreadsheet model should not allow assumption values to combine in ways that would be impossible or unlikely in the real world.

Simple Sensitivity Analysis

The dynamic model is a powerful tool for asking "What if?" questions. The model allows authors and recipients to ask directly: what happens to predicted results if this or that assumption changes? For that reason, it is helpful to build a summary section at the top of each cash flow statement that looks something like Figure 6.14 below. The analysis period dates and length are taken from the set up page, but all other information is derived directly from a cash flow statement directly beneath the box. Users can change assumptions elsewhere in the model, and then check the financial metrics here to see how results change.

Summary of Financial Results and Assumptions
The estimated net benefit (cost) over the evaluation period is as follows:

Net Cash Flow.. $	1,989,185	
8.0% discounting, Net Present Value........$	1,508,331	Discounting at
15.0% discounting, Net Present Value........$	1,252,529	year end
Simple ROI... $	374.4%	
Payback Period	1.3 Years	
Total Benefits / Productivity Gains.................$	2,457,185	
Total Costs... $	518,000	
Internal Rate of Return (IRR)..........................	152.6%	
Analysis Period..	15 Aug 02 ..to.. 14 Aug 06	
Analysis Period Length..	4 Years	

Figure 6.14 Summary box for the top of a cash flow statement. All information in the box except for analysis period information is derived automatically from cash flow results on the same worksheet. Users can change assumptions elsewhere in the model and then check here to see the result.

Figure 2.6. Simple sensitivity
analysis: Results are very
sensitive to assumptions A
and D, slightly sensitive to
assumption C, and completely
insensitive to assumption B.

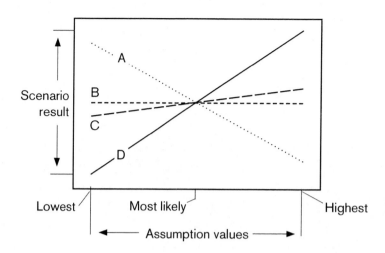

Simple sensitivity analysis
plays a valuable role, even
though the real world does not
behave like a simple sensitivity
test.

Simple sensitivity analysis is the process of checking the model's assumptions, one by one, to determine how each controls overall results (such as total net cash flow). The objective, in other words, is to assess the *sensitivity* of results to each assumption. Figure 6.15 above illustrates the principles involved: for each assumption, determine the lowest value that could reasonably occur and the highest value that could occur. The most likely value will be somewhere between these extremes. To examine the impact of one assumption, watch the effect on an important scenario result (for example, total net cash flow) as the assumption is changed from its lowest to its highest reasonable value. At the same time, keep all other assumptions at their most likely value. If you plot the scenario result as a function of assumption values, the graph will probably look like one of the curves in Figure 2.6. For the four assumptions tested, it is clear that scenario results are indeed sensitive to changes in assumptions A and D, because those curves have a steep slope. By the same criterion, results are only slightly sensitive to changes in assumption C and completely insensitive to assumption D.

Figure 6.16 (next page) shows what a real analysis might look like (the Figure first appeared on p. 40 as Figure 2.6). In this case, net cash flow results are much more sensitive to an assumption about business volume than to the assumption about the price of oil. Notice, by the way, that the business volume curve is not a straight line, but that sensitivity tends to decrease at the extreme ends of the curve. This means that the author programmed formulas to use the assumption with a certain degree of non-linear behavior. Business volume above a certain point might bring diminishing returns as the company's ability to meet demand is exceeded.

In fact, however, the real world does not behave like a simple sensitivity test. All assumptions are likely to change at the same time and, as we saw above under "GIGO," some assumptions are likely to be correlated with others. For these reasons, the simple approach has limited

Figure 2.6. Simple sensitivity analysis of two assumptions in a dynamic financial model.

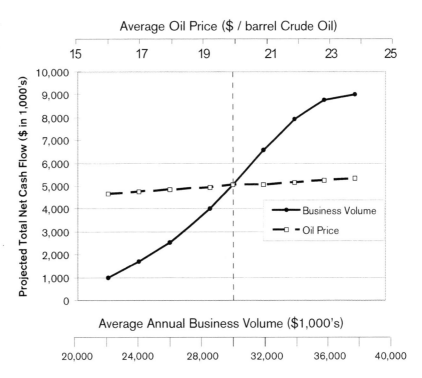

value in predicting real world outcomes for a scenario. Nevertheless, simple sensitivity analysis plays an important role in developing, communicating, and using the case. This kind of analysis:

- Helps identify the response of results to changes in assumptions
- Helps validate the behavior of the model
- Helps the author decide which assumptions should be included in more rigorous sensitivity and risk analysis, and which can be omitted.

Monte Carlo Simulation: The Future Played Out Thousands of Times

Business case results are predictions, and like all predictions, they come with uncertainties. "Uncertain" does not mean "unknown" or "indescribable," however. We can use probability analysis to measure the uncertainties that come with our results, and in so doing, we provide the basis for recipients to use the results with confidence.

Monte Carlo simulation with the dynamic model provides a more useful sensitivity analysis than the simple approach described above, and it also produces a risk analysis at the same time. The approach is called "Monte Carlo" because it uses the same probability concepts that operate on the gaming tables at the Grand Casino in Monaco.

Microsoft Excel and Lotus 1-2-3 cannot perform the simulation alone, however, without a substantial programming effort in the spreadsheet's macro language. Instead of trying to program the simulation yourself, I recommend using one of the several commercial Monte Carlo simulation products available as "add-ins" for Excel or 1-2-3. Two such products that work well for people who are not professional statisticians, and which are well suited for business case analysis as presented in this *Guide*, are Crystal Ball® from Decisioneering, Inc., and @RISK from Palisade Corporation.[1] This section illustrates the concept using Crystal Ball with Excel, but the approach is similar with any other good analysis package.

An Example for Simulation

The best way to show what Monte Carlo simulation does is to examine an example. Figure 6.17 below has the very simple summary box from the top of an incremental cash flow statement. The statement represents the difference between a full value proposal scenario and a full value business as usual scenario. Below the summary box there is a complete cash flow statement which is not shown in the figure. The "After Tax Net Cash Flow figure of $987,200" in the summary box at top is read from a "Grand Total" cell at the bottom of the cash flow statement below. You can be sure that case readers will notice immediately that the author projects a net gain worth $987,200 over the five year analysis period.

Figure 6.17 Summary box and table of assumptions for an incremental cash flow statement. The subject is of the case is a proposed marketing program.

Proposed Marketing Program: "Millenium Takeoff"
Summary of Financial Results and Assumptions
Incremental Analysis: Proposal Scenario - Business as Usual

The estimated net benefit (cost) over the evaluation period is as follows:
After Tax Net Cash Flow...................... **$987.2**   ($ in 1,000's)
Evaluation period............................. 1 Sep 2002 - 31 Aug 2007
Evaluation period length..................... 60 Months

Table of Assumptions

		Name
Annual inflation rate.............................	3.0%	INFL_RATE
Annual salary increase rate....................	5.0%	SAL_INC
Annual advertising price change: Internet	-20.0%	ADV_NET_CHG
Annual advertising price change: Print......	11.5%	ADV_PRNT_CHG
Annual market share growth rate.............	10.0%	MKT_SHARE_CHANGE
Annual market size growth rate..............	20.0%	MKT_SIZE_CHANGE
Average hiring cost per employee............	$23.2	AVG_HIRE_COST
Annual comm volume growth..................	15.0%	COMM_GROW

1. More information about Crystal Ball can be found on the Decisioneering web site at www.decisioneering.com. For more information about @RISK, see the Palisade Corporation web site at www.palisade.com.

No sooner do recipients read the "bottom line," then questions arise: What happens to predicted results if *market share* does not grow as assumed? What happens if *market size* grows faster than predicted? What happens of the assumed *price trends* for hardware do not appear? Management also says that the predicted $987,200 gain is attractive but they want to be very sure the program brings gains of *at least* $500,000. Otherwise, the required funds could be used to better purpose elsewhere. How does the author answer such questions? How confident is the author that the program will bring at least $500,000? Answers to such questions come from *assumptions*, especially from assumptions that we make about assumptions.

Notice the "Table of Assumptions" below the summary box in Figure 6.17. Most serious cases will have many more than eight assumptions as shown here, but to keep the example simple we will focus only on these.

Notice especially the names of assumptions listed to the right of each assumed value. Cost and benefit estimates in the spreadsheet use these names in formulas in order to produce the cash flow figures. For instance, there is a cost item called "Communications Costs." On the surface, the cash flow statement line item looks like this:

For the year ending... $ in 1,000s	Year 1 31-Aug 2003	Year 2 31-Aug 2004	Year 3 31-Aug 2005	Year 4 31-Aug 2006	Year 5 31-Aug 2007	TOTAL
Communications Costs	(348.0)	(412.2)	(496.7)	(588.3)	(716.5)	**(2,561.7)**

Beneath the surface, however, lie formulas. The Excel worksheet cell that holds Year 2 communication costs, (412.2), has this formula:

$$= 354 * (1+COMM\_GROW)^2 * (1+INFL\_RATE)^2 * (-1)$$

The spreadsheet author modeled the cost by taking the current year's communication costs, $354,000, and then applying two growth rate assumptions. (This is the second year of the analysis period, so the growth rates are applied twice by the ^2 exponents. The final factor, –1, turns the cost figure into a cash outflow). The author can use names like COMM_GROW and INFL_RATE in the formulas, because these names were assigned to cells in the table of assumptions that hold values for these assumptions.

In order to answer questions about changing assumptions and the likelihood of other results, we could change values in the Table of Assumptions ourselves (as in simple sensitivity analysis), but the better approach is to allow the Monte Carlo simulation program to change assumptions: the program will select new values for the 8 assumptions, plug them into the assumption table in place of the values we see there now, and then check to see what happens to the

Answers to risk and sensitivity questions come from the assumptions we make about assumptions.

overall result (net cash flow). It will repeat that process a few thousand times and then show us the relative frequency with which different results appear.

The key to making all of this information useful comes from the way that the simulation program selects new values for assumptions. In order to see what is going on, we will walk through a simulation, step by step, using an Excel-based dynamic model and the Crystal Ball add-in program.

Setting up the Simulation

▣ The heart of the process is thinking carefully about what we know or expect for each assumption.

Decision makers and planners might very well pay close attention to several financial metrics, such as total cost, payback period, net cash flow, and others. For this example, the simulation focuses only on net cash flow, but remember that we could in fact examine how a number of different metrics behave when assumptions change.

In order to tell the simulation program which cell holds the forecast that we want to watch, select the net cash flow cell in the summary box, and click on a Crystal Ball tool bar icon to "Define Forecast." The dialog box appears as shown in Figure 6.18. Giving the forecast a name and specifying units sets up labels for the graphs and tables that will come out of the analysis. Clicking OK marks the selected cell as the forecast.

Figure 6.18 Defining the forecast cell for the simulation.

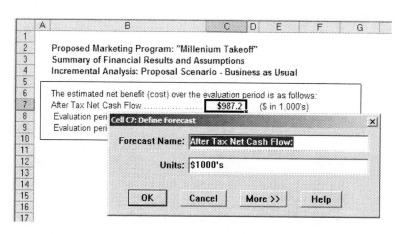

The heart of the set up process comes next, as we think carefully about what we know or expect for each assumption. In Figure 6.17, the first assumption is "Annual inflation rate," after which the value of 3.0% appears as our best estimate of the average rate to expect across the analysis period. The simulation program asks for more information, however, in order to fully define the assumption. In order to complete this process, we select the cell holding the first assumption value as shown in Figure 6.19, next page, and then click

Figure 6.19 Defining an assumption for the simulation program. This means, essentially, defining the range of possible values for the assumption and the likelihood (probability density function) that different values appear.

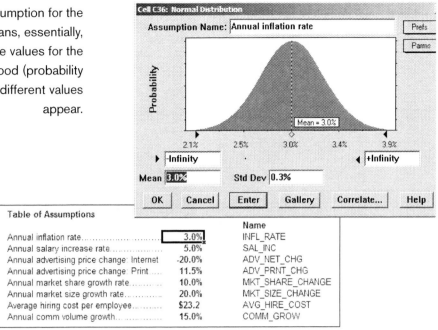

another tool bar icon to "define forecast." What we see removes any doubt—if there ever was any—that we are engaged in a *statistical* exercise.

The Crystal Ball dialog box in Figure 6.19, floating over the Table of Assumptions, asks for statistical properties of the selected assumption. The horizontal axis in the figure represents possible values of the assumption, and you can see that the tabled value (3.0%) is at the center of the display. Standing over the horizontal axis is a bell shaped curve. If you have an elementary statistics or probability course in your background, you should recognize this picture as a probability density function over a continuous random variable (in this case, inflation rate). The curve is put to practical use by assuming that the total area under the curve (the green area) equals 1.0 and the probably that the variable falls in any horizontal axis interval (say, 2.5% to 3.4%) is equal to the area under the curve, over that interval (about 0.837 in this case, or 83.7%).

If you are wondering now just how far into the statistical jungle we have to go in order to set up a simulation, the answer is "not far." However, it is necessary to have a very minimal familiarity with basic concepts in statistics and probability. If the paragraph above this one makes no sense to you at all, then you should expect to spend a little extra time reading the Crystal Ball or @RISK user manual (the manuals do not assume any statistical background).

In brief, defining an assumption means specifying a probability density function for the assumption:

▣ A very minimal familiarity with basic concepts in statistics and probability is unavoidably necessary for setting up the Monte Carlo simulation.

- Choosing the appropriate shape probability curve (this author chose a symmetric normal distribution).

- Specifying the curve's parameters (once a curve is identified as a symmetric normal curve, it is completely specified by two parameters, a mean and a standard deviation). The mean locates the center of the curve and the standard deviation determines the "spread."

The set up for simulation is completed when each assumption has been defined in those terms. Suffice it to say there are some subtleties involved that are not covered here: your assumptions will represent different kinds of variables and choosing the appropriate curve for each assumption requires a little knowledge of which kinds of processes are best described by normal, binomial, Poisson, exponential, and other kinds of probability functions. This book's purpose, however, is to illustrate the simulation concept in principle, not teach the process, so we will leave the set up at this point and get on with the simulation.

Running the simulation

The simulation program essentially "runs" the future a few thousand times and then displays the likelihood of different outcomes (projected net cash flow, in this case). For each run, or trial, it uses the probability rules we gave it to select a new value for each assumption. When it selects a new value for inflation rate, for instance, the value will almost certainly be somewhere between 2.1% and 3.9% (plus or minus three standard deviations from the normal curve mean of 3.0%). Values closer to the mean are more likely than values further from the mean. Selecting and plugging in new values for all defined assumptions completes the trial, and program records the value of the forecast that we told it to watch.

Figure 6.20 (next page) shows how 10,000 such trials are summarized. The horizontal axis represents values for the net cash flow figure that appeared on various trials. The vertical axis is scaled both as frequency (right) and probability (left), showing how often or how likely different outcomes appear in the simulation trials. Remember that the original analysis predicted a net cash inflow of $987,200 over five years. You can see that a very few trials produced results over $4,000,000, and a few trials actual produced a net *outflow* result. The majority of trials, however, are grouped in the 600,000–1,000,000 range. Based on the behavior of the author's spreadsheet model, and based on the assumptions about assumptions that set up the simulation program, it looks like a wide range of results are certainly possible.

▣ The simulation essentially "runs" the future a few thousand times, and then displays the likelihood of different outcomes.

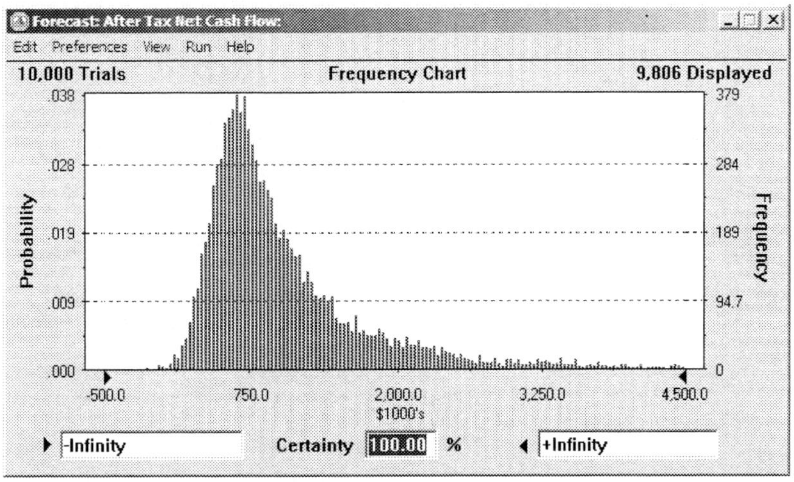

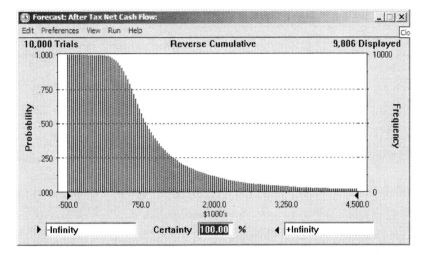

Figure 6.20 The relative frequency of different outcomes from the Monte Carlo simulation (from Crystal Ball). The range of net cash flow values extends far above and below the initial predicted value of $987.2 thousand.

Figure 6.21 The relative frequency results of Figure 6.20, plotted as a reverse cumulative curve (from Crystal Ball). The curve in this form shows the probability of obtaining results as high as a given value or higher.

What can we say about management's need to gain at least $500,000 from the program? We can use these results to speak to that issue by replotting the data from Figure 6.20 as the reverse cumulative probability curve shown in Figure 6.21. Do not let the curve's name frighten you: *reverse cumulative* means one minus the probability of getting a result higher than a given value on the horizontal axis. That means that the curve shows the probability of getting *at least* to any point on the horizontal axis. Although it may not be easy to calibrate the graph image very precisely here, the $500,000 point (to the left of the 750.0 figure) has a probability coordinate of about 0.87. That means there is an 87% chance of realizing at least $500,000 gain from the program.

This kind of risk information is far more useful than a simple prediction that $987,200 is our best estimate for coming results.

Sensitivity Analysis from the Simulation

While the Crystal Ball Monte Carlo program was plugging in different assumptions and counting net cash flow outcomes it was also measuring something else in the background: the correlation between changes in each assumption and changes in the forecast results. In other words, the program was performing a statistically respectable sensitivity analysis. The sensitivity of results to changes in assumptions was measured while all other assumptions were changing, simu-

Figure 6.22 Sensitivity analysis performed during the Monte Carlo simulation. The figures and the bars show the measured correlation between each assumption and the net cash flow results.

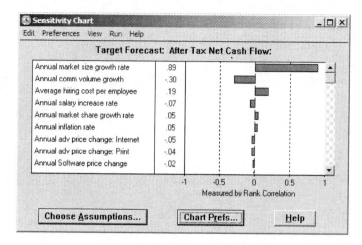

lating combinations of assumptions that could be expected in the real world. Crystal Ball summarized its sensitivity analysis with the bar chart shown in Figure 6.22, above.

The table in Figure 6.22 has the same list of assumptions as Figure 6.17. The table above, however, was assembled by the simulation program, not by the spreadsheet author. It lists the assumptions in decreasing order of importance, that is, in terms of controlling the forecast results. The figures are correlation coefficients. If you have had an elementary statistics course, you should remember that a correlation coefficient is the measure of association, or co-relation between two variables. Annual market size growth rate, for instance stands at the top of the list with a rank order correlation coefficient of 0.89. This means that increases in the assumed market size are followed very closely by increases in predicted net cash flow.

The next highest correlation is for the assumption about communications volume growth. The negative value of this correlation coefficient (–0.30) means that as the growth rate in communications volume increases, the forecasted cash flow tends to decrease.

This kind of information about the relative importance of assumptions will be crucial to the recommendations and conclusions we will shortly write into the case report.

Comparing Financial and Non Financial Benefits

We are almost ready to begin packaging the case for publication and presentation, but there is still an important loose end to be tied up at this point: What do we do with important benefits that could not be measured in financial terms? Do we have to walk away from them, leaving them out of report and presentation? Or do we simply mention them and hope that recipients give them fair consideration in making decisions and planning? Is there a credible way to compare the non financial benefits with financial benefits?

This section presents one approach for making the comparison. The result can provide a basis for making a strong statement about important non financial benefits: "These benefits are real and they are as important as some of the financial benefits in this case!" To illustrate how this works, consider again an example that we first saw from 3,000 feet in Chapter 2. Now, at ground level, we are ready to step through the process. The walk begins where most work having to do with benefits begins–with business objectives.

As you may recall, an IT director for a commercial bank had proposed upgrades to local area networks in the branch offices, along with software enhancements designed to provide loan officers and sales people with better access to customer data, economic data, and the bank's own decision-support software. The immediate business objectives for the proposed action were to:

- Improve the quality of decision making (reduce losses from bad loan decisions).
- Reduce loan-processing time from an average ten days to three days.
- Improve the sales team's performance selling the more profitable financial services.

These were indeed the immediate operational and sales performance goals. However, in order to fully understand the benefits as well as the costs from the proposal, we had to bring the full range of important strategic objectives into view. This bank operates in an intensely competitive industry, in which it is clear that banks that do not thrive and grow will either fail or be absorbed by their more successful rivals. It was not surprising that this bank's *strategic* objectives were constantly on the minds of senior management.

- Increase market share from 23% TO 40%
- Become the bank of choice for the largest and most prestigious commercial customers
- Increase the share price of the bank's stock
- Increase after-tax profits from the current 8% to 15%
- Attract and retain talented employees

You may also remember that the Director's business case proposal actually found five benefits to expect under the primary proposal scenario:

- **Increased revenues.** ($ quantified)
  From increased sales productivity and more success selling the bank's higher-priced services.
- **Increased customer satisfaction.** (Non financial)
  From decreased loan processing time and better support of customer service staff.
- **An enhanced corporate image.** (Non financial)
  By promoting the improved customer service, and by "repackaging" the bank's product line.
- **A more professional work environment.** (Non financial)
  By enabling professionals to give more attention to the creative aspects of their jobs.
- **Cost savings.** ($ quantified)
  By reducing a range of information-gathering communications costs, by avoided hiring of new staff, and by reducing losses from bad loans.

I mentioned also in Chapter 2 that we only managed to assign financial value to two of the benefits, increased revenues and cost savings. That left three very important benefits that had no visibility at all in the financial analysis.

Figure 6.23 below is the core team consensus of the relative importance of the *five* benefits (this graph appeared earlier as Figure 2.9). "Importance, relative to what?" you may ask. The scale at the bottom represents the consensus view of the importance of these benefits to the full set of strategic business objectives. Surprisingly the two top ratings went to non financial benefits, namely increased customer satisfaction and enhanced corporate image. With the results shown in the figure, the IT director could say to management: "I do not know the exact financial value of the customer satisfaction or corporate image benefits from the proposal, but I am confident that they are more important to us than the increased revenues or cost savings which we *have* measured in financial terms."

To understand the exercise that produced this comparison, remember a few basic characteristics of business benefits:

Consensus: Importance of Benefit

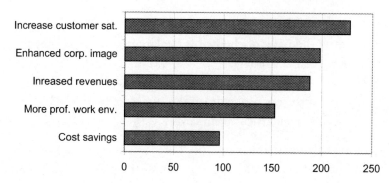

Figure 6.23 Comparison of all benefits in the case, using the score and weight method explained in the text. According to this group's consensus view, increased customer satisfaction is more important than increased revenues or cost savings.

- Benefits are business impacts that contribute to meeting business objectives.
- The benefit and the objective are not necessarily the same thing:
- One benefit can contribute to several business objectives.
- One objective can be supported by several benefits.

The kind of relationship between the business benefits and business objectives was suggested earlier in Figure 4.8, repeated here as Figure 6.24.

Figure 6.24 The relationship between benefits and business objectives is not always one-to-one.

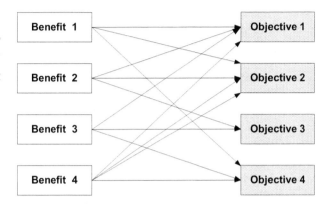

In order to compare all benefits in the case, we will put the above relationship into a framework more suitable for analysis. Figure 6.25, is the worksheet for this exercise. The process we will use is called "score and weight."

The benefit comparison has the most value and the most credibility when it is completed as group exercise with either the case building project team, the core team, or both. One person working alone can of course complete the mechanics of the exercise, but the real contributions to understanding benefits come from discussions between participants as they work through to a consensus viewpoint. Ideally, the case author or a skilled outside facilitator leads participants through the exercise.

Business Objective	Weight	Benefit 1 Incr. Revenues		Benefit 2 Enhanced Image		Benefit 3 Incr. Cust. Sat		Benefit 4 Cost Savings		Benefit 5 Prof. Environment	
		Score	Wt*score	Score	Wt*score	Score	Wt*score	Score	Wt*score	Score	Wt*score
Increase market share											
Become bank of choice											
Increase share price											
Increased profits											
Talented employees											
		Total		Total		Total		Total		Total	

Figure 6.25 Blank worksheet for the score and weight exercise to compare benefits.

Every participant receives a copy of the blank worksheet shown in Figure 6.25. The case's five business benefits are written in columns of the grid, and the five strategic business objectives are listed in the rows.

The consensus building exercise begins in fact with some individual work. Steps 1–4 are completed individually, that is, with no discussion among participants. The facilitator directs them to do the following:

1. Select the one business objective the individual considers the most important for the company. Assign that objective the weight 10 (write it in the "weight" column).

2. Select the business objective that the individual considers the least important for the company. Assign that objective a weight of 1.

3. Assign weights to the remaining 3 objectives, using the scale 1–10, in terms of their importance relative to the least and most important objectives already identified. Individuals may assign more than one 1, or more than one 10. The only requirement is that there be at least one 1 and one 10.

4. Score each benefit rating its contribution to each business objective. This time use the scale 0–10 where:
   0 = No contribution to the business objective
   10 = Very major contribution to the business objective

In steps 1 through 4, participants work individually to produce five weights for the business objectives, and 25 scores, rating the contribution of each benefit to each objective (it is important to rate the benefit contribution to the objective, not the reverse). The reason for insisting that participants finish these steps *individually* is to ensure that everyone starts with their own subjective judgements, not influenced by other participants. They are not to fill in the "score * weight" column yet.

The assignment for step 5 is to reach a group consensus on the weights for each objective, and then a consensus on the scores. The number of objectives and benefits in this example would typically require at least two hours for debate and discussion. Once the group does have consensus, the "score * weight" products can be filled in. The relative importance of each benefit is taken as the sum of its "score * weight" values. Figure 6.26 (next page) shows how the table might look after consensus is reached. The five totals at bottom are the horizontal axis points on the bar graph of Figure 6.23.

The score and weight exercise has value for participants, even if a results graph like Figure 6.23 does not make it into the final case

Business Objective	Weight	Benefit 1 Incr. Revenues		Benefit 2 Enhanced Image		Benefit 3 Incr. Cust. Sat		Benefit 4 Cost Savings		Benefit 5 Prof. Environment	
		Score	Wt*score	Score	Wt*score	Score	Wt*score	Score	Wt*score	Score	Wt*score
Increase market share	10	6	60	7	70	8	80	1	10	5	50
Become bank of choice	8	4	32	8	64	9	72	3	24	7	56
Increase share price	1	8	8	6	6	4	4	8	8	3	3
Increased profits	6	10	60	5	30	8	48	9	54	2	12
Talented employees	4	7	28	7	28	6	24	0	0	8	32
		Total	188	Total	198	Total	228	Total	96	Total	153

Figure 6.26 Score and weight worksheet for comparing benefits after group consensus is reached. The five totals at bottom are the horizontal axis data points for the bar graph in Figure 6.24.

report. By having to think carefully about the importance of business objectives, and then the connection between benefits and objectives, participants are much better prepared to explain or defend the case and its conclusions in a critical review. The full value of the score and weight exercise comes, moreover, in the consensus building process, where different views are aired and debated.

Conclusions and Recommendations

The Conclusions and Recommendation Section of the your business case report will probably be the second most frequently read part of the document (after the Executive Summary). There may be some recipients in fact who skip everything in between. If the business case is to be effective, this section has to be effective. Here are some guidelines for achieving that goal.

- Organize the conclusions and recommendations section around business objectives, not as a serial walk through of all the financial results. The objectives in view should be the same objectives that were highlighted in the introductory section.

- Try to take the recipient's viewpoint. Ask: what do recipients need to know in order for the case to achieve its purpose?

- Use the results of sensitivity and risk analysis to support recommendations for maximizing results or minimizing problems during the analysis period. As suggested in Chapter 2, the sensitivity analysis results should allow you to divide assumptions into two groups: those that are important (play a significant role in controlling results) and those that are not. Further divide the important assumptions into two groups:

  ○ Assumptions that can be controlled or managed, at least to some extent (For example, assuming that salary increases will not exceed a certain level, or that employees will ramp up to 100% on new skills by a certain date). Recommendations on these items are called *contingencies*: things that must be managed if expected results are to arrive.

○ Assumptions that cannot be controlled or managed, but which can still have important impact on predicted results (such as assumed market size, competitor's actions, or currency exchange rates). The recommendation here is to monitor these factors closely. These assumptions are *risks* that need to be anticipated.

• Highlight any unexpected or surprising results that might be important to recipients.

• Finally, discuss any results that could be misinterpreted

Building on Experience

We have now crossed the business case landscape three times: at 39,000 feet (Chapter 1), at 3,000 feet (Chapter 2), and at ground level (Chapters 3 through 6). To bring this trek to a close, to help explain why experiential learning is so important, we finish by visiting once more a theme that runs throughout the *Guide*—success and failure. Improving the success rate with business case practices requires a good understanding of why cases fail.

Business cases can fail in two ways. Either they meet with skepticism or a cold shoulder from management and fail to achieve the immediate objective—obtaining funding, for instance. Or, they fail when the proposal or plan is implemented and the real costs and benefits turn out to be very different from the business case estimates. From my experience, I believe that both kinds of failure usually have the same root cause.

The cause of failure might be called "lack of history." Many organizations do not save and use the experience of previous business case exercises to improve current efforts. Every case builder has to re-invent the methodology, the structure, and the format of the case. Every recipient has to work to get oriented to the author's unique approach. The problem, as you know by now, is that cases in complex settings require arbitrary and subjective judgments (when evaluating costs, or valuing benefits, for instance); they may require new data and information that do not exist in current budgets, business plans, or financial statements; they will very likely need cost and benefit models tailored to fit the action or acquisition under consideration (to determine what belongs in the analysis and what does not). These requirements can be very hard to meet adequately on a "first pass" business case, even if the best methods and expertise are used without reference to earlier cases.

The author's ability to build and recipients' ability to understand improve when the business case approach is validated and fine-tuned over and over again, through cycles of business case analysis and implementation. The data and results will change from case to case, but the methodology, rationale, structure, and presentation format should be consistent, and should be continually improved.

I believe This is the single most effective way to improve business case accuracy. It is also the single most effective way to counter skepticism and improve credibility. A business case may be challenged on many different fronts, but primarily the following two:

- In terms of *methodology*
  Critics may say ...

  "The choice of cost/benefit items was biased."
  "The scope of coverage was inadequate"
  "Too much credit was given to 'soft' benefits."
  "The data are incorrect, out of date, or incomplete."
  "IRR is a misleading metric for this kind of scenario"

- In terms of *analysis*
  Critics may say ...

  "The benefit stream needs a longer 'ramp up' or 'learning curve."
  "Not enough weight was given to risk factors"
  "The projected gains are too optimistic"

Clearly, the business case sponsor has an uphill battle if both the methodology and the analysis have to be explained, sold, and defended at the same time. Methodology, at least, should not be an issue if it has been established, explained, improved, and accepted through previous business case exercises.

The next business case you build will probably not be your best one. The case you build after the next one should be better. And the one after that, still better. Individuals and organizations alike need to learn how to apply the methods presented here in their own environment. Your skill in estimating costs and benefits will improve as you validate previous cases, discard methods that do not work for you, and refine those that do. In brief, your ability to build successful cases will improve if you manage to learn from experience.

What's the Difference?

Planning vs. Decision Support

What is the difference between a case built for decision support and a case built to support business planning? The methods, structure, and case building process presented in this *Guide* apply to both kinds of cases. Nevertheless, there are some fundamental differences between them that impact every section of the case report.

Decision Support Case	Planning Case
Almost always includes two or more scenarios.	May include many scenarios or only one scenario.
May omit items that are the same in all scenarios.	Will include all cost and benefit items, even if they are the same in all scenarios.
Attempts to create "apples to apples" comparisons between scenarios.	Attempts to predict actual financial results accurately
May not build in long term trends for such things as price changes and inflation.	Will attempt to anticipate trends, so as to predict accurately
May include benefits whose value is arbitrarily assigned cash flow value.	Will include benefits only if they are expected to result in real cash inflow

In Summary

The chapter focuses on methods for bringing out all the useful information available in business case results, and for developing practical guidance for decision makers and planners.

- The spreadsheet model is a key tool in making business case analysis approachable and for making results useful to recipients.

- The spreadsheet model is structured to support either a full value analysis or an incremental data analysis.

- Cost and benefit values in the dynamic model are derived from three kinds of assumptions: global assumptions, which apply to all scenarios, scenario assumptions, and item-specific assumptions.

- The spreadsheet model makes possible sensitivity and risk analysis. It also helps establish the credibility of the case, provides authors and recipients with an easy means for asking "What if?" questions, and can serve as a template or example for other business case authors.

- Each cost and benefit item can be a small modeling system in its own right. The cash flow statement is not the best place to model individual cash flow estimates. Separate worksheet pages for cost and benefit line item estimates are the recommended solution.

- The financial model should be implemented so that users enter data only on set up pages, line item worksheet pages, and pages for assumptions. Cash flow statements, graphs, and other results should be developed automatically as users enter data on assumptions pages.

- The most fundamental financial metric in the case is net cash flow. This tells recipients the total expected value of results over the analysis period.

- Cumulative cash flow figures show the net result through the end of each period time segment of the analysis period.

- Discounted cash flow (and net present value) adjusts the value of expected cash flow to reflect the time value of money. Inflows or outflows expected in the distant future have a lower present value than expected near-term financial events.

- Payback period is a financial metric that measures the amount of time required for an investment to cover its own costs.

- Cost analysis in the cost model framework can reveal spending patterns and potential problem areas that are not apparent from the cash flow statement.

- Sensitivity analysis shows which assumptions have a strong influence on results. Risk analysis shows the likelihood of other results, besides the central predicted result.

- The cost model helps case builders identify every relevant cost item, assure recipients that every relevant item is included, and that different scenarios are comparable. The model also serves as a cost analysis tool in its own right.

- Monte Carlo simulation uses the dynamic financial model and the author's assumptions about the important assumptions to perform sensitivity and risk analysis.

- Non financial benefits can gain legitimacy and carry weight in decision making if the author compares them directly to financial benefits.

Appendix A
Sample Business Case

Business Case Analysis
Proposed Design Software Acquisition

Contents

About this Case

This case is meant only to illustrate the structure and content of a complete business case analysis, appropriate for supporting a decision to acquire a complex hardware and software solution.

This example case is based on a real system acquisition decision undertaken by an aerospace company in 2001. However, names of people, products, and companies used in this case are fictional. Prices, resource requirements, assumptions, and business case results are adjusted so as to preserve anonymity, and are not meant to represent the actual situation for any real company or organization. The business results for any company or organization will vary and must be developed on an individual basis, using information current and applicable to the specific situation.

Business Case Analysis: Proposed Design Software Acquisition

To: Kurt Andersen, Chairman, Aerofirma Capital Review Committee
From: Robert Arndt, Aerofirma Business Case Analysis Team
        Robert Ritter, Avanti Corporation
Date: 24 July 2003

Executive Summary

This business case estimates expected benefits and costs to Aerofirma that would result from a decision to equip members of the design engineering staff (40 engineers) with DesignMax, as proposed by Avanti Corporation on 15 June 2003. Aerofirma is considering the move to DesignMax as a step towards reducing costs significantly in several areas, improving responsiveness to customers and to changing design requirements, and to shortening product development times.

Based on the known costs in Design Engineering under the current design systems, and based on the experience of other Aerospace companies in moving to DesignMax, we project a net gain of $3.87 million over three years (after covering total costs of $0.98 million). This represents an expected three-year ROI (return on investment) of more than 395%, and a payback period of about 0.5 years. The figure below summarizes the annual cumulative cash flow result.

These expected results depend on several assumptions, including the need to train engineers, and necessary changes to workflow and process be executed smoothly, without disruption to current customer projects, and that the benefits to our customers are communicated effectively by Sales, Marketing, and Services personnel. Based on the very favorable financial projections outlined in this case, we recommend that the Aerofirma Capital Review Committee accept the Avanti DesignMax proposal, and take steps to begin implementation immediately.

Aerofirma Aircraft Assemblies, Inc.
Proposed DesignMax Implementation for Design Engineering
Currency: $

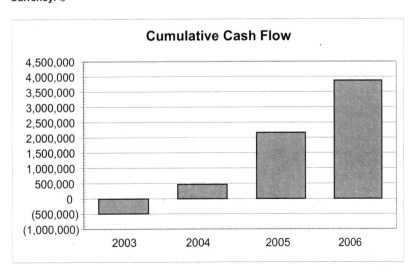

A. Introduction

A.1. Background

Aerofirma Aircraft Assemblies, AG, is a leading supplier of aircraft sub assemblies to major aircraft manufacturers in six European countries. Last year the company earned $15.5 million, after taxes, on sales revenues of $148.0 million.

Increasing competition and rising costs have resulted in "flat" earnings over the last three years, even though sales revenues grew at an average of 3% per year over that period. Market growth averaged 7% per year during that time. Cash flow is still adequate to allow for modest investments in new resources, but management has given high priority to several planned actions designed to improve the company's financial performance, improve competitiveness and market share, and ensure long term viability and growth of the company.

Aerofirma's strategy for improving earnings, winning new business, and regaining market share, addresses three kinds of business objectives:

- Reducing costs in several targeted areas within product design and manufacturing
- Meeting the more complex needs of aerospace industry customers (more customized designs, faster response to change requests, etc.)
- Reducing product development lead time (time to market)

Engineering management believes that all of these objectives can be addressed by enhancing the productivity and capabilities of the Product Design Engineering Department. Key to this enhancement, we believe, is a move to 3D design capabilities, the use of virtual prototype building and testing, significant improvements to the product data management system, and better communication and collaboration between engineering, manufacturing, and sub-contractors. For this reason, on 15 June 2003, Design Engineering invited the Avanti Corporation to submit a proposal for equipping Aerofirma with the DesignMax system.

During the first two weeks of July, Avanti met for discussions with members of the Aerofirma Business Case Analysis team, Design Engineering Staff, and key individuals in Manufacturing Engineering, Quality Management, Marketing, and Customer relations, in order to better understand Aerofirma needs and objectives. On 15 July, Avanti delivered a proposal for a 40-seat implementation of DesignMax. The proposal assumed a start date for implementation within two months of proposal acceptance, and realization of full capabilities no more than six months later.

A.2. Subject of the Case

This business case examines the likely benefits and costs to Aerofirma Aircraft Assemblies, resulting from a decision to implement the Avanti DesignMax proposal of 15 June 2003. The main elements of the proposal call for 40 single-user licenses of the DesignMax module, database licenses, training for the Design engineers involved, and installation and integration services. Additionally, implementing the proposal will call for additional hardware resources purchased during the second and third years of implementation.

The benefits and costs that follow from a decision to implement the DesignMax proposal will very likely continue at least five years into the future. In view of the company's very pressing financial situation, however, this case limits the period of analysis to three years, beginning with an assumed implementation start in mid-September 2003.

The value of DesignMax benefits derives directly from expected contributions to the business objectives identified above, namely, reducing costs in several specific areas, better meeting the complex needs of our customers, and reducing product lead times. Expected increases in design engineer productivity will also contribute to the overall benefits projections.

A.3. Purpose of the Case

This case is designed to provide members of the Capital Review Committee with the necessary financial projections, financial metrics, and assessment of contingencies and risks, to support a decision either to accept or not accept the Avanti DesignMax proposal. This decision will be made at the Capital Review Committee meeting to be held 7 August 2003.

B. Methods and Assumptions

B.1. Scenarios and Data

The value of expected DesignMax benefits and costs was developed from a comparison of two scenarios: A "DesignMax implementation" scenario, and a "business as usual scenario." The DesignMax implementation scenario estimates operational performance and other factors, assuming that Design Engineering implements DesignMax as proposed, while the business as usual scenario estimates the same factors over the analysis period assuming the proposal is not implemented, and that current systems and practices remain in place.

Benefit and cost values for the cash flow summary represent the *incremental impact* of the DesignMax proposal, that is, the differences between results in the two scenarios.

B.2. Scope of the Case

Time

The business case analysis covers a three-year period, beginning with 15 September 2003, and extending through 14 September 2006. It is assumed that Aerofirma will begin DesignMax implementation in mid-September 2003, that the firm will begin to incur costs at that time, and that the "ramp up" to full utilization of the new software would also begin at that time.

Organizations

The case includes expected improvements in business performance for Aerofirma AG, including increased profits and increased market share. Cost impacts (Cost increases and cost savings) for this analysis cover the following organizations: Design Engineering, Manufacturing, IT, and Human Resources (primarily training expenses).

Technologies

Benefit and cost estimates are restricted to impacts resulting from or directly supporting the DesignMax system, the design engineering data base system, and electronic communications in support of those systems. Other computing costs and benefits within the company are assumed to be equal under either scenario, and therefore not relevant to this case.

B.3. Financial Metrics

Cash flow estimates in euro ($) for individual benefit items are developed for each of the three years in the analysis period (Years 1 to 3). A "Year-0" is also included at the start of the analysis period to capture the initial expenditures for software and a few other items that will occur immediately, in September 2003. Expected cash flow results are summarized on a standard format cash flow statement. Cash flow estimates form the basis, moreover, for several financial metrics:

Net cash flow

The combined result of all estimated inflows and outflows. Net cash flow is presented in $ for the three year period. Cumulative net cash flow for each year of the analysis period is also presented in the cash flow summary.

Net Present Value (NPV)

The value of cash flows discounted at a rate of 8.0 % p.a., and a second NPV reflecting discounting at a rate of 15.0% p.a. NPV is presented in $ for the three year period.

Simple ROI

The "Return on Investment," taken as projected incremental gains from this investment (net of investment costs), divided by investment costs. ROI is presented as a percentage, in which all values over 0% represent a net gain from the investment.

Payback Period

The number of years required for the initial investment costs to be recovered from the gains.

Internal Rate of Return (IRR)

The interest rate that yields an NPV of 0 for this investment. IRR is given as a percentage.

B.4. Benefits

Important benefits under DesignMax identified and analyzed for this case included the following items.

Decreased lead time

This means that the company can design new products and bring them to market in less time than is currently required. The impact is measured as a reduction in time (average time required under the current system, less the expected time required under DesignMax).

A more fluid design environment

This means that designers respond more quickly and more easily to changing needs. Changes are thus made at an earlier stage of the design process (e.g., in concept design instead of the detailed design phase), lower change costs.

Improved change propagation

This impact is a benefit when design dependencies are understood and managed more efficiently. Automated "Publish and Subscribe" under DesignMax ensures that change effects propagate correctly. Also, MML (Multi-Model Links) ensure that models, meshes, and drawings are consistent.

Better clash management

Improvements in clash management mean that design clashes are understood, managed, captured, and communicated more effectively. The prototype works on the first build.

Ability to design in context

This means that designers always work with the correct configuration (using the right data at the right time). Under DesignMax, the design can be viewed in the context of functional zone. Maturity management will also improve under DesignMax.

Improved collaborative design

Easier (faster, more accurate, more efficient) collaboration between designers and groups within the company should result when DesignMax is fully operational.

Increased Productivity

In addition to the above benefits, the case estimates increases in overall designer productivity (measured in time to complete design assignments, number of designers required to complete design assignments of a given complexity, and scope of work undertaken by individual designers). The value of this impact derives either from reduced need to hire new design staff, or from increased output per designer, or both.

B.5. Costs

Cost impacts for this business case included asset and expense items in the areas summarized by the business case cost model:

Cost impacts under both scenarios		DesignMax Life-Cycle Phase	
		DesignMax Acquisition and Start Up Year 0 and Year 1	**DesignMax Operational Phase Year 2 and Year 3**
Resources	Software	• One-time license - Design SW • One-time license - Database SW • One-time license – Admin SW • SW Maintenance costs	• SW Maintenance costs
	Hardware	• Server system upgrades • Client system (desktop) purchase	• Server system upgrades • Client system (desktop) purchase
	Personnel	• Initial training • Designer productivity	• Continuing training • Designer productivity
	Services	• SW installation and integration services	• SW integration services

B.6. Major Assumptions

The DesignMax scenario underlying this case analysis assumes that:

- DesignMax implementation will begin in mid-September 2003.

- All 40 members of the Design Engineering Department will receive DesignMax licenses and training during the period September – December 2003.

- Design engineers will reach their maximum proficiency with DesignMax no later than September 2004, a 12-month "ramp up," and that realization of most benefits to their maximum level will follow the same ramp up profile.

- Any turnover (departure and replacement) of design engineering staff during the analysis period would be equal under both the DesignMax scenario and the Business as Usual scenario.

- No additional hiring or expansion of the engineering staff is anticipated during the analysis period.

- Design engineer salaries and overhead costs average $54 per hour now, and will increase at a rate of 4% over the next 3 years.

- There are 212 work days per year.

C. Business Impacts

C. 1. Overall Results

The expected cash flow results from the DesignMax implementation (compared to business as usual) are summarized in Table 1 (page A-12) and Figures 1 and 2 (pages A-13 and A-14).

In brief, the analysis predicts a positive net cash flow of more than $3.87 million over the three year analysis period. This return is projected based on a total expected cost of $ 0.98 million over the same period, making a simple ROI (return on investment) of 395.2% (see the summary box at the top of Table 1).

Other financial metrics are also very positive: Payback period for the DesignMax investment is projected as 0.5 years, and internal rate of return (IRR) at 211.7%. Following is a brief discussion on the major benefit and cost items contributing to these results.

C. 2. Benefits

The largest projected benefit from the DesignMax implementation comes from gains in **improved collaborative design**. The total benefit of $2,125,000 is based on the assumption that the costs of achieving collaborative design (now totaling $6.8 million per year, in aggregate) can be reduced by 25% under the DesignMax implementation, and that DesignMax itself should receive 50% of the benefit value for this reduction (the other 50% "credit" appropriately goes to changes in design process, workflow patterns, and management). This results in an annual DesignMax benefit of $850,000 once the full benefit impact level is achieved (year 2 in the present case).

The second largest benefit in table 1 appears under "**Personnel staffing cost productivity gains**" (in Costs and Cost Savings). The projected cost savings of $1,146,252 is based on the assumption that 40 designers will become at least 10% more productive under DesignMax (this assumption is a very conservative estimate, based on experience in similar design organizations at other companies during the last year). The productivity gain is expected through more efficient variation management, more efficient building and testing of prototypes (virtual prototypes instead of physical prototypes in many cases), and more effective task management throughout all phases of design. The benefit value represents 10% of 40 designer salaries across the next 3 years (assuming 4.0% per annum pay increases).

Improved ability to **design in context** leads to a projected three-year benefit of $793,728. This is based on evidence that shows that DesignMax can change the creation of an analysis environment for digital mock up units (DMUs) from a 45-minute task to a 10-minute task. This is a 78% improvement in a task that now consumes $47,040 worth of engineering labor per year. We assume that these savings will be translated directly into increased productivity and reduced need for additional hiring.

The nearly continuous need to implement design changes is a costly process for Aerofirma, targeted for cost reductions under DesignMax. The goal is to identify necessary changes as early as possible, in the concept design phase, where the average cost per change is $ 200, rather than the detailed design phase ($ 1,200 per change), the testing-prototype phase ($9,600 per change), or, in the worst case, after start of production (where change costs average $24,000 per change at Aerofirma). Based on an estimated 500 design changes per year, the more fluid design environment under DesignMax is expected to produce a redistribution of change events, as summarized in Table 2 below (page A-15):

Aerofirma Aircraft Assemblies, Inc
Proposed DesignMax Implementation for Design Engineering

Summary of Financial Results and Assumptions
Incremental cash inflows (outlflows) with DesignMax

The estimated net benefit (cost) over the evaluation period is as follows:

Net Cash Flow	$	3,872,473	
8.0% discounting, Net Present Value	$	3,206,316	
15.0% discounting, Net Present Value	$	2,747,076	
Simple ROI*	$	395.2%	
Payback Period		0.5 Years	
Internal Rate of Return		211.7%	
Total Benefits / Gains	$	4,852,466	
Total DesignMax Costs	$	979,992	
Analysis Period		14 Sep 003	to 14 Sep 06
Analsis Period Length		3 Years	

* Simple ROI = (Net Cash flow - DesignMax costs)/ DesignMax costs

CASH FLOW STATEMENT

	Year 0 Sep 2003	Year 1 Sep 2004	Year 2 Sep 2005	Year 3 Sep 2006	TOTAL
BENEFITS / GAINS					
Cash inflows (outflows)					
Decreased lead time	N/A	7,000	14,000	14,000	35,000
More fluid design enviornment	N/A	82,000	164,000	164,000	410,000
Change propagation	N/A	53,233	106,466	106,466	266,166
Clash management	N/A	15,264	30,528	30,528	76,320
Design in context	N/A	158,746	317,491	317,491	793,728
Collaborative design / Concurrent Engr.	N/A	425,000	850,000	850,000	2,125,000
Total Benefits/Gains	$ N/A	741,243	1,482,486	1,482,486	**3,706,214**
COSTS AND COST SAVINGS					
Cash inflows (outflows)					
Software					
Software One-time Charges	(450,092)	0	0	0	**(450,092)**
Software Maintenance and Operations	N/A	(52,367)	(52,367)	(52,367)	**(157,100)**
Total Software	$ (450,092)	(52,367)	(52,367)	(52,367)	**(607,192)**
Hardware					
Server and server-related costs	0	(25,000)	(71,400)	(92,000)	**(188,400)**
Client and client-related costs	(15,400)	(8,300)	(22,000)	(12,000)	**(57,700)**
Hardware Maintenance	0	(1,800)	(1,800)	(1,800)	**(5,400)**
Total Hardware	$ (15,400)	(35,100)	(95,200)	(105,800)	**(251,500)**
Personnel and Services					
Personnel staffing cost productivity gains	N/A	367,200	381,888	397,164	1,146,252
Training costs	(34,000)	(15,000)	(8,000)	(9,000)	**(66,000)**
Services costs	0	(42,000)	(10,300)	(3,000)	**(55,300)**
Total Personnel and Services	$ (34,000)	310,200	363,588	385,164	1,024,952
Total Costs and Cost Savings	$ (499,492)	222,733	216,021	226,997	166,259
CASH FLOW SUMMARY					
Cash inflows (outflows)					
Benefits	N/A	741,243	1,482,486	1,482,486	3,706,214
Costs and Cost Savings	(499,492)	222,733	216,021	226,997	166,259
NET CASH FLOW	$ (499,492)	963,976	1,698,507	1,709,482	3,872,473
Cumulative Net Cash Flow	$ (499,492)	464,484	2,162,991	3,872,473	
Discounted Cash Flow					
8.0% Discounted cash flow	$ (499,492)	892,570	1,456,196	1,357,043	3,206,317
15.0% Discounted cash flow	$ (499,492)	838,240	1,284,315	1,124,013	2,747,076

Table 1. Projected cash flow results expected under DesignMax scenario compared to business as usual.

Aerofirma Aircraft Assemblies, Inc.
Proposed DesignMax Implementation for Design Engineering
Currency $
:

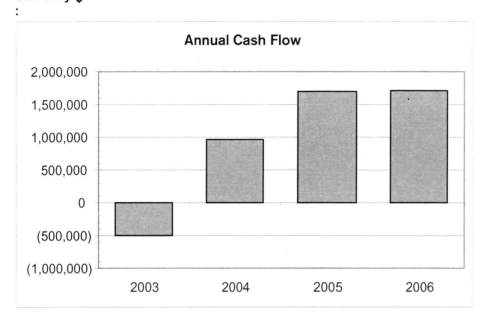

Aerofirma Aircraft Assemblies, Inc.
Proposed DesignMax Implementation for Design Engineering
Currency $
:

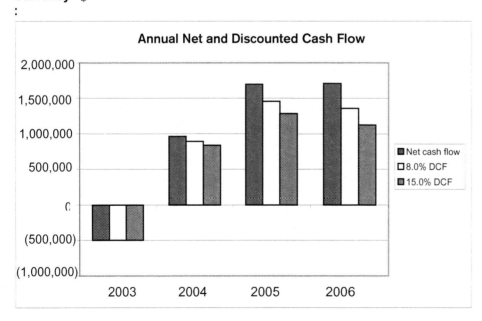

Figure 1. Annual cash flow projections shown as simple net cash flow (top) and as discounted cash flow (bottom). The year-0 net (2003) immediate impacts at the start of year 1 is negative, but net cash flow becomes positive for each subsequent year as the benefits ramp up."

Aerofirma Aircraft Assemblies Inc.
Prroposed DesignMax Implementation for Design Engineering
Currency $
:

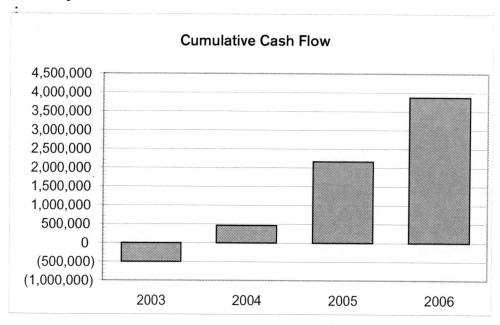

Aerofirma Aircraft Assemblies Inc.
Proposed DesignMax Implementation for Design Engineering
Currency $
:

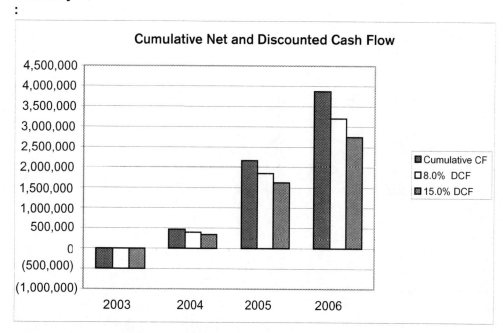

Figure 2. Cash flow projections on a cumulative basis. The net positive cash flow at the end of year one (2004) indicates that payback occurs during that year.

	% of Total Changes Now	%Total Changes with Design Max	Average $ Cost per Change	Net $ Difference
Concept design phase...........................	41.0%	51.0%	200	(10,000)
Detailed design phase..........................	30.0%	21.0%	1,200	54,000
Testing - Prototype phase	19.0%	19.0%	9,600	0
After start of production......................	10.0%	9.0%	24,000	120,000

Table 2. Expected re-distribution of change events under DesignMax.

Moving 10% of the total design changes into the concept design phase increases change costs during that phase by $10,000, but that increase is more than offset by reducing the number of more costly changes occurring in later phases. Therefore, we estimate the total benefit from a **more fluid design environment** to be worth $410,000 over the 3 years.

A related but different benefit arises from improvements in **change propagation** under DesignMax is valued at a total of $266,166 over the three year analysis period. We know from experience that change events occur about once every two days for the typical engineering project, and we estimate that the time requirements for these can be reduced from 30 minutes to 2 minutes, on average, under DesignMax. This is a 93% improvement in change activity time requirements, that now cost Aerofirma $114,480 each year in labor costs. The net annual savings (when the benefit reaches full impact level in year 2) is therefore valued at 93% of the current cost, or $106,466 per year. The total 3-year impact of this benefit is $266,166, assuming a 12-month ramp up to full benefits.

Other benefits included in this case include an estimated savings of $76,320 in **improved clash management** over three years, and an estimated increase of $35,000 in profits due directly to **reduced lead times** under DesignMax. We expect that product lead times will drop from the current average 18 months to an average of 12 months, once Design Engineering gains full proficiency with DesignMax. The very modest benefit credited here (less than 3% of profits last year) recognizes that reduced lead time also calls for significant changes in manufacturing and other functional areas, in addition to shorter design times under DesignMax.

C. 3. Costs

Table 1 also summarizes the expected cost consequences of implementing the DesignMax proposal. The major cost impacts include software acquisition ($450,092 in one-time purchase costs), software maintenance ($157,100 over three years), as well as hardware costs totaling $251,500 (for server and client upgrades and acquisitions, and hardware maintenance for the incremental hardware purchases). Additional training costs ($66,000) and services costs ($55,300, primarily for additional integration consulting) complete the cost picture.

Total incremental costs for the DesignMax implementation are estimated at $979,992, which are expected to bring in total benefits and gains of $4,852,466.

D. Sensitivities, Risks and Contingencies

Engineering management can play a very critical role in maximizing returns from this investment in a new design environment. This is shown in a sensitivity analysis of financial model underlying the projected results. For instance, the projected three-year net gain of $3.87 million is based on many assumptions, including these:

- Collaborative engineering costs will be reduced 12.5%
- Overall designer productivity (for 40 design engineers) will improve by 10%

Improvements or decrements from these values have a strong influence on projected results. For instance:

- If Collaborative engineering cost reductions are only half the expected amount (6.25% instead of 12.5%), estimated cash flow for the entire investment drops from of $3.87 million of $2.81, an overall reduction of 27%.

- If, on the other hand, collaborative engineering cost reductions are even larger, say 25% below the current levels, the overall expected returns rise by 54% to of $6.00 million.

- If individual designer productivity improves only 5% (instead of the assumed 10%), projected results fall 15% to $3.30 million.

- An average increase in designer productivity of 20% (instead of 10%) increases expected investment results by 54% to of $6.00 million

Improvements in collaborative engineering individual productivity, we believe, especially require effective management in Design Engineering.

The projected results are also sensitive to other benefits assumptions, but to a lesser degree. For instance, these results assume that the time required to create a design context will drop from 45 minutes to 10 minutes (based on DesignMax experience at other companies). If this design time can be reduced even further to 5 minutes, the resulting productivity gains bring projected results of $3.98 million, a 3% increase over the total presented here.

Overall, most assumptions that account for the very favorable expected results of this investment rest on four more basic assumptions:

(1) Acrofirma design engineers will be trained and become proficient DesignMax users during the first year of implementation.

(2) The transition from the current design environment to the DesignMax environment will be effected smoothly, that is, with no disruptions in work flow or project scheduling

(3) Aerofirma's customers are appraised as soon as possible of the specific improvements in design capability, responsiveness, and customer service expected under DesignMax. These changes represent substantial benefits to our customers which should lead to improved business volume, cost of sales, and quality of communication with our entire customer base.

(4) Aerofirma's cost structure and business model will adhere to current plans and predictions. This means, essentially, that there are no significant, unplanned cost increases or extraordinary financial events that interfere with the full realization of expected benefits.

Basic assumptions (1) and (2) put a special responsibility on Aerofirma IT management and engineering management, to ensure that training is scheduled and utilized quickly and effectively, and that the transition between design environments runs smoothly.

Assumption (3) requires that sales, marketing, and services management take an active role during the transition to the DesignMax design environment, to ensure that our sales people, consultants, and marketers begin setting customer expectations appropriately.

If the decision is taken to implement the DesignMax proposal, the Aerofirma Engineering Steering Committee will produce a transition plan during the month of August, outlining the tasks and responsibilities necessary to ensure that assumptions 1 – 3 are met.

Assumption (4) refers to events largely beyond the control of Aerofirma management, but which must be monitored closely. Regardless of external events in the market or the economy in general, it is especially important that the DesignMax program receive all expected resources and management support during the first year of implementation, to ensure that benefit "ramp up" occurs on schedule.

E. Recommendations and Conclusions

Based on the analysis presented above, the DesignMax Business Case Analysis Team recommends that Aerofirma Capital Review Committee accept the Avanti DesignMax proposal of 15 July 2003.

We further recommend that the Autofirma Executive Steering Committee take several steps to ensure successful implementation and realization of the business objectives that provide the motivation for this action:

- Begin working with the Avanti Services consultant immediately to outline the main features of the implementation and integration project, and to ensure that proposed hardware and software delivery schedules are in place.

- Ensure that IT staff and resources are available and dedicated to the DesignMax installation and integration requirements during the remainder of year 2003.

- Review the design project transition plan to be presented by the Director of Design Engineering, to ensure that existing customer projects are completed on time, without disruption during the transition.

- Request and review quarterly reports on the financial measures outlined in this business case and progress toward the important business objectives outlined in the introduction of this report:

  (1) Cost reductions (identified under "Benefits" above)
  (2) Improved responsiveness to customers and to change requirements
  (3) Reduced product lead time.

Appendix B
Financial Metrics

Appendix B
Financial Metrics

Those who know the basics of accounting, bookkeeping, or finance know there are many different ways to count money and measure the value of financial events. The most basic *financial metric* (financial measure) for the business case is *cash flow*, for instance, which means something different from other financial measures such as income, revenue, debit, or credit, cost, or expense. Cash flow—and special methods designed to analyze cash flow events—are the heart of most business case results, and for that reason, anyone intending to build or evaluate the business case needs to understand at least a few basic financial terms related to cash flow analysis.

This appendix presents a brief overview of several well-known financial metrics commonly used in business case analysis. Each says something different about the overall pattern of cash flow events in the results, and each carries a different message:

- Cash flow, net cash flow, cash flow stream
- Payback period
- Return on investment (ROI)
- Discounted cash flow (DCF) and net present value (NPV)
- Internal rate of return (IRR)

Cash Flow, Net Cash Flow, Cash Flow Stream

The most basic metric or measurement in the business case is *cash flow*. This means the cash that actually flows into the company (or organization) or actually flows out. All of the business case design efforts are directed toward producing a cash flow summary, describing the full set of cash outflows and inflows that follow from the subject of the case. All of the other financial metrics in this appendix are designed to extract certain information from these cash flow results.

Part of the business case design works to establish the rationale for deciding just what constitutes cash flow: cost savings, for instance are usually treated as a cash inflows. The benefits rationale for *some* cases, moreover, may use cash flow as a metric for assigning financial value to real benefits, such as tangible improvements in customer satisfaction ratings, or shorter time to market, or lower risks of various kinds, even though this real value is first measured in something other than currency. (see Chapters 4 and 5).

The case builder's task is to build a cash flow summary table, or financial model, where cash flow estimates for each cost or benefit item are presented, for each time period in the analysis period.

Cash flow is different from income (or earnings, or profits). *Income* is an income statement term and it is based on some accounting conventions that do not represent real cash flow. Depreciation expenses, and allocated costs, for instance, are accounting conventions that impact the bottom line (income) on the income statement; they do not impact cash flow directly. Cash flow is also something different from sales revenues. Under accrual accounting practices used by most companies, revenues are claimed when the sale is closed—even though the customer may not actually send cash payment (the cash flow event) for 30 days or some other longer period.

Net cash flow is the "bottom line" result of the cash flow summary statement. Net cash flow is simply the difference between money coming in and money going out over a time period:

Net Cash Flow = Cash Inflows - Cash Outflows

Lining up the net cash flow results of several time periods produces a *cash flow stream*, for example the right column of Table B-1, below:

Business Case Results			
Timing	Cash Inflows	Cash Outflow	Net Cash Flow
Now	$0	($100)	($100)
Year 1	$40	($20)	$20
Year 2	$50	($30)	$20
Year 3	$75	($35)	$40
Year 4	$90	($30)	$60
Year 5	$100	($40)	$60
Total	$355	($255)	$100

Table B-1. Derivation of cash flow stream results from a business case analysis. The cash flow stream is the series of "Net Cash Flow" values at right. Figures in parenthesis are negative values, that is, cash outflows.

The action or acquisition under consideration (the subject of the business case) is expected to bring a net cash flow of $100 over five years. But does this represent a good business decision? Can the returns be improved? Where are the risks? The level of detail in this table is the minimum data needed to begin answering such questions.

Each column and row tells a story: Inflows continue to rise throughout the 5-year period, but so do total outflows. Management will want to use this understanding and the data behind it, for instance, to apply the financial tactics to reduce costs, increase gains, and accelerate gains.

In a nutshell, a business case summary should always include a net cash flow stream because it:

- Shows actual inflow and outflow figures, which are important for budgeting and business planning
- Provides the basis for calculating other financial metrics, such as DCF, IRR, and payback
- Is the beginning point for management actions to manage and optimize overall results

Payback Period

The Payback Period metric takes an "Investment" view of the action, plan, or scenario, and its estimated cash flow stream. Payback period is the length of time required to recover the cost of an investment (e.g. investment in a new marketing program, or purchase of computer software). Payback period is usually expressed in years (such as, "Payback = 4.2 years"). When comparing different scenarios or competing investments, other things being equal, the better choice is the one with the shorter payback period.

Most of us run into the payback concept when someone tries to sell us something, based on the idea that it "pays for itself" in cost savings over a short time. There is nothing wrong with the payback concept, as long as you understand its limits, and as long as you are confident that the project cost savings or increased income under an "investment" scenario are real.

Payback periods are also used sometimes used as a way of comparing alternative investments with respect to *risk*: other things being equal, the investment with the shorter payback period is considered less risky. You may sometimes hear management say something like this: "We will *not* invest in assets or programs that have an expected payback over 2 years." The thinking is simply that longer payback periods are too risky to make investment advisable.

As an example, Table B-2 summarizes the information necessary to evaluate payback for a $150 software purchase that is expected to bring productivity improvements valued at $60 per year for the three years:

	Paid Out	Paid Back	Total Paid Back
Year 1	($150)	$60	$60
Year 2	$0	$60	$120
Year 3	$0	$60	$180

Table B-2. Cash flow (Paid Out and Paid Back) for a simple investment scenario. The investment pays for itself sometime in year 3. Figures in parenthesis are cash outflows.

Payback obviously occurs in Year 3, but where, precisely? With no other information about the timing of cash flows in year 3, we have to proceed as if the total inflow for that year is spread evenly throughout the year. (However, if you *do* have information on the exact dates and amounts of cash flows, you *can* pin down payback to the day on which it actually occurs. When you do not have exact dates, you have to interpolate, as illustrated here).

The "formula" for payback period is simple to follow (but surprisingly cumbersome to implement as a formula within a single spreadsheet cell).

First find the payback year. Here, the total paid back does not cover the investment after year 2, and the total paid pack more than covers the investment by the end of year 3. Year 3 is thus the payback year. Then determine how much remains to be paid back *during* the payback year:

Amount to be paid back during payback year
= Total investment − total paid back at end of previous year
= $150 − $120
= $30

Payback period will be 2 years plus some fraction of year 3. Since we have to assume the $60 year 3 cash inflow is spread evenly across the year:

Payback Period = 2 + 30/60 = 2.5 Years

Payback period is an appealing financial metric because almost everyone understands the concept. It is easy to derive graphically, by plotting cumulative cash flow from an investment over time (payback occurs when the curve first makes a transition from negative cumulative total to positive). If the cash flow stream in view consists of just a few figures like Table B-2, you can probably estimate payback period roughly just from visual inspection of the figures.

Despite its simplicity and appeal, however, there are some points to keep in mind when using payback to summarize your business case cash flow results:

- Payback (like IRR) is of no use unless you have cash inflows somewhere in the investment period. In fact, payback cannot be calculated if the positive cash inflows do not eventually outweigh the cash outflows.
- Payback calculation ordinarily does not recognize the time value of money in a discounting sense. Two alternative purchases or investments might have identical payback periods, yet one might achieve most of the payback early, while the other achieves most at a later time, just before the payback date. The payback period by itself does not distinguish between two.
- The measure of payback period does not reflect money coming in or going out *after* the payback event occurs. If you compare two investments or decision alternatives on the basis of payback only, anything that happens from either investment after payback is ignored.

Return on Investment (ROI)

The term "Return on Investment" (ROI) is so familiar and used so often, that many people use the term "ROI analysis" interchangeably with "business case analysis" (see "What's the Difference: Cost/Benefit vs. ROI vs. Justification vs. TCO," pp. 48-49). In fact, ROI is better thought of as one financial metric, among several possible financial metrics, for evaluating business case cash flow projections.

More accurately, ROI is better thought of as *several* financial metrics, all of which are designed to compare returns from an investment, to the investment costs. Because ROI has several meanings, at least, it is prudent to be sure that everyone involved with the case has the same meaning in mind.

The most frequently used and simplest ROI for an investment (or set of business case results), is simply the "Return" (incremental gain) from an action, divided by the cost of that action. That is "simple ROI". For example, suppose that an investment in new telecommunications systems is expected to add $1,000,000 in costs over the next five years, but deliver an additional $1,400,000 in productivity gains and increased profits during the same time. What is the simple ROI on that investment?

$$
\begin{aligned}
\text{Simple ROI} \quad &= \text{(Gains - Investment Costs) / Investment Costs} \\
&= \text{(Incremental Gain) / Investment costs} \\
&= (\$1,400,000 - \$1,000,000) \, / \, \$1,000,000 \\
&= (\$400,000) \, / \, \$1,000,000 \\
&= 40\%
\end{aligned}
$$

Simple ROI works well where both the gains and the costs of an investment or other action are easily known and where they clearly result from the action. In complex business settings, however, it is not always easy to match specific returns (such as increased sales) with specific costs that brought them. Simple ROI becomes less trustworthy as a useful metric, moreover, when the cost figures include *allocated* or *indirect* costs, which are probably not caused directly by the action or the investment.

Other commonly used "financial ratios" are also treated as ROI figures at times. "Return on Invested Capital," "Return on Capital Employed," "Return on Total Assets," "Return on Equity," and "Return on Net Worth," are sometimes called "return on investment." Return on Total Assets, for instance, is sometimes (but not always) simply the ratio of net profit to total assets. "Return on Capital Employed is sometimes (but not always) net profit divided by working capital. If you discover that managers asking for an ROI in your business case really expect one of these latter metrics, be sure you work with a financial specialist to understand how it is developed. This is one more good reason to have a financial specialist on your business case core team (see pp. 19–23)

Discounted Cash Flow (DCF) and Net Present Value (NPV)

If your business case is reviewed by someone trained in finance, expect to be asked for a *discounted cash flow analysis*. Discounting and time-value-of-money concepts are central to modern finance, and financial professionals will almost certainly consider discounting when evaluating financial events that extend across more than one year into the future. In brief, discounting adjusts the value of future cash flows, so as to give more weight to near term cash flow and relatively less weight to distant future events.

Put another way, the discounted cash flow (DCF) is a cash flow summary that has been adjusted to reflect the time value of money. When the discounted values of a cash flow stream extending across time are added together, the total is called *net present value* (NPV). NPV for a cash flow stream is the financial metric; DCF methods produce the NPV.

NPV is an important criterion in evaluating or comparing decisions, investments or purchases. Other things being equal, the purchase or investment associated with the larger NPV is the better decision.

The DCF methods is based on the idea that money you have now should be valued more than an identical amount you would receive in the future Why? Money you have now, could (in principle) be invested now for gain or interest, between now and the future time. Money you will not have until some future time cannot be used now. Therefore, the future money's value is *discounted* in financial evaluation, to reflect its lesser value.

What that future money is worth today is called its *present value*, and what it will be worth when it finally arrives in the future is called not surprisingly its *future value*. Just how much present value should be discounted from future value is determined by two things: the amount of time between now and future payment, and an interest rate. (For rough estimates, think of the interest rate as the return rate we would expect if we had the money now and invested it). For a future payment coming in one year:

Present Value = (Future Value) / (1.0 + Interest Rate)

What is the present value of $100 we will not have for a full year? If we use an annual interest rate of, say, 10%, then

Present Value = ($100)/(1.0 +0.10) = $90.91

The $100 that you will not receive for a year is worth (has a present value of) only $90.91. The present value of that $100 decreases, moreover, as the payment date goes farther into the future. What is the present value if the payment were not coming for 3 years? For multiple periods, the present value calculation becomes:

Present Value = (Future Value) / $(1.0 + \text{Interest rate})^n$

The exponent n is simply the number of periods, or years, in this case 3. The present value of $100 to be received in 3 years, using a 10% interest rate is thus:

Present Value = $100 / $(1.0 +0.10)^3$ = $100 / $(1.1)^3$ = $75.13

"Periods" for these calculations can actually be years, months, or any other time. In any case, be sure that the interest rate represents interest for that period. (When calculating DCF on a monthly basis, for instance, use the annual interest rate divided by 12).

241

As the payment gets further into the future, its present value drops. Also, as you can see, increasing the interest rate would further reduce the present value. Only where interest rates were assumed to be 0% (an economy with no investment possibility and no inflation) would present value always equal future value.

Now consider two competing investments in computer equipment. Each calls for an initial cash outlay of $100, and each returns a total a $200 over the next 5 years making net cash flow gain of $100. But the timing of the returns is different, as shown in Table B-3 below (Case A and Case B), and therefore the present value of each year's return is different.

Timing	Net Cash Flow - A	Present Value - A	Net Cash Flow- B	Present Value B
Now	($100.00)	($100.00)	($100.00)	($100.00)
Year 1	$60.00	$54.54	$20.00	$18.18
Year 2	$60.00	$49.59	$20.00	$16.52
Year 3	$40.00	$30.05	$40.00	$20.05
Year 4	$20.00	$13.70	$60.00	$41.10
Year 5	$20.00	$12.42	$60.00	$37.27
Total (NPV)	$100.00	$60.30	$100.00	$43.12

Table B-3. Expected net cash flow and discounted cash flow (present value) from two case scenarios, A and B. Discounting is performed at a 10% annual interest rate. Figures in parenthesis are cash *outflows*.

The sum of each investment's present values is called net present value for the cash flow stream (discounting for these calculations was performed using the formulas above and a 10% annual interest rate).

Evaluating only the net cash flows, both investments have an identical five-year result. Comparing the discounted values (NPVs) of the two investments, you can see that the early large returns in Case A lead to a better NPV than the later large returns in Case B. When choosing alternative investments or actions, other things being equal, the one with the higher NPV is the better investment.

You may wonder at this point, just how the interest is decided for discounting calculations. The higher the interest rate, the greater the discounting effect (the greater the difference between present value and future value). The best advice for most business case authors is simply to *find out* the rate recommended by your organization's financial specialists, or by established policy. Normally this will be a few points above the current inflation rate, somewhere around the "cost of capital" figure used by the organization. If for some reason you cannot get guidance on finding the interest rate, use the current cost (rate) for borrowing that would apply to you or your organization.

In brief, a discounted view of the cash flow stream should probably be included with your business case results when:

- The business case deals with an "investment" scenario of any kind, in which different uses for money are being compared
- The business case covers long periods of time (two or more years)
- Inflows and outflows change differently over time (e.g., the largest inflows come at a different time from the largest outflows)
- Two or more alternative scenarios are being compared and they differ with respect to cash flow timing within the analysis period

Internal Rate of Return (IRR)

The final financial metric in this appendix is the least familiar to non financial specialists, but is, nevertheless a mainstay of modern finance: the internal rate of return, or IRR. If there is a financial specialist on the recipient list for your business case, and if your business case subject is competing for funding with other alternatives, you may very well be asked for an IRR.

Very roughly speaking, the expected IRR for an investment or expenditure helps address questions like these: Is this a good use of the money? Or, should we simply loan out the money at current interest rates? IRR, like discounted cash flow analysis and the NPV, takes into account the magnitude and timing of future cash flows. The higher an investment's IRR, the better the investment's return relative to its cost.

IRR has a simply stated definition: The IRR for an investment is the discount rate for which the total present value of future cash inflows equals the cost of the investment. It is the interest rate, that is that produces a 0% NPV. You may still wonder just how to evaluate that, or how to apply it to a specific investment or purchase. Probably the best way to grasp IRR quickly is with the help of the graph in Figure B-1 (next page).

These curves are based on the same Case A and Case B cash flow scenarios presented in Table B-3 above to illustrate NPV. Here, however, we have used nine different interest rates, including 0.0 and 0.10, on up through 0.80. Clearly, as the interest rate for calculating NPV increases, the resulting NPV decreases. For Case A, an interest rate of 0.38 produces NPV = 0, whereas Case B has NPV = 0 with an interest rate of 0.22. Case A therefore has an IRR of 38%, and the IRR for case

Net Present Value of Cash Flow

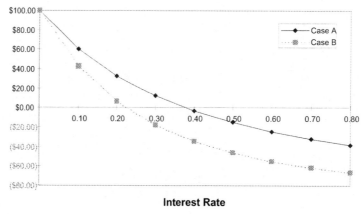

Figure 3.1 Finding the IRR for two different investments by graphing. Ea curve shows the NPV of a cash flow stream from Table **b-3**. NPVs for eac stream are plotted at nine different interest rates. The point on the hori: axis where NPV = 0 represents the internal rate of return. Clearly, Case A has a higher IRR than Case B.

B is 22%. Which is the better Investment? Other things being equal, the one with the higher IRR.

Now, would an investment with an IRR of, say 75% be a better investment? The answer is *yes*. Another way to think of IRR is this: IRR tells you just how high interest rates would have to go in order to "zero" the gain from the this investment, compared to simply loaning out the money at prevailing interest rates. For Case A cash flow, the interest rate would have to rise all the way to 38% to make this investment have zero gain over loaning out the money. The Case **B** investment would cease to be the best use of money if interest rates rose only to 22%.

For these reasons, IRR for a prospective investment is sometimes compared to an internal "hurdle rate," which can be arbitrarily set at any value. If the organization's financial management sets the hurdle rate at, say 40%, than any proposed investment must project an estimated IRR over that rate in order to be approved.

How do you actually calculate IRR? The graphical approach illustrated above can give you a rough estimate of IRR. Beyond that you may be surprised to learn there is no simple analytic solution. What you would have to do, essentially, is write an equation for NPV for the cash flow stream, set NPV = 0, and solve for the interest rate. Instead, however, spreadsheets, calculators, and humans armed with simple calculators solve by trial and error, repeatedly trying different interest rates in the NPV calculation, and checking to see if the result approaches zero NPV. Spreadsheets such as Microsoft Excel and

Lotus 123, and more advanced financial calculators of all kinds have easy-to-use built in functions that do the trial and error work for you. Input a series of numbers representing the cash flow stream, and the program or calculator delivers the IRR.

Choosing financial metrics

Which of these financial metrics should you use to summarize a business case? The best answer—repeated several times in this *Guide*—is to find out what recipients need and want to see before starting your case. Find out which criteria were used to guide similar decisions in the past.

Beyond this, the best advice is to develop all of these financial metrics and present all of them–if their values have meaning. The real issue then is to decide which of them should become primary decision criteria, or which should carry the most weight in comparing alternatives. There is no universal answer to that question, but here some factors to consider.

- Each financial metric measures, or says something different about the cash flow stream:
  - **Net cash flow** measures the total cash flow result in non-discounted currency units (dollars, euro, yen, pounds, etc.)
  - **Payback period** measures time (e.g, Payback = 4.2 years)
  - Simple **return on investment** (ROI) shows the relative size of the returns compared to the investment in percentage (e.g., Simple ROI = 60.0%
  - **Net present value** (NPV) shows the magnitude of the cash flow result in currency units (like net cash flow), but these are discounted to reflect the time value of money. (e.g., npv = $74.40).
  - **Internal rate of return** (IRR) finds the interest rate that gives the investment zero gain (zero NPV), compared to loaning out the money at the same rate.
- All financial metrics have meaning only when described for a specific time period. (See Figure 2.3, p. 24, for instance, which shows how financial metrics can change, depending on the time period in view).
- Different financial metrics for different scenarios or decision options can carry conflicting messages. Case A might have a shorter payback period than Case B, for instance, but case B might have a much large NPV or IRR. When different financial metrics carry different messages, it is up to someone (perhaps you) to decide which metric's message is most important for the current situation.

- IRR has the most meaning when there is an initial net cash outflow, followed by inflows or gains that are large, relative to the initial cash outflow. IRR an be quite misleading if there is no large initial cash outflow. That is why IRR is not a good metric for making "lease vs. buy" decisions: the relatively small initial expenditure for the "lease" option generally leads to a huge IRR, compared to a similar "buy" option that *does* have a large initial purchase outlay. In brief, IRR is a valid basis for comparing competing investment scenarios, if all scenarios have roughly similar cash flow patterns over time.
- The cash flow stream must have a positive inflows somewhere, in order for IRR, ROI, or payback to have meaning.
- NPV results are sensitive to the interest rate (discounting rate) used in the calculation, and choice of rate is arbitrary. When using NPV, be sure to use a rate that matches your audience's common practices and expectations.

References

Online References

The internet is a rich source of useful, practical information for the case-builder. The availability of material is constantly changing of course, and the best reference to online sources that can be provided here is itself an online source. Solution Matrix Ltd. maintains a "Knowledge Base" that provides links and free downloads of example cases from hundreds of sources, salary and price information, government guides and guidelines (from Australia, Canada, New Zealand, the United Kingdom, and the United States), tax information, and business case related articles and publications.

The Business Case Knowledge Base is available at:

http://www.solutionmatrix.com/business-case-knowledge-base.html

Books

Brent, R.J. *Applied Cost-Benefit Analysis*, Cheltenham, Edward Edgar, 1996.

Dasgupta, A.K. and Pearce, D. *Cost Benefit Analysis: Theory and Practice*, London, Macmillan, 1987.

Irvine G, 1978, *Modern Cost-Benefit Methods*, London, Macmillan.

Kempis, Rolf-Dieter, and RInkbeck, Jürgen *Do IT Smart*, New York, The Free Press, 1999.

Layard R, (ed), *Cost-Benefit Analysis*, Harmondsworth, Penguin, 1972.

Mishan, E.J. *Cost-Benefit Analysis*, 4th ed., London, George Allen and Unwin, 1988.

Piesello, Thomas, Return on Investment for Information Technology Providers: Using ROI as a Selling and Management Tool, New Canaan, CT, Information Economics Press, 2002.

Phillips, Jack J. *Return on Investment in Training and Performance Improvement Programs*, Houston, Gulf Publishing Company, 1997.

Sinden, J.A. AND Thampapillai, D.J. *Introduction to Benefit-Cost Analysis*, Longman, Melbourne, 1995.

Strassman, Paul A. The Business Value of Computers, New Canaan, CT, Information Economics Press, 1990.

Strassmann, Paul A. *Information Payoff*, New York, The Free Press, 1985

Sugden, Robert and Williams, Alan *The Principles of Practical Cost-Benefit Analysis*, Oxford University Press, 1985.

Index

A

accounting statements 117–118
analysis period 23–25
"as is" scenario 26, 84
assumptions 81–83
  clarification 82
  and cost estimation 130–140
  and dynamic model 37–39
  global 86
  item-specific 86
  for prediction 81–82
  and risk analysis 42–43
  scenario 86
  and sensitivity analysis 40–41
  for simplification 82
Authors 57–59
avoided cost 173

B

background information 52–54
before tax vs after tax 119–121
benefit 31–34, 99–106
  avoided cost 141
  benefits rationale 33–34, 104, 145–150
  and business objectives 31–34
  contributions to business objectives 100–103, 145–150, 173–175
  cost savings 100, 141–143
  estimating 140–150, 173–175
  hard benefit 9, 143–144
  increased income 100, 144–145, 173
  intangible 108
  non financial 9, 44–47
  soft benefit 9, 145
boundary. *See* scope and boundary
budget 53–54
business as usual scenario 26, 87
business case
  vs. accounting statements 117
  defined 1
  design 16–19, 54–55
  history 73–74
  previous 53
  structure 16–20
  vs. business plan 12
business impact 27–34, 90–91
  defined 27
  direct financial impact 27–28
business objective 53, 65–69
business plan 12, 54

C

D